English Literature

for the IB Diploma

David James and Nic Amy

Cambridge University Press's mission is to advance learning, knowledge and research worldwide.

Our IB Diploma resources aim to:
- encourage learners to explore concepts, ideas and topics that have local and global significance
- help students develop a positive attitude to learning in preparation for higher education
- assist students in approaching complex questions, applying critical-thinking skills and forming reasoned answers.

CAMBRIDGE
UNIVERSITY PRESS

CAMBRIDGE
UNIVERSITY PRESS

University Printing House, Cambridge CB2 8BS, United Kingdom

Cambridge University Press is part of the University of Cambridge.

It furthers the University's mission by disseminating knowledge in the pursuit of education, learning and research at the highest international levels of excellence.

www.cambridge.org
Information on this title: www.cambridge.org/9781107402232

© Cambridge University Press 2011

First published 2011
4th printing 2014

Printed in the United Kingdom by Cambrian Printers Ltd

A catalogue record for this publication is available from the British Library

ISBN 978-1-107-40223-2 Paperback

Content

Introduction: starting out on an IB Literature course

Using your Literature coursebook

This coursebook is written for IB English Literature students by highly experienced IB English Literature teachers. In writing this book we had many different objectives, but we were clear about one fundamental aim: that this coursebook should help you to become a more self-confident student of English Literature. We hope this book proves helpful, challenging and – importantly – interesting and enjoyable. The activities you will find in each chapter are not only varied, but also clearly linked to your course and its different methods of assessment. This coursebook will support you throughout your course, offering advice and guidance about all the different aspects of the English Literature programme. At the end of this introduction you will find a section on how to use this coursebook most effectively.

What this coursebook *isn't* is a short cut to gaining outstanding grades. You will need to put in the hours reading, writing and thinking. English Literature is an important subject, but it is only one among six which, taken with the Core (Theory of Knowledge, the Extended Essay, and Creativity, Action, Service), add up to an integrated, holistic programme of study. That said, being able to read analytically and to write clearly (qualities that are integral to studying literature at this level) will no doubt help you in other subjects. If you do your very best, and if you are organised, motivated and prepared, then you could achieve your full potential.

How does this Literature course work?

In studying the Language A: Literature course in the IB Diploma you are following an exciting and challenging programme which provides both Standard Level and Higher Level students with a broad and in-depth knowledge of the subject. In following this course, not only will you study some of the finest literature in English, but you will also read, discuss and write about works of literature from other cultures and traditions.

Importantly, you are assessed in a number of different ways: there are formal literary essays (both in coursework and in two exams), you will also give a presentation to other students in your class and discuss, one-to-one, works of literature that you have studied in-depth. This flexibility marks this course out as not only hugely stimulating and rewarding, but also ideal preparation for studying literature in higher education. Other elements of the course add to its richness: both Theory of Knowledge and the Extended Essay allow students to stretch their understanding of literature in new ways; these elements of the Diploma Programme will bring added scope and sophistication to your work.

We refer to the Language A: Literature course as **English Literature** throughout this coursebook in order to distinguish it from the companion **English Language and Literature** course (and its accompanying Cambridge coursebook). It is also useful to bear in mind that there are literature courses available in other languages within Language A: Literature and, although you will study works in translation, the focus for this course is very much literature originally written in English.

Standard Level and Higher Level courses

This coursebook is written for both Standard Level and Higher Level (referred to as SL and HL throughout this coursebook) Literature students. The courses are structured in the same way, but with some important differences. HL students study 13 texts and SL students study 10; HL students have more teaching time to complete their studies; the courses are also assessed using slightly different criteria. Other differences are perhaps not so obvious at first (such as the fact that HL students have a discussion as part of their individual oral commentary whereas SL students do not).

The differences between the SL and HL courses are summarised here:

Part of the course	Standard Level	Higher Level
Part 1: Works in translation	Study of two works in translation from the prescribed literature in translation (PLT) list	Study of three works in translation from the prescribed literature in translation (PLT) list
Part 2: Detailed study	Study of two works, each of a different genre, chosen from the prescribed list of authors (PLA)	Study of three works, each of a different genre (one of which must be poetry), chosen from the prescribed list of authors (PLA)
Part 3: Literary genres	Study of three works of the same genre, chosen from the PLA	Study of four works of the same genre, chosen from the PLA
Part 4: Options	Study of three works freely chosen	Study of three works freely chosen
External assessment		
Paper 1: Commentary	A literary analysis of a previously unseen passage in response to two guiding questions	A literary commentary on a previously unseen passage
Internal assessment		
Individual oral commentary	A 10-minute oral commentary based on an extract from one of the works studied in Part 2	A 10-minute oral commentary on poetry studied in Part 2, followed by a discussion based on one of the other two works studied

These distinctions are clearly mapped out for you in the following chapters.

What are the skills you need to study Literature?

This coursebook aims to support you in all aspects of your study of the IB Literature course. It provides you with detailed information about assessment and the structure of the course; more importantly, it also aims to help you to develop very important skills. The study of English Literature teaches you to read carefully and analytically; it helps you to become a more confident writer and it encourages you to think deeply about the world around you.

As you develop as a student of English Literature you will be looking to widen your critical vocabulary; however, it is important to understand that simply 'spotting' literary features in a text does not guarantee marks from examiners. Throughout this coursebook we will encourage you to:

- think about *why* and *how* a writer uses a literary technique, rather than just talking and writing about *what* it is and *when* it is used

- discuss the effect of writers' choices of language, structure and form on the text as a whole and, in turn, the reader
- get to know a range of specialist words and phrases; we have provided you with key terms boxes and a Glossary at the end of the coursebook to ensure that your knowledge in this area is as secure as it can be.

A sophisticated response goes beyond an unthinking regurgitation of knowledge. You will have to show, at every stage, that you understand and that you can interpret and analyse.

How is this coursebook organised?

In writing this book, we have followed closely the structure of the 2011 IB Language A: Literature syllabus and so the emphasis placed on certain criteria reflects the distribution of marks available in the various components of the course. This book will help you to understand exactly how each part of the course is assessed so that you always know the desired outcome, in terms of both the required content and the marks that are available. Please refer to the IB Guide for the latest information. Each chapter of this book deals with a separate component of the course, as follows.

This **introductory chapter** gives you an overview of the course requirements, as well as the assessment criteria. At the end of this chapter you will find a section entitled 'How to use this coursebook' which will help you to understand how you can best use the various chapters and activities to support your study of literature.

Chapter 1 provides a detailed exploration of Part 1: Works in translation; in this chapter extra emphasis is placed on appreciating how context shapes a text's meaning.

Chapter 2 introduces you to Part 2: Detailed study. In this part of the course you will study some of the most important texts in English literature. Particular emphasis is placed here on developing close reading skills which enable you to 'drill down' into the various meanings of different texts. You will also work on tasks that will help secure your knowledge of different genres.

Chapter 3 is focused on Part 3: Literary genres. In this chapter you will build on the work you did in Chapter 2 to explore the different conventions and techniques used by writers to achieve particular effects in different genres. Understanding the conventions that govern a writer's choices is essential to a course which tests not only your understanding but also your knowledge of the subject. Your knowledge base – for both SL and HL – has to be broad, but it also has to be deep if it is to sustain you in your studies over two hugely stimulating years.

Chapter 4 covers the most varied – and distinctive – part of the English Literature course. Part 4 of the course consists of school-based choices; you are given the opportunity to study prose other than fiction – hypertexts, graphic novels, new media, literature and film, amongst other genres. It would probably be impossible for any coursebook to cover the range of options available to schools in this part of the course and so the focus here is on further developing your writing technique and your presentational skills – qualities that are required if you are to make the most of this school-assessed component.

Chapter 5 shifts the focus to Paper 1: Commentary (known as the guided literary analysis at SL and the literary commentary at HL). To help you to prepare for this key component a number of activities – including timed essays – are included which will help you to practise for the examination. You will have been developing many of the skills required for this paper over the two years of your studies, and in many ways this paper is a 'synoptic' exam – a test of how well those skills have become firmly embedded. By the time you take this exam (and Paper 2 – the genre paper) you will have a secure

tip

This book guides you through each part of the course; however, you may find it useful to begin at Chapter 5 because it focuses on the essential skills you will need to develop throughout the course.

understanding of how to write an effective literary essay. This coursebook will support you in getting to that point, and Chapter 5 gives you detailed advice on what a good literary essay looks like.

An overview of your IB English Literature course

The course you are studying is divided into four parts. The IB syllabus allows your school the flexibility to study these parts in any order. You should not expect your course to start with Part 1 and proceed through to Part 4 in the second year of your studies (indeed, many schools begin the course with Part 4, for reasons we will explain in Chapter 4).

Here is an overview of the course:

	Standard Level	Higher Level
Part 1: Works in translation *All works chosen from the titles in the prescribed literature in translation (PLT) list*	2 works	3 works
Part 2: Detailed study *All works chosen from the prescribed list of authors (PLA), chosen from* **different** *genres*	2 works	3 works
Part 3: Literary genres *All works chosen from the prescribed list of authors (PLA), chosen from the* **same** *genre*	3 works	4 works
Part 4: Options *Works freely chosen in any combination*	3 works	3 works
Total	**10 works**	**13 works**

Note: Additionally all students take Paper 1: Commentary.

What do we mean by a 'work'?

A 'work' can be defined quite broadly but, according to the IB syllabus, it can be:

- a single major text
- two or more shorter texts (novellas for example)
- a selection of short stories
- a selection of poems
- a selection of essays
- a selection of letters.

When more than one text is used your teacher will have thought very carefully about how appropriate the selection is: it will be comparable to one full-length play or novel.

What will you need to do for each part of the course?

What follows is a more detailed breakdown of each part of the course you will study. Look carefully at how much each part of the course is worth as a percentage of the final mark: knowing each component's weighting can help focus your thoughts as you prepare to study it.

Part 1: Works in translation

In this part of the course you are encouraged to understand the ways that literature represents and interacts with the culture in which it was written. Placing works of literature in a wider context – and making connections between the texts you study and the worlds they engage with – is a hugely rewarding experience. As well as showing that you understand various cultural contexts you will also have to analyse how time and place affect your understanding of a text and in what ways these may affect its meaning.

You should always keep in mind that this is a Literature course, not a History course: the focus is on the work itself, rather than the period or the writer. All the works in Part 1 of the syllabus are studied in translation and although the texts you are studying are translated you will still need to focus on the words on the page, rather than evaluate the success of the translator's work, or how much it differs from the original.

How is Part 1 assessed?

SL and HL	You have to write one coursework essay of between 1200 and 1500 words, with a reflective statement of 300–400 words.	Worth 25% of your final mark in English Literature

Part 2: Detailed study

Each work studied in this part of the course must come from a different genre; at HL one of the genres must be poetry.

Close reading of a text is a fundamental part of your course, but here in particular you are required to spend a substantial amount of time looking at key passages in real depth. Having a strong grasp of literary terms that are appropriate to these genres will make your analysis even more focused. In Part 2 of the course the focus is on detailed analysis of a work, in terms of both content and technique.

How is Part 2 assessed?

SL	**Individual oral commentary** In this part of the course you will be given about 30 lines from a text (which you will have studied before) and be asked to mark it up for 20 minutes. You will then talk about this text for 8 minutes, followed by 2 minutes discussing questions asked by your teacher. There will be guiding questions provided.	
HL	**Individual oral commentary and discussion** In this part of the course you will be given a poetry text (which you have studied before) and be asked to mark it up for 20 minutes. You will then talk about this text for 8 minutes, followed by 2 minutes discussing questions asked by your teacher. Following this you will have a discussion with your teacher on an additional text you have studied in this part of the course. This will also last 10 minutes.	Worth 15% of your final mark in English Literature

Part 3: Literary genres

Each of the works studied in this part of the course must come from the same literary genre. As in Part 2, a secure knowledge of the literary conventions of the genre you are studying is required if you are to get as much as possible out of your studies. Comparing and contrasting how these conventions are used by different writers will deepen your understanding of the texts you study.

How is Part 3 assessed?

SL	**Exam: Paper 2 (1½ hours)** One essay based on at least two works studied in Part 3. Three essay questions for each literary genre. You are not allowed to take the texts you have studied into the exam.	Worth 25% of your final mark in English Literature
HL	**Exam: Paper 2 (2 hours)** One essay based on at least two works studied in Part 3. Three essay questions for each literary genre. You are not allowed to take the texts you have studied into the exam.	

Part 4: Options

Part 4 of the course gives the school a free choice and your teacher will decide what best suits the group you are working with. There is great flexibility here: works may be chosen freely, and they can have been written originally in English or translated into English. Teachers can choose texts from different periods, regions or genres from the texts you study for other parts of the course. Your school may wish to focus on literature that is local to your area or culture.

There are three options available in Part 4, although they should be viewed as *suggestions* or *examples*, rather than something prescriptive. They share the same aims: each student is expected to develop knowledge and understanding of the works studied and to give a presentation on an aspect of these works, clearly and with confidence, to an audience. Developing presentational skills will form a vital part of your preparation for assessment.

- **Option 1: The study of prose other than fiction**
  This option provides you with an opportunity to read genres other than novels and short stories. You could choose travel writing, autobiography, letters, essays or speeches, amongst many other examples of types of writing. The aim is for you to understand the various conventions that organise and shape these important genres and to explore the cultural contexts they were written in. This option also gives you the opportunity to practise and produce writing in the forms you have studied and, in self-analysing your work, to produce an individual presentation to a group of fellow students.

- **Option 2: New textualities**
  This option allows you to study any of a number of rapidly evolving text forms. You could choose graphic novels, hypertext narratives, blogs, fan fiction, or media texts that defy easy categorisation. All of the texts used should be original, and should have genuine – and evident – literary merit. It is important to remember that these texts should be original, rather than adaptations of existing literary texts.

- **Option 3: Literature and film**
  Whilst this is not a media studies unit, and three works in this study must be in printed form, you may wish to concentrate on analysing how a literary work has been adapted for the screen. The aim is for you to become a more critical 'reader' of film and television. Other avenues to explore include looking at how symbolism can work in two different media. Other devices used in film could also be explored here in relation to the literary texts being studied.

Remember that the three 'Options' should be seen as example Part 4 courses; schools can still choose freely from other areas should they wish to, although it is advisable to

check with the IB if in doubt about the suitability of any particular genre or text. Each
of these three Options provides schools with ideas about what can be taught as part of
a modern IB programme. In doing so, it is hoped that the Options will provide some
additional structure and focus should it be required.

How is Part 4 assessed?

SL and HL	Individual oral presentation Your presentation should last 10–15 minutes. It is assessed by your school.	Worth 15% of your final mark in English Literature

Paper 1: Commentary

In addition to the exams and written and oral assessments for each of the four
parts, you will also sit Paper 1: Commentary. This paper assesses your ability to
analyse a previously unseen text and, as such, tests the skills you have learned over
the two-year course. Remember that only SL students will have guiding questions
in this exam.

How is Paper 1 assessed?

SL	Guided literary analysis (1½ hours) Literary analysis of one unseen text (you will choose either poetry or prose) in response to guiding questions	Worth 20% of your final mark in English Literature
HL	Literary commentary (2 hours) Literary analysis of one unseen text (you will choose either poetry or prose)	

How will you be assessed?

This coursebook will help and encourage you to become familiar with the ways in
which your work will be assessed. Put simply, the assessment criteria tell you how you
are marked, and the more familiar you become with the different criteria for each part
of your course the more confident you will feel as a student and the better prepared
you will be for your exams. Such awareness can make a great difference in both exams
and your coursework, and each chapter will look specifically at where you can pick up
marks – and show you how to avoid the places where they can sometimes be lost! At
all times we would encourage you to discuss your work with your teacher (and indeed
with anybody whose judgement you trust).

In each chapter you will find activities specifically focused on key assessment
criteria. You will also find 'tips' which give you extra hints about how to make the
most of each piece of work, both written and oral, throughout the course, in the
exams or when you are writing your coursework. See page vii for an example of
a tip.

How do the assessment criteria work?

This section gives you a clear overview of the assessment criteria for each part of your
course, as well as advice on how to be as well prepared as possible for each criterion.
Being well prepared and thoroughly organised is crucial in enabling you to devote
enough time to each part of the Literature course, as well as to the other subjects you
are studying for the Diploma.

For **Part 1: Works in translation** you are assessed in this way:

	Summary of descriptors	Marks available
Criterion A	*Fulfilling the requirements of the reflective statement* Show that you have reflected with sensitivity and insight on your interactive oral, and that you have extended your understanding of the cultural and contextual elements.	3
Criterion B	*Knowledge and understanding* Show that you know the texts really well, and provide a strong and coherent interpretation of them. Your analysis should be valid and consistently well argued. Show that you clearly understand the cultural and historical contexts in which the text was written. Important though cultural, biographical and historical factors are, it is important to keep the literary text central to your analysis.	6
Criterion C	*Appreciation of the writer's choices* Look carefully at the writer's use of language, giving examples with short quotations; keep in mind that nothing is put on paper 'by chance', and that a sensitive reading of the possible different meanings is important here. Don't avoid 'difficult passages': they may be the key parts of the text.	6
Criterion D	*Organisation and development* Your essay should be well organised, containing a clear introduction, carefully linked arguments, and an unambiguous conclusion. Planning your essay is important here, and although some students go through a number of drafts it is often better to plan effectively and write a good first draft than try to re-write an essay several times because your thesis was not worked out in advance. Your teacher's help will be invaluable at this stage of the essay.	5
Criterion E	*Language* Make your language as clear as possible, ensuring that every word choice is working well for you. Do not forget to use literary terms, but only use them when they are appropriate and give a specific example by using a short quotation from the text. Also remember that if you use a good, varied and sophisticated general vocabulary this can be rewarded here as well.	5
Total		**25**

It is essential that you remember that throughout this and each part of the course you need to show appropriate and succinct evidence from the texts you are studying to support your points. Knowing how to quote primary and secondary quotations is a key skill in the study of literature. You will find out more about how to do this in Chapter 1.

For **Part 2: Detailed study** SL candidates are assessed on their commentary in this way:

	Summary of descriptors	Marks available
Criterion A	*Knowledge and understanding of the extract* Show that you know the passage really well, and link it to other passages, or works, you have studied by this author. It is important that you show a very secure understanding of the conventions of the genre you have studied. You will be given guiding questions in the exam and you should use them.	10
Criterion B	*Appreciation of the writer's choices* Ask yourself to what extent the choices made by the author are informed by the conventions of the genre. Are you aware of alternative interpretations? How valid are these different views? Showing such awareness is important, but remember that your personal response is vital.	10
Criterion C	*Organisation and presentation* Your planning time is crucial and is the starting point for good organisation and presentation. Your commentary should be organised as an essay, with a beginning, middle and conclusion, and a coherent argument running throughout; your presentation skills should be secure so that you do not repeat yourself, or sound uncertain. Again, use the guiding questions you are provided with if they help you structure your analysis.	5
Criterion D	*Language* Make sure your use of critical vocabulary is clear and precise, think carefully about the words and phrases you use. Don't repeat yourself, and use literary terms where appropriate. A wide, sophisticated vocabulary is more important than simply regurgitating a list of literary terms.	5
Total		**30**

For **Part 2: Detailed study** HL candidates are assessed on both the commentary and discussion in this way:

	Summary of descriptors	Marks available
Criterion A	*Knowledge and understanding of the poem* Show that you know the poem's main themes very well, and link it to other poems you have studied by this author if appropriate. It is advisable not to go through the poem line by line; instead, focus on verses, or sections, being very aware of the main ideas, and the images that bring those ideas to life.	5

Criterion B	*Appreciation of the writer's choices* You will have a discussion on a work other than the one you have just completed your commentary on, so be prepared for this. Show that you understand how the word choices made by the writer affect your interpretation of the work. Again, an understanding of the conventions of the genre the work is taken from will be a good foundation for your analysis.	5
Criterion C	*Organisation and presentation of the commentary* Planning time is crucial here: your analysis should be as well organised as an essay. Make sure your commentary is well structured: you should develop and link ideas, showing your examiner that you are fully aware of the writer's aims. Be enthusiastic: a flat delivery, even when the ideas are good, might weaken your commentary.	5
Criterion D	*Knowledge and understanding of the work used in the discussion* Make sure that you have a sound understanding of the work used, and that you are familiar with the conventions that organise it. Remember, engage with the work.	5
Criterion E	*Response to the discussion questions* Remember to answer the questions asked, not the questions you would prefer to answer; try to keep your answers clear and succinct and, again, avoid repeating yourself. Try to enjoy the experience, and do not be afraid of showing enthusiasm for the work. Do not be afraid to voice your opinion, but remember to support your points with references to the text.	5
Criterion F	*Language* Make sure your use of critical vocabulary is clear and accurate; think carefully about the words and phrases you use to explain your points. Ensure that the critical vocabulary you have spent time becoming more comfortable with over the course is used effectively here.	5
Total		**30**

For **Part 3: Literary genres** SL and HL students are assessed in this way for the exam (Paper 2):

	Summary of descriptors	**Marks available**
Criterion A	*Knowledge and understanding* How well do you know the texts you have studied? Do not spend valuable time providing unnecessary biographical context on each writer. Your essay should analyse the texts you have studied and consider their literary merits.	5

Criterion B	*Response to the question* Have you completely understood the question? Strong answers come from students who have read the question carefully and interpreted it accurately. Look at the wording, underline the key parts of the question, and satisfy yourself that you are comfortable with what is being asked of you.	5
Criterion C	*Appreciation of the literary conventions of the genre* Do you understand the conventions of the genre you are writing about? Do you appreciate how these conventions shape meaning? This is an opportunity to show the examiner how much you have learned over the last two years, so use it.	5
Criterion D	*Organisation and development* How well structured is your essay? There should be a clear, concise and direct introduction, followed by a full development of the key ideas (which are linked); and there should be an unambiguous conclusion which neatly summarises your thesis.	5
Criterion E	*Language* Your language should be precise, varied and clear. This book will advise you repeatedly to use literary terms; make sure that they are used accurately, and that in using them you focus on the effect of the technique under analysis. Your language use is, inevitably, fundamental to conveying your meaning, and although it is tempting to try to impress an examiner with elaborate phrasing it is often advisable to concentrate on making your ideas as clear as they can be. In other words, say something clever but say it as simply as possible.	5
Total		**25**

For **Part 4: Options** SL and HL students are assessed on the individual oral presentation in this way:

	Summary of descriptors	Marks available
Criterion A	*Knowledge and understanding of the work(s)* Remember that this is not a media component and the majority of the texts used have to be in written form. Make sure you know these texts as well as you would for any other assessed work, and also know how they relate to each other (through genre, ideas, aims, and so on).	10
Criterion B	*Presentation* Your presentation should be carefully researched, and your subject area very focused (be very careful you do not choose an area that is too broad). Engage with the audience, and do not read from a pre-prepared script, or over-use tools such as PowerPoint or Keynote.	10

Criterion C	*Language* As with every part of the course, your use of language is crucial, and as in Part 2, the presentation should be prepared as carefully as any written coursework. Make sure that you have not only a very secure knowledge of the literary terms required for analysing non-fiction (including graphic novels and media texts amongst others), but also the technical vocabulary required for studying different genres, including film and television.	10
Total		**30**

For **Paper 1:** Commentary SL and HL students are assessed in this way:

	Summary of descriptors	**Marks available**
Criterion A	*Understanding and interpretation* A clear understanding and interpretation of a text you have not seen before is key to succeeding in this paper. Use your reading time constructively, and mark up carefully and quickly after that reading time is up. There is more on how you do this in Chapter 5.	5
Criterion B	*Appreciation of the ways in which the writer's choices shape meanings* The examiner will want to see that you clearly understand how vocabulary choices made by the writer inform the meaning of the text; you will need to demonstrate an awareness of how the main themes are developed, and how the text's structure and form affect your reading of it.	5
Criterion C	*Organisation* It is vital that you plan your essay clearly before you start to write it. Decide upon your key points, sequence them if you are happy to do that, and regularly check on this plan as you write. A short overview of your thesis can also help you clarify your thoughts so that the meaning is clear before you begin to write.	5
Criterion D	*Language* A varied vocabulary is important here: use words carefully, and when you do use literary terms make sure that they are accurate and they advance your meaning: simply putting literary terms into an essay does not guarantee you extra marks.	5
Total		**20**

How to use this coursebook

This coursebook will support you throughout the two years of your IB Literature course. You will find that each chapter provides you with an in-depth insight into each part of the course. Within each of these chapters you will find activities for you to work on and additional features to deepen your knowledge and understanding of the subject, as well as a variety of different approaches which, we hope, will help you develop the skills that are essential for the successful study of literature. The additional features which you will find throughout the coursebook are as follows.

Objectives

Each chapter contains:

- a list of clear objectives; you should keep these in mind, and keep referring to them as you work through the chapter
- a clear outline of the assessment objectives for this part of the course, as well as – importantly – how they relate to the activities in the chapter; at the end of each activity you should have a clear understanding of how you will be marked for each piece of work, whether it is marked by an examiner or by your teachers.

Tips, Theory of Knowledge and Extended Essay features

- **Tips**: the tip boxes are simple, clear pieces of advice that you should find helpful and memorable.
- **TOK ideas**: Theory of Knowledge (TOK) is not only a distinct and assessed part of your course; it should also be integrated into every subject in your Diploma programme. Our TOK boxes will ask you to think about an idea as a knowledge issue, and to question its value from an informed, critical and enquiring perspective. Approaching certain texts within a TOK framework can add real depth to your understanding of the text you are studying.
- **Extended Essay ideas**: English Literature is one of the most popular subjects for the extended essay, and the Extended Essay boxes provide you with a number of possible ideas for further research. Suggestions for further reading are given; however, you should remember that much of the work for the Extended Essay is independent research: we can provide you with starting points, but the momentum must come from you, and how much you do is up to you (and in cooperation with your teacher).

Activities

One of the most important features of the book is the suggestions for activities which you will find in every chapter. The activity features are clearly marked. One of the many strengths of your course is its variety: although you are formally assessed through your writing, there are many opportunities to write and present in a number of different styles. The activities in this coursebook reflect that variety: we hope they stimulate you, challenge you, and keep you interested throughout your studies.

Each activity has clear objectives, and may also include:

- discussion points for pair and group work
- assessment opportunities which clearly explain how your work is linked to the assessment criteria.

Key terms and Glossary

Key terms are highlighted in bold green, and near by, on the same page or spread, you will find a clear definition of the key terms in the margin. You will also be able to refer to the Glossary at the end of the coursebook to check any terms you are still uncertain about.

Further resources

Further resources boxes suggest where to go for a deeper understanding of a particular feature. Because different resources suit different students, you will find suggestions for a wide range of media, including books, websites, anthologies and documentaries.

Sample student responses

Throughout the coursebook you will also find examples of sample student responses. You will be able to read real IB students' attempts at essays and assess the transcripts of their oral responses to Parts 2 and 4 of the course. We hope you will read these in conjunction with the assessment criteria for each part so that you can make your own judgements about what is successful and where these students need to improve. Some of the sample material has been marked up to show you where the response has met the criteria; others have been left blank for you to arrive at your own conclusions. We hope that this real-life material will support you in your preparations for the exams and the orals.

It is important to point out that you should always be honest in all your work. In practice, this means you mustn't plagiarise. Plagiarism is when you pass off someone else's work as your own. It happens a lot, and often because students simply don't understand what is expected. There are very serious consequences for IB students who are caught plagiarising and the software that spots cheating is becoming ever more powerful and effective: if you cheat it is likely that you will be caught. We would strongly advise you to follow this advice:

- Whenever you are using words that were said or written by someone else you must put quotation marks around them to acknowledge that they are not your own.
- If you make reference to an idea that isn't originally yours, make sure you clearly acknowledge whose idea it is and where you read or heard about it.
- Use a system for referencing you work and use it consistently and accurately.
- When you are reading and researching take careful notes so that you can always acknowledge the source of a quotation or an idea.

You should always reference your work. Think positively about all this: if you have researched a topic or an author, and you show where you have used their thoughts and ideas, then you are likely to be rewarded for doing so; furthermore, using secondary sources will inform your work, and deepen your understanding of the subject.

You are now ready to start – so dive in!

If you are at the beginning of your studies all this information may appear rather daunting. It shouldn't be. Remember: you have already started preparing for this course. You have read books you love; you have read poems that have moved you; and you have seen plays that perhaps made you laugh or cry (or both). You will have seen films and liked the plot and script, you may have recommended an article in a newspaper to a friend, discussed a piece from a favourite magazine, thought about an advertisement you saw on the side of the road, sung a song with a favourite lyric, recalled an unusual phrase that somebody might have said to you … all this experience – this exposure to words – prepares you very well for the study of this course. Use that knowledge, and the skills you already have, as you work with this book, and as you develop as students of English, and you will achieve your best.

We hope this coursebook supplements your studies in English Literature, but don't forget that it does not – and could not – replace the other invaluable work you do in other contexts – in class, at home, in a library, with your teachers, tutors, family or with your friends. The study of literature is developmental, and working with others – so that you get that interchange of ideas and emotions – is essential. We will provide you with stimulating ideas, and a new wealth of material, but you will provide the spark that makes the subject come alive.

1 Works in translation

How is this chapter structured?

This chapter follows the shape of Part 1: Works in translation. There are four quite distinct stages in this part of the course which lead up to and include the written assignment, and each tests quite different skills.

1 In the first unit, Unit 1.1, you will look at what we mean by a 'text in translation', as well as the importance of **context**. Getting the balance right in these areas can make a substantial difference to how you will be assessed.

2 Unit 1.2 looks closely at how you should prepare for Part 1 of the course, and explains in clear English what you are being asked to do and how you will be assessed. Suggestions about how to make the most of this crucial stage of your coursework are provided.

3 Unit 1.3 is an analysis of the four stages of this part of the course: the interactive oral, the reflective statement, developing a topic through supervised writing and the final essay. There is a lot to absorb here, and you will be taken through this step by step.

4 Unit 1.4 offers practical advice on how to structure the final essay for the written assignment. This lengthy essay will be one of the most demanding – but, we hope, rewarding – parts of your English Literature course and it is very important that you prepare for it appropriately. You will focus on essential skills here (including how to quote correctly). There is also feedback from examiners.

You will also be asked to consider how you should prepare for analysing texts that may be quite different – in subject matter, style and cultural content – from anything you have studied before.

Throughout the chapter you will have to consider how the assessment criteria are applied. We will also look at the issue of contextualisation (a key part of this course). However, it should be stressed that this is, first and foremost, a *literature* course, and important though historical, biographical and sociological aspects undoubtedly are,

Key term

Context The surrounding circumstances of an event or text.

they should only be used to support your understanding of the texts you are studying. We will also consider the role of the translator.

To exemplify the analyses we will use examples of actual work by students. The IB syllabus recommends that the teacher should only give feedback on the first draft of the final Part 1 essay before it is submitted for assessment, and this expectation of independent learning should be respected. Of course, you can redraft your essay as many times as you like, and indeed this process of looking at your own work objectively is another important skill you should try to develop.

Unit 1.1 What is Part 1: Works in translation?

Part 1 of the English Literature course is called 'Works in translation'. The IB Diploma is not just an international qualification, it is also a qualification with *international-mindedness* at its heart: it requires you to study literature in translation so that you enrich your appreciation of writers and the contexts they work in. In doing so you will deepen your understanding of their art and develop a more profound understanding of how human experience, although highly individualistic, has a universality which is often most effectively expressed through literature. Ultimately, and in line with the IB learner profile, it is hoped that in studying literature from other cultures you will deepen your tolerance of, empathy with and respect for those with perspectives other than your own.

TOK

In his essay, Judt goes on to write: 'If words fall into disrepair, what will substitute? They are all we have.' To what extent would you agree with Judt's statement? Is there anything beyond language? Are our identities wholly defined by the words we use? Are words all we have?

A note on translated texts

The historian Tony Judt once described the use of language as 'translating being into thought, thought into words and words into communication'. It is a complex process that we all use, and it could be argued that writers are more skilled at it than most. But what happens to that process when a text is translated? How does that process change? Does the writer become more distant from the reader? Is the original meaning of the text lost, or diluted?

Consider, for example, these opening sentences from one of the most popular text choices in Part 1: Franz Kafka's *The Metamorphosis.* Here it is in its original German:

> Als Gregor Samsa eines Morgens aus unruhigen Träumen erwachte, fand er sich in seinem Bett zu einem ungeheuren Ungeziefer verwandelt.

And here is a literal translation:

> As Gregor Samsa one morning from restless dreams awoke, found he himself in his bed into an enormous vermin transformed.

And here are four alternative translations:
1   As Gregor Samsa awoke one morning from uneasy dreams he found himself transformed in his bed into a gigantic insect.
2   Gregory Samsa woke from uneasy dreams one morning to find himself changed into a giant bug.
3   One morning, upon awakening from agitated dreams, Gregor Samsa found himself, in his bed, transformed into a monstrous vermin.
4   When Gregor Samsa awoke from troubled dreams one morning he found that he had been transformed in his bed into an enormous bug.

We can see that each sentence is different, but that the writer's *sense* – his main intention – is preserved. But consider the following questions:

- Which translation is the most memorable, or vivid?
- Which is the weakest (and why)?
- Is the literal translation closest to Kafka's voice?
- What is lost in this version, and what is gained?
- In the other examples, are you reading the translator's words, or Kafka's?

Such questions seem extremely difficult to answer and although you should be aware of many of the issues surrounding translated texts, it is advisable to focus almost entirely on the words in that translation. Each of the tasks you are set – and this includes the final Part 1 essay – should be concerned with the translated text as the *primary* literary text.

Let us return to Kafka: by considering the different translations of a particularly emotive word ('insect', 'bug', 'vermin') a student is able to explore very subtle – but important – differences of meaning which influence our understanding of not only the character of Gregor Samsa, but also how other characters respond to him (which in turn affects our interpretation of these characters). If his family views him as 'vermin' then that is quite different from the more neutral 'insect' and the even less threatening 'bug'. As you can see, considering such word choices – and showing an awareness of the translator's craft – can be effective. And these word choices, despite being those of the translator, have to be seen as the author's choice.

Text and context

To get the most out of Part 1 of the course you will have to keep everything in balance: if you concentrate too much on just one aspect of this part you risk neglecting key areas which contribute to your final piece of work: the essay for the written assignment It would be a mistake to spend too much time focusing on producing this if it meant that you neglected the interactive orals. each step is important. But, as we have seen, it would also be a mistake to concentrate on linguistic issues such as translation at the cost of the work you are studying: focus on the words in front of you, but be aware of some of the issues behind certain word choices.

The same goes for context. Your final essay for the written assignment should be a strong literary analysis, but that there should also be an implicit sense of the context of the works studied. That word *implicit* – is important: your essay should show an understanding of the conditions that influence a work, and you have to show the examiner that you know a text cannot be written or read in isolation, removed from the world the writer or the reader lives in. The IB syllabus states that:

'This part of the course is a literary study of works in translation, based on close reading of the *works themselves*. Students are encouraged to appreciate the different perspectives of people from other cultures and to consider the role that culture plays in making sense of literary works.

Part 1 of the course aims to deepen the students' understanding of works as being products of a time and place. Artistic, philosophical, sociological, historical and biographical considerations are possible areas of study to *enhance* understanding of the works.' [our italics]

In other words, unless the context extends your analysis and understanding of the work then, at best, it won't gain you any marks, and if you spend too long on the work's background it may, at worst, lose you marks.

Extended essay

The Russian critic Viktor Shklovsky has written that 'the purpose of art is to impart the sensation of things as they are perceived and not as they are known … Art is a way of experiencing the artfulness of an object; the object is not important.' In other words it is the writer's job to make the object secondary to the sensation of experiencing that object, and writers – such as Kafka – do this through **defamiliarisation**. You could research this area of literary aesthetics in an extended essay.

TOK

The three-way relationship between writer, translator and reader is a complex one. Students of TOK may wish to do their presentations on this area: the knowledge issue is very clear – to what extent is the translator the 'author' of the work?

Key terms

Literal Language that is used and interpreted in its primary meaning.

Character A 'person' in a play, novel or poem.

Linguistic Of or belonging to language.

Biography/biographical An account of a life written by someone else.

Defamiliarisation A process in which a writer can make a reader perceive something in a new way, sometimes making them feel uncomfortable.

> **Key term**
>
> **Theme** In literature an idea that is explored and developed by the writer; for example, a theme in *Macbeth* is ambition.

There are many ways in which an understanding of a wider context can deepen and enrich your understanding of a literary text. You could, for example, happily read and discuss Stendhal's *Scarlet and Black* without a knowledge of 19th century France, but the events in the novel would resonate much more if you did have an understanding of these events; similarly, you could argue that you can only appreciate Lorca if you are familiar with Spanish society at the beginning of the 20th century, or that Brecht only makes sense if you know about German and Marxist politics, or that Murakami's themes only really make sense if you have an insight into modern Japanese society. These are all no doubt true. But you also have to be realistic: this is a literature course, and you have a limited period of time to study often challenging texts. Be selective in your use of context, and ask your teacher for guidance. You should be aware that there are writers who lend themselves more to a political or biographical reading than others.

Let's look at one such example.

Figure 1.1 The Russian writer Fydor Dostoyevsky (1821–1881).

Fydor Dostoyevsky

The Russian writer Fydor Dostoyevsky was imprisoned in Siberia in 1849 for belonging to a group of political dissidents. He was sentenced to death. After a mock execution he was sent for four years of hard labour in exile. When he was released from prison his view of life had changed, both politically and spiritually (he gained a profound Christian faith). Such changes he viewed positively, and he wrote about them in various novels. He began to value instinctive thought as well as intellectual arguments, and promoted traditional values over those which he perceived as 'Western' and corrosive. His most famous novel, *Crime and Punishment*, was published in 1866. It tells the story of Raskolnikov, a young man who rejects the society he lives in and murders two women in a symbolic gesture of rebellion against it. He, like the book's author, is sentenced to imprisonment, and he too finds redemption, through both his love of Sonia (a woman saved from prostitution by her faith) and God.

Now read this passage:

> On the evening of the same day, when the barracks were locked, Raskolnikov lay on his plank bed and thought of her. He had even fancied that day that all the convicts who had been his enemies looked at him differently; he had even entered into talk with them and they answered him in a friendly way. He remembered that now, and thought it was bound to be so. Wasn't everything now bound to be changed?
>
> He thought of her. He remembered how continually he had tormented her and wounded her heart. He remembered her pale and thin little face. But these recollections scarcely troubled him now; he knew with what infinite love he would now repay all her sufferings. And what were all the agonies of the past! Everything, even his crime, his sentence and imprisonment, seemed to him now in the first rush of feeling an external, strange fact with which he had no concern. But he could not think for long together of anything that evening, and he could not have analysed anything consciously; he was simply feeling. Life had stepped into the place of theory and something quite different would work itself out in his mind.
>
> Under his pillow lay the New Testament. He took it up mechanically. The book belonged to Sonia; it was the one from which she had read the raising of

Lazarus to him. At first he was afraid that she would worry him about religion, would talk about the gospel and pester him with books. But to his great surprise she had not once approached the subject and had not even offered him the Testament. He had asked her for it himself not long before his illness and she brought him the book without a word. Till now he had not opened it.

It is clear that if you were studying this text, then an understanding of the author's life would be invaluable: linking Dostoyevsky's life with his art is a valid process for a student; but if that life begins to obscure the literature itself, then it stops being an essay of literary analysis. If you were to use this passage as a key extract for your final essay, you would use what you know of the author's life to inform your argument, but the focus would still be on the development of character and the themes of love, spiritual awakening and transformation, and you would look closely at the language used – the imagery employed – as well as the biblical allusions which are clearly linked to Raskolnikov's 'resurrection' to further your points. The text remains central, and the life and other contexts should be used to enhance our understanding of the work.

Unit 1.2 **How and what will you study for Part 1?**

Part 1 of the course could be characterised by the *differences* in context and perspective you are expected to explore. Here you are exposed to writers from outside your culture, and you are encouraged to read texts written originally in a language other than the language of instruction (in this case, English). All the writers you study for Part 1 must come from the prescribed literature in translation (PLT) list.
- In Part 1 SL students study *two* works; HL students study *three* works.
- You can study texts from a variety of different languages.
- You can study texts from the same genre or different genres.
- Place is roughly defined as a geocultural region, such as a province, country or continent.

The advantage of studying works from the same genre is that you gain a more secure understanding of that genre's conventions. However, you or your teacher may wish to widen your knowledge base by choosing texts from different genres. Remember that you have to talk about all the texts you have studied, but your written assignment is on only *one* of those texts.

How is Part 1 assessed?

At both SL and HL the assessment of Part 1 counts for 25% of your total marks for English Literature. The marks for the written assignment are distributed as follows (you can find a more detailed explanation of these criteria in the Introduction on page xii):

Criterion A	Fulfilling the requirements of the reflective statement	3 marks
Criterion B	Knowledge and understanding	6 marks
Criterion C	Appreciation of the writer's choices	6 marks
Criterion D	Organisation and development	5 marks
Criterion E	Language	5 marks
Total		25 marks

Key term

Argument There are several definitions of *argument*: in literature it can mean the summary of a plot; in literary criticism it means a position taken by the writer.

Read as much about other cultures and traditions as you can, and try to understand – and question – the ideas behind the issues. Question too your own preconceptions about the cultures you are reading about. Read writers who come from cultures about which you have no previous knowledge. You don't have to read just novels: poems, short stories or even articles from trusted and reputable websites or newspapers can widen your understanding of the world around you and prepare you for the pronounced international flavour of this course.

Students, as well as teachers, should have access to the prescribed literature in translation list, provided by the IB, so that you are completely confident that the authors you are studying have been approved.

There are four stages to the assessment for Part 1 of the course (a more detailed analysis of this structure is given in Unit 1.3).

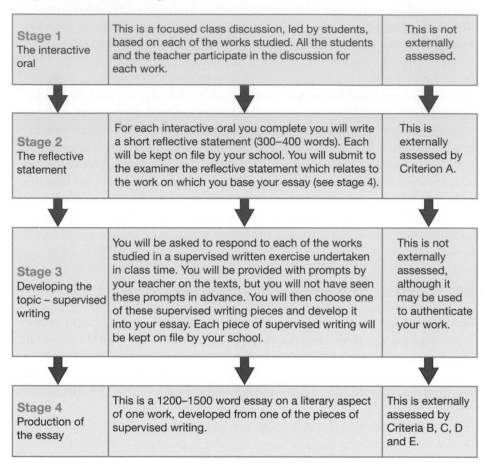

Stage 1 The interactive oral	This is a focused class discussion, led by students, based on each of the works studied. All the students and the teacher participate in the discussion for each work.	This is not externally assessed.
Stage 2 The reflective statement	For each interactive oral you complete you will write a short reflective statement (300–400 words). Each will be kept on file by your school. You will submit to the examiner the reflective statement which relates to the work on which you base your essay (see stage 4).	This is externally assessed by Criterion A.
Stage 3 Developing the topic – supervised writing	You will be asked to respond to each of the works studied in a supervised written exercise undertaken in class time. You will be provided with prompts by your teacher on the texts, but you will not have seen these prompts in advance. You will then choose one of these supervised writing pieces and develop it into your essay. Each piece of supervised writing will be kept on file by your school.	This is not externally assessed, although it may be used to authenticate your work.
Stage 4 Production of the essay	This is a 1200–1500 word essay on a literary aspect of one work, developed from one of the pieces of supervised writing.	This is externally assessed by Criteria B, C, D and E.

Figure 1.2 Your essay is likely to evolve over several different stages.

As you can see, the aim is for you to engage with each text you are studying, and to move from a wide and collaboratively understood exploration towards an increasingly focused and individual analysis of a particular aspect of one work. The interactive orals you do in lessons should allow you to explore a number of areas that have interested you in class, and the short, reflective statements provide you with an opportunity to articulate your thoughts still further, but this time on paper. One of the supervised writing pieces will form the basis of your essay for assessment, and this sustained piece of analysis, along with the reflective statement, completes your assessed work in Part 1. This progressive structure allows you, your teacher and the examiner an opportunity to see how your responses to texts develop over time, moving from the general to the specific.

How should I prepare for Part 1?

This part of the course is diverse in content, structure and assessment. It will challenge you, not only in what you think about other cultures and traditions, but also in how you work. In some respect it a micro-course in itself, condensing a wide range of approaches into a small number of teaching weeks (the IB syllabus states that SL students should have 40 hours of teaching on this part of the course, and HL students should have 65). There is an emphasis on independent learning, with the most important work being done, unsupervised, by you, but with guidance from your teacher.

Be organised

As this course moves from the general to the specific it really is important that you do not discard any ideas or notes which may help you in your final essay for the written assignment. Might that comment a classmate made about transcendence in a novel by Gabriel García Márquez be useful later on? It could be, so don't ignore it. From the very first lesson you have on your Part 1 texts you should take notes, and use every opportunity to speak as practice for the interactive orals. Develop your note-taking skills, and your speaking and listening skills.

Be open-minded

In the IB's mission statement, 'intercultural understanding and respect' are placed at the forefront of its aims, and it also states that a main objective of the IB's mission is to encourage students to realise that 'other people, with their differences, can also be right'. This is not to say that we should not judge others, or that there are no moral absolutes but only moral **relativism**; it means that it often pays to listen to others and, importantly, to understand their contexts and backgrounds before condemning their actions. Harper Lee, the author of *To Kill a Mockingbird*, puts it more vividly when she writes that 'you never really understand a person until you consider things from his point of view – until you climb into his skin and walk around in it', which is both admirable and aspirational. You cannot hope to empathise with each character or writer you read about, or every person you meet, but that movement away from the self is inherently healthy.

Open-mindedness will benefit you at a more 'local' level as well. listen to your classmates (and your teacher of course), and you will be listened to in turn. Ask questions and evaluate the answers you hear before questioning their validity. And as you absorb their thoughts, and listen to your own developing ideas, you will learn and grow as a student.

Unit 1.3 **The four stages: a step-by-step guide**

The IB syllabus states that in Part 1 of the course teachers should aim to develop the student's ability to:
* understand the content of the work and the qualities of the work as literature
* recognise the role played by context and **conventions** in literary works
* respond independently to the works studied by connecting the individual and cultural experience of the reader with the text.

The ultimate aim of Part 1 is to produce a well-informed essay, but a closely linked aim is to study each text carefully, and each step of this part of the course contributes to that written assignment. To ensure that your understanding of technique and context is as secure as it can be, you are set a number of different tasks; if you prepare yourself properly you will both enjoy them and gain a great deal from completing them. Once you have studied your texts, the first stage of the four-step process is the interactive oral.

Stage 1: The interactive oral

What is the interactive oral?
* It is a class discussion led by students in which all the students and the teacher participate.
* SL students will discuss their two texts, and HL students will discuss their three texts.
* A minimum time required for discussion is 30 minutes for each work, but class sizes may mean that this is adjusted so that each student is given an active role.

Key terms

Relativism A belief that morality and knowledge (among other contentious areas) are dependent on the value system they originate from and function within.

Quotation An extract from a text used in another text.

Convention An accepted format, structure, mode, style or behaviour.

tip

You will see that the **quotations** given here are embedded. This is an important skill to try to develop, and although it can take time, it is worth practising it at every opportunity. It should be possible to take away the quotation marks without altering the 'flow' or sense of your sentence.

- Remember, there is an expectation for every student to *initiate* an aspect of the discussion in at least one interactive oral.
- It is not recorded.

Although there is considerable room for spontaneous and informed discussion, all students should address the key cultural and contextual considerations. In this sense each interactive oral is perhaps a more structured and targeted everyday class discussion.

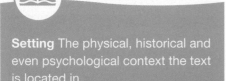

Key terms

Setting The physical, historical and even psychological context the text is located in.

Characterisation The process by which an author creates a character's distinctive qualities.

Plot What happens in the narrative.

The questions	Some questions to think about and use in the interactive oral
1 In what ways do time and place matter in this work?	• To what extent does the period, and the setting, affect our understanding of the work? • Are the characters' actions, their language, and the ideas that the writer explores through them principally shaped by the time they were written in? • Is this different from the period the work is set in? • To what extent does the work's location shape the characters' actions as well as our understanding of the work itself? • Does the writer describe something that is localised, both in time and place, or is there a greater universality in what he or she is describing?
2 What was easy to understand and what was difficult in relation to the social and cultural context and issues?	• What were the major challenges you found in trying to understand works of literature which were outside your usual cultural and social experiences? • Did these differences surprise you? What did you find relatively easy to grasp? Why?
3 What connections did you find between issues in the work and your own culture and experience?	• What similarities did you discover between your own social and cultural context and the work you have been studying? • How could you explain these? Were these connections specific to a particular perspective or idea, or were they more universal in scope?
4 What aspects of technique are interesting in the work?	• What is it about the writer's style that has caught your attention? Is it the subject matter? The way that language is used? The characterisation or plot? The skills you have developed in other areas of the course will help you here.

These are both broad and exacting questions, but as you know them in advance you should be able to plan some good responses. Remember, though, that this is an *interactive* oral, which means that you listen and contribute to the whole discussion: you should not read from a prepared script or expect to give a presentation to class.

You could reduce these key questions down to a more manageable form: by doing so you can keep them in mind as you read any text from a culture and tradition that is not immediately familiar:

1 Time and place
2 Easy and difficult
3 Connections
4 Technique

Or think about it as a simple mnemonic: TECT.

Let's try to apply this to Kafka's *The Metamorphosis.* Read the following three extracts from this novella and then do the activities that follow.

Time and place: early in the morning, domestic setting. A new dawn, a new beginning. The seemingly innocent opening is in stark contrast to what is to come.

Easy and difficult: in itself this is very easy to picture – a large vermin lying on the bed – but it is initially difficult to understand as well because it is so unusual.

Text 1.1 Extracts from *The Metamorphosis*, Franz Kafka, 1915

Opening paragraph, Chapter 1

One morning,[1] when Gregor Samsa woke from troubled dreams, he found himself transformed in his bed into a horrible vermin.[2] He lay on his armour-like back, and if he lifted his head a little he could see his brown belly, slightly domed and divided by arches into stiff sections.[3] The bedding was hardly able to cover it and seemed ready to slide off any moment.[4] His many legs, pitifully thin compared with the size of the rest of him, waved about helplessly as he looked.

Second paragraph, Chapter 1

'What's happened to me?' he thought. It wasn't a dream. His room, a proper human room although a little too small, lay peacefully between its four familiar walls. A collection of textile samples lay spread out on the table – Samsa was a travelling salesman – and above it there hung a picture that he had recently cut out of an illustrated magazine and housed in a nice, gilded frame. It showed a lady fitted out with a fur hat and fur boa who sat upright, raising a heavy fur muff that covered the whole of her lower arm towards the viewer.

Opening paragraph, Chapter 2

It was not until it was getting dark that evening that Gregor awoke from his deep and coma-like sleep. He would have woken soon afterwards anyway even if he hadn't been disturbed, as he had had enough sleep and felt fully rested. But he had the impression that some hurried steps and the sound of the door leading into the front room being carefully shut had woken him. The light from the electric street lamps shone palely here and there onto the ceiling and tops of the furniture, but down below, where Gregor was, it was dark. He pushed himself over to the door, feeling his way clumsily with his antennae – of which he was now beginning to learn the value – in order to see what had been happening there. The whole of his left side seemed like one, painfully stretched scar, and he limped badly on his two rows of legs. One of the legs had been badly injured in the events of that morning – it was nearly a miracle that only one of them had been – and dragged along lifelessly.

Figure 1.3 *The Metamorphosis*, directed by Derek Goldman, Synetic Theater, USA, 2010.

Technique: this long, descriptive sentence adopts a very matter-of-fact tone; in doing so it defamiliarises the character, and the action, even more from the reader.

Connections: strange though the passage is, it is referencing an ordinary scene, and one that we can all empathise with: we have all woken up in the morning feeling disoriented, with the blanket about to slide to the floor.

tip

You might find your meaning becomes clearer if you consult the Glossary at the back of the book. In particular look at the definitions for the following literary terms and see if you can use them here: **rhetorical question**, **simple sentence**, **complex sentence**, **tone**, and characterisation.

Key terms

Rhetorical question A question that is framed for effect, not necessarily for an answer.

Simple sentence A sentence that contains only one independent clause.

Complex sentence A sentence that contains two or more clauses.

Tone The emotional aspect of the voice of a text (for example, friendly, cold, intimate).

Paragraph A section of a piece of writing that is often concerned with one theme or key point.

Alienated/alienation The condition of being isolated from other people or a place; being removed from society.

Transfiguration The changing from one form to another.

Fable From the Latin word for 'discourse, a story'; a short story in poetry or prose that has a strong moral message.

Conclusion The final part of a process; in an essay it usually contains a 'summing up' of the arguments.

Discussion

Discuss with another student whether Gregor has really changed into a vermin. Obviously this is impossible, and if we begin to follow this line of argument we end up asking ourselves as critics what Kafka really means. Is this just a **fable**, a story that illuminates another, deeper, moral truth about the human condition?

Activity 1.1

1 Read the mark ups for the first paragraph of *The Metamorphosis* in Text 1.1 and think about how an interpretation has begun to be formed from this initial process. Ask yourself the following questions:
   - How helpful has the TECT mnemonic been here (see page 8)? Did you find it helped you structure your response?
   - What role has context played in adding to your understanding of the text?
   - Do you have a better understanding of Kafka's technique after analysing this text in this way?

2 Now try to apply the same structured marking-up process to the second paragraph (your teacher may be able to provide you with a clean copy of the passage which you will be able to mark up), asking the same short questions: look for differences and connections, and think about the writer's technique as well as the time and place explored in the text.

3 By the beginning of the second chapter Gregor's family are turning against him as they feel increasingly alienated by their son's alarming transformation; at the end of the previous chapter Gregor's father has locked him in his bedroom. Again, your teacher may be able to provide you with a copy of the passage.

   Complete this activity either with another classmate or in a group.
   - Read the opening paragraph of Chapter 2 of *The Metamorphosis* (Text 1.1) twice.
   - Mark it up using the four-point mnemonic.
   - In addition to thinking of some answers to the four questions, jot down some questions you could ask your classmate(s). Once you have all done this, initiate a really meaningful discussion amongst yourselves.
   - Listen to your classmates' answers carefully, and try to write down some brief follow-up questions (for example: 'Why do you think Kafka does this?', 'What is the main theme being explored here?' and so on).

There are obvious parallels between the first paragraphs of Chapters 1 and 2 of Text 1.1: both have domestic settings, and both, initially at least, seem to describe an everyday scene. But a key word – 'antennae' – alerts us to the unreality of what is being described, just as 'vermin' did in the very first paragraph of the novel. Kafka then goes on to describe the rows of legs, which further emphasises the transfiguration Gregor has undergone.

You can practise very short, interactive orals with your classmates with any text, translated or not, and in doing so you will develop critical reading skills – as well as speaking and listening skills – which are invaluable in this part of the course. We would advise that in order to prepare for Part 1 you choose texts that are outside your usual cultural and social contexts, and these very often include texts in translation.

Text 1.2 is another opening to a well-known text. For this activity we are not going to tell you anything about the text, its context or any other background information. Focus instead on the language: analyse the writer's technique, the imagery used, the tone of voice employed and the detail revealed, as well as the historical references.

Text 1.2

On August 16, 1968, I was handed a book written by a certain Abbé Vallet, *Le Manuscrit de Dom Adson de Melk, traduit en français d'après l'édition de Dom J. Mabillon* (Aux Presses de l'Abbaye de la Source, Paris 1842). Supplemented by historical information that was actually quite scant, the book claimed to reproduce faithfully a fourteenth-century manuscript that, in its turn, had been found in the monastery of Melk by the great eighteenth-century man of learning, to whom we owe so much information about the history of the Benedictine order. The scholarly discovery (I mean mine, the third in chronological order) entertained me while I was in Prague, waiting for a dear friend. Six days later Soviet troops invaded that unhappy city. I managed, not without adventure, to reach the Austrian border at Linz, and from there I journeyed to Vienna, where I met my beloved, and together we sailed up the Danube.

Activity 1.2

1   Once you have written some notes on the language used in Text 1.2, begin to widen your analysis, keeping in mind the four guiding questions we have already discussed (the TECT questions):
    • Time & place
    • Easy & difficult
    • Connections
    • Technique
2   Now try to write one question relating to this text for every member of your class, including your teacher; if your class is quite large write one question for each pair of students. You don't need to provide the answers to the questions: the aim is to *initiate* a stimulating conversation. With your teacher's agreement you could chair the debate, listening to every question and prompting fellow classmates to respond.

We have looked at several very different openings, but now let's consider the **conclusion** of *The Unbearable Lightness of Being* by Milan Kundera, originally published in Czech in 1985.

Text 1.3 *The Unbearable Lightness of Being*, Milan Kundera, 1984

On they danced to the strains of the piano and violin. Tereza leaned her head on Tomas's shoulder. Just as she had when they flew together in the airplane through the storm clouds. She was experiencing the same odd happiness and odd sadness as then. The sadness meant: we are at the last station. The happiness meant: we are together. The sadness was form, the happiness content. Happiness filled the space of sadness.

tip

If you are doing any of these activities on your own then record yourself talking about the passage and play it back later on. Try to be objective about your delivery. Did you hesitate too much? Did you say 'um', 'er' or other linguistic fillers? Does the tone of your voice remain the same throughout? How could you vary it so that it sounds more interested and more interesting? Many people do not like listening to themselves, but try to get over this reluctance. Put bluntly: are *you* interested in what you say? If not, how do you change that?

Extended essay

EE

Modernism was a movement in art which began in response to the destruction of World War One. Kafka was among many writers and artists – including T.S. Eliot, Ezra Pound, James Joyce, George Grosz, Arnold Schoenberg – who re-interpreted the world for their audiences, often using alarming imagery which showed how society had become dislocated. Although it would be a misrepresentation to say these artists shared a coherent world view, it is fair to say that they all interpreted man's role in the world as having been profoundly altered by the conflict. There are a great number of resources, published online and in books and journals, on Modernism being a response to the war, and students of Visual Art, History and English Literature might find it an interesting area to research.

tip

You might find it helpful to consult the Glossary at the back of the book. In particular, think about how this author's tone is affected by the use of the **first person narrative**, and how this in turn influences the characterisation.

They went back to their table. She danced twice more with the collective farm chairman and once with the young man, who was so drunk he fell with her on the dance floor.

Then they all went upstairs and to their two separate rooms.

Tomas turned the key and switched on the ceiling light. Tereza saw two beds pushed together, one of them flanked by a bedside table and lamp. Up out of the lampshade, startled by the overhead light, flew a large nocturnal butterfly that began circling the room. The strains of the piano and violin rose up weakly from below.

Figure 1.4 A still from the 1988 film adaptation of *The Unbearable Lightness of Being*, directed by Philip Kaufman.

tip

Remember that the *minimum* time for discussion for each work is 30 minutes, but this does not have to be completed in one session. When you begin to practise interactive orals, both with classmates outside lesson time as well as with students and your teacher in class, try to build on the time you are able to spend discussing the text in relation to the four guiding questions. In doing so you will not only prepare yourself for the next stage of Part 1, but you will also develop skills essential for Parts 2 and 4 of the English Literature course.

Activity 1.3

Remember that developing your ability to discuss literature with others is an important part of the English Literature course. Take some time now to discuss this passage with another student. Here are some questions you could ask each other:

1   How important is the setting here? Are there any suggestions about where the text is located? How does it contribute to our understanding of the text? What about time? Are there any clues that locate it within a particular historical period? It seems to be set in a dance hall or hotel: does that affect the characters' behaviour?

2   What did you find easy to understand and what did you find that was more difficult? Was it the action, or was it something more abstract, such as the themes which are developed at the end of the first paragraph?

3   What connections can you make between your own experiences and the context of this text? What links are there between your own culture and experience and those described in this text? A personal response is favoured here.

4   What did you find particularly memorable about the writer's technique? Did you find the descriptions vivid? Is the characterisation clear? What about the use of symbolism in the final paragraph: how do you think this might tie in with the lives of the characters, and perhaps with life itself?

There are many other questions you could ask. Again, try to use short follow-up questions with your classmates if you do this short exercise with them.

Stage 2: The reflective statement

What is the reflective statement?

- The reflective statement is a short piece of writing of between 300 and 400 words. It is assessed using Criterion A (Fulfilling the requirements of the reflective statement).
- Although this is assessed, the reflective statement can be done outside class time.
- It can be revised before it is submitted to the IB examiner.

You will be asked to reflect on every interactive oral you complete; this is called the reflective statement. The only reflective statement that goes forward to the examiner is the one that has *relevance* to your final essay for the written assignment. The reasoning behind this is that the IB examiner wants to see how the final essay has evolved, and to what extent you have followed the four steps of Part 1 of the course.

Like the interactive oral, there is a lot of scope for personal expression in the reflective statement, but also like the interactive oral, questions will be provided that will help you structure your response. Examples of the types of guiding question you might receive are given below, along with some points you might consider when planning your reflective statement.

	The questions	Some points to think about for your reflective statement	Optional or required?
1	What elements of the role played by context were illuminated or developed by you?	To what extent did you *understand* the different contexts (biographical, social, historical, artistic) which helped shape the work? How satisfactorily did you articulate these in the interactive oral? Think about the 'what' and the 'when'. To what extent did you *interpret* these different contexts? Think about the 'why' and the 'how'.	Required
2	What aspects of the discussion most interested you?	A personal response is required here, what stimulated you most of all, and why? Relate your points to the work under discussion; make the connections between your experiences and those explored in the text relevant and appropriate.	Optional
3	What new angles on the work did the discussion provoke for you?	These new angles could come from your classmates (remember, it is 'interactive' and you should show how you are learning from others) as well as yourself. Again, keep the text at the centre of your writing here.	Optional

How does the reflective statement work in practice?

Perhaps the best way to explain how this works in practice is to look at some student samples. Alex is an SL student who studied the following texts for Part 1 of the course:

Henrik Ibsen   *A Doll's House*
Anton Chekhov   *Three Sisters*

After Alex's class had studied both texts over a number of weeks the teacher felt it appropriate to prepare them for their first interactive oral. The focus was on *A Doll's House*. This play, written in 1879, was originally written in Norwegian. It tells the story of a stultifying marriage: the husband, Torvald, infantilises his wife Nora until, unable to live so restrictively, she decides to leave him and their children and establish a new life alone. When it was first performed it caused uproar: it was seen as radically subversive,

Key terms

First person narrative The use of a character as the narrator of a story, which provides a fixed perspective.

Figurative language A story told from the perspective of its teller. The narrative will often use language that uses imagery and is not literal.

Juxtaposition The placing of several things close together; in literature done deliberately for contrast and purpose.

Symbolism The representing of things using symbols.

For any interactive oral the primary focus is on the analysis of literature, but you are also looking for cultural differences and similarities, and your response to these has to be rooted in the personal experience you have gained from your own cultural and social contexts. It is perfectly acceptable to respond here in the first person ('I', 'for me', and so on). You can only respond strongly to literature if it speaks directly to you. Don't ignore that vital connection. Equally, don't ignore differences: engage with these and articulate why and how they are different from your own views.

championing women's rights and rejecting accepted or 'conventional' (and patriarchal) social norms.

The class had been reminded of the four guiding questions (remember, TECT) in a previous lesson and, overall, the teacher felt that the students performed well in their first interactive oral. The students were then asked to write a reflective statement on this interactive oral for homework. The teacher also reminded them that although only one of the three guiding questions was required, they might find the optional questions useful too. This is Alex's first draft:

My first interactive oral was on Henrik Ibsen's *A Doll's House*. The play is one of the most powerful pieces of literature I have ever read, and I hope that my interest in it – and the themes Ibsen explores – were clearly conveyed to the group. Much of the discussion focused on the importance of context in understanding the power of Ibsen's ideas, and it would be impossible to really appreciate the full implications of Nora's final actions if we did not understand the society the play was written and performed in. Norway (and indeed Western Europe) in the late 19th century was a deeply conservative and patriarchal society; although it is a generalisation, middle class women like Nora were not expected to work. Instead, their role was to look after the children and attend to their husbands.

I argued that Ibsen's presentation of Nora was more radical than a simple rejection of the 'stay-at-home mother': in fact, what Nora rejects is still difficult to accept in many cultures: for a man to leave his wife *and* children is not unusual, but for a woman to do so is seen by many as immoral and unnatural. Understanding this position goes some way to explaining why it caused such a scandal when it was first performed (and why Ibsen was forced to change the ending for the German audience).

I found the ideas that other classmates contributed very stimulating although I did not agree with them all: other students judged Nora's actions less sympathetically than me, and argued that Ibsen did not necessarily intend us to unequivocally favour Nora's actions, despite Torvald's behaviour. Others felt the characterisation was weak, or inconsistent, and that the transformation of Nora to an early, radical feminist was unconvincing. I could sympathise with the latter point because if we compare her to the Nora of Act I there is little similarity; but I could not agree that Ibsen was not clear about how we should view her actions. It is clear that Ibsen did intend us to sympathise with Nora (and indeed for many women in the audience to empathise with her), and to think otherwise shows an unwillingness to accept the subversiveness of his message. It led to a stimulating discussion which, I hope, will inform my later written work.

383 words

This is a good reflective statement: it shows a strong, personal response to the text, and although the opinions Alex holds about Ibsen's ideas and characters are firm, it is clear that he has listened and engaged with his classmates about certain differences of interpretation. It is also evident that Alex has a good contextual understanding of the play, but this does not get in the way of the text itself. Importantly, there are strands of thought in here which could be developed in Stage 3 of Part 1 (Developing the topic – supervised writing), and Alex is aware of this potential.

Let's look at another reflective statement from the same class. Katja was involved in the same interactive oral as Alex, and this is her reflective statement:

I don't think I did very well in this interactive oral. I don't really understand the play, and to be honest I didn't feel confident enough to make many contributions. I was probably the quietest member of the class, but others did dominate and didn't allow me to speak very much. The teacher asked me if I thought that the context of the play was important, and I said it was because without understanding when the play was written we couldn't really understand what the writer meant to say. I know that Nora is seen as a heroine for many women, and that Torvald, her husband, is guilty of imprisoning her. I'm not sure about this though: if Nora is such a strong character why does she allow Torvald to treat her like this to begin with? It doesn't make sense. Also, when she leaves her children, isn't she guilty of the same sort of selfishness that she accuses Torvald of throughout the play? The point I made, when I was allowed to speak, was that Nora is selfish and manipulative throughout the play, and her final action – leaving her family – is not a surprise because it is in character with everything else she does. I'm not sure if we're expected to agree with her action, but there were many in the class who argued that we were, and they made some good points. Overall, as I say, I think I could have done better in this interactive oral; hopefully, in the next one I will be better prepared and will be allowed to speak more.

265 words

How would you rate this reflective statement? Is it weaker than Alex's? If so, why? Try to be clear and honest but not unduly harsh about your evaluation. Look at the three guiding questions: are they all answered? How well did Katja do in exploring the role of context in the play? What are the strengths of this statement?

Reflective statements such as Katja's are not uncommon. It should be noted that there are some strong points here which could, with some work and encouragement, be developed in the final essay for the written assignment: Katja's interpretation of Nora as being essentially manipulative and selfish, rather than a heroine, deserves further work because it is a valid and intelligent point to make. But she has not reflected enough on this before writing down her thoughts.

Text 1.4 *No, I'm not afraid*, Irina Ratushinskaya, 1984

This poem was originally written in Russian. In 1983 Ratushinskaya was imprisoned for seven years in the Soviet 'strict regime' labour camp at Barashevo for distributing her poetry. There, she was beaten frequently, starved, force fed, and kept in solitary confinement. After a worldwide campaign she was released after three years. This poem was written one year into her sentence.

Look at your classmate's work and encourage them to look at yours. Know the assessment criteria and the guiding questions. Begin to think like a teacher or an examiner: in doing so you will begin to gain a vital objectivity about your work which will, in turn, make your reflective statements easier to write and your work, overall, more mature.

Remember, the IB syllabus stresses the need for students to use their initiative. Understandable though it is that some students are more reticent than others, it is important that you make your ideas heard in these orals. You should be proactive rather than reactive: make clear your position. Katja's tone here is defensive: she seems to be blaming others for not allowing her to talk. The onus is on you to assert yourself, as well as to listen to what others say. Don't always rely on your teacher to bring you into the discussion.

Figure 1.5 A Soviet labour camp.

tip

You may find that your analysis benefits from using specific literary terms: in this way you are able to get a better understanding of the writer's technique. Using the Glossary at the back of this book, see if you can find where Ratushinskaya uses the following devices: first person narrative, **enjambement**, **end-stopped line**, **verse**, **metaphor**, **simile**, **ellipsis**, **rhythm**.

No, I'm not afraid: after a year
Of breathing these prison nights
I will survive into the sadness
To name which is escape.

The cockerel will weep freedom for me
And here – knee-deep in mire –
My gardens shed their water
And the northern air blows in draughts.

And how am I to carry to an alien planet
What are almost tears, as though towards home...
It isn't true, I *am* afraid, my darling!
But make it look as though you haven't noticed.

Key terms

Enjambement A term used in poetry for when the sense of a line carries on to the line – or verse – that follows.

End-stopped line A term used in poetry for when the sense and metre of a line coincide with a full stop or pause at the end of the line.

Verse This can be a general term for poetry, or it can be used as another word for a stanza.

Metaphor From the Greek word for carrying from one place to another; a figure of speech in which something is said to be something else.

Simile A figure of speech which frequently uses *like* or *as* to compare one thing to another.

Ellipsis The omission of a word or words from a sentence in order to aid clarity through compression.

Rhythm From the Greek word for 'flowing'; the metrical patterns in prose and poetry.

Stanza An organised grouping of a number of lines in poetry.

Activity 1.4

In pairs or groups, read the poem *No, I'm not afraid* by Irina Ratushinskaya. Try to do a condensed interactive oral and reflective statement based on this poem.

Some questions for the interactive oral:
1   In what ways do time and place matter in this work?
2   What was easy to understand and what was difficult in relation to the social and cultural context and issues?
3   What connections did you find between issues in the work and your own culture and experience?
4   What aspects of technique are interesting in the work?

Some questions for the reflective statement:
1   To what extent does understanding the context of this poem help you understand its meaning?
2   How does the poet convey the importance of the setting in this poem? Give examples.
3   Comment on the use of contrasting imagery in the second stanza: how does this shape your understanding of the poem?
4   What did you most strongly respond to in this poem?
5   What new angles and insights did others provide in the oral?

Stage 3: Developing the topic – supervised writing

What is supervised writing?
* As well as responding orally to each work studied and writing a reflective statement, you will also have to write an essay in class time on each work. These essays are known as the 'supervised writing'. They will be completed under exam conditions, although you will be allowed to refer to copies of the works.
* HL students will write three supervised pieces; SL students will write two.

- The recommended time for each piece of writing is 40–50 minutes.
- At the end of the lesson the essay must be handed in; you should not re-draft it or correct it after the allocated time.
- You will choose one of these pieces to develop into your final essay, and the original piece of writing will be kept on file for reference, but will not be given a mark.
- You will be provided with prompts by your teacher. These can be generic questions, or they can be appropriate to specific works. You will not see these prompts before you write the essays: the IB syllabus states that these prompts are designed 'to encourage independent critical writing and to stimulate thinking about an assignment topic'.

Here are some examples of the sort of prompts you might get for supervised writing:

- What is the impact on the work of a major choice and/or decision made by the characters?
- Are different voices used to express thoughts and feelings in the poems of X? What effect do these have on your responses to the poems?
- Do you think there are some characters in the work whose chief role is to convey cultural values?
- To what extent do time and place influence your reading of the work?
- Would you agree that this work reinforces stereotypes more than it challenges them?
- Is the world view presented in X's plays pessimistic rather than hopeful?
- Are the female characters in X's novels better role models than the male characters?
- Are the short stories of X closer to propaganda than real art?
- To what extent would you agree that after reading the poetry of X we have a clear – but less happy – view of the world?

You can view these supervised essays in several ways:

- They allow you to build on the work you have already achieved in the interactive oral and the reflective statement. In that sense they consolidate what you have already learned.
- Your essays will benefit from the additional prompts provided by your teacher: they will be clearer, and more focused on specific subject areas.
- Should you do well in these supervised essays you will certainly have a solid foundation for the final essay, which is the main goal for Part 1 of the course.

Remember that Part 1 of the English Literature course can be characterised by a phased and selective focusing of ideas. you move from studying two or three texts in class, and from discussing them as a group, to working on a reflective statement on your own; now, with the supervised writing, you have to drill down even further into your texts before choosing one aspect to concentrate on in the final essay. This is a transitional point in your studies of Part 1: Works in translation; read the prompts carefully and keep in mind the possibility that you might develop one of these essays into an essay of between 1200 and 1500 words.

Think about the texts you have studied, either for Part 1 of the English Literature course or for another part of the course; if you have just started studying for the Diploma then also think about the literary texts you have studied over the last two years. It is possible to write generic questions on any text, and it is also possible to write very focused questions on specific texts. Neither type, however, is desirable for these essays: if the questions are too general then your answers could be vague; if the questions are too narrow you could be guided away from the main themes the writer wants you to think about, and which is required at this level.

Key term

Generic Something that is characteristic of a collection of things; often used to mean 'non-specific'.

Extended essay

EE

If you are studying History as part of your Diploma you may wish to think about exploring the treatment of dissident writers in the last years of the Soviet Union: writers such as Aleksandr Solzhenitsyn graphically described their time in Stalin's gulags (the labour camps used in the Soviet Union to hold political prisoners), but less is known about writers such as Ratushinskaya and her treatment in a more modern Soviet system. How much did their voices contribute to *glasnost* (the more open form of government introduced in the Soviet Union in the mid 1980s) and, eventually, to the dismantling of the Soviet system?

Activity 1.5

Here are ten prompts: which do you think are acceptable for this part of the course, and why? If you finish this task quickly, think about re-writing these questions so that they are suited to your texts.

1. 'Frank Kafka's *The Metamorphosis* is not concerned with a giant insect: instead, it charts the decline of man into something less than human. In that sense it is a fable of modern times.' Would you agree with this statement?
2. Would you agree that Frank Kafka's *The Metamorphosis* is completely without hope?
3. To what extent does Irina Ratushinskaya's poetry provide us with a human, rather than purely political, insight into the Soviet Union?
4. Which books have you most enjoyed studying for Part 1 of your course?
5. 'Kundera's *The Unbearable Lightness of Being* is only concerned with the Prague Spring of 1968.' Would you agree?
6. Discuss the importance of inanimate objects in *A Doll's House*.
7. 'All literature is a lie.' Do you agree?
8. Which context has been the most important to your study of X? The biographical? The sociological? The political? The historical? Or the geographical? Explain your answer.
9. 'The surrealism of *The Metamorphosis* rests not in Gregor's transformation but in the ordinary way Kafka describes it.' Would you agree?
10. 'In *A Doll's House* Ibsen describes not just the tragedy of women, but also the tragedy of men: they are as trapped by society's expectations as the females he describes.' Would you agree?

As you can see, getting the balance right in such questions can be difficult.

Let's look at how Alex and Katja got on with this stage of the course. They have completed their interactive orals and are now ready to work on their first piece of supervised writing, again on *A Doll's House* by Henrik Ibsen. Although the play may not be familiar to you, it is still useful to see how each student approached this task. We will look at their introductory paragraphs and their concluding paragraphs.

Katja and Alex both wrote an essay on this text, and were given 40 minutes to write it in. They decided to have a copy of the play with them, but did not use any notes written before the assignment. At the end of the lesson the written work was handed in to the teacher. They were given the following prompts by their teacher on the day of the supervised writing task:

1. To what extent would you agree that Nora's decision to leave her husband and children is morally right?
2. Would you agree that Torvald, as much as Nora, symbolises the cultural and social conditions of the time?
3. Would you agree that Ibsen's play, although bleak in its portrayal of marriage, is ultimately hopeful?

tip

You are allowed to have your texts with you when you do these supervised pieces. If you choose to do so, make sure that you have short, important quotations marked to support your points.

Activity 1.6

Read the opening paragraphs of both essays below and discuss with a classmate, or your teacher, their strengths and weaknesses in relation to the prompts given. It should be noted that both students have English as a first language.

This is Alex's opening paragraph:

Nora's decision to leave both her husband, Torvald, and her children is the only logical and morally defensible action she could take at the end of the play. From the very opening scene, Ibsen's characterisation clearly shows us how Nora has been reduced to nothing more than an extension of her husband's identity: in order for her to move from being his 'songbird' or 'doll' to a woman in her own right she has to leave him. Torvald – the ambitious bank manager – is preoccupied with his reputation and controls everything about him – his career, his family, his reputation, even what his wife is allowed to eat – and he does so with a ruthlessness that the audience cannot help but find alienating. Nora's references to herself as his doll might sound odd, and to some perhaps even endearing, but *he* calls her his 'squanderbird', a wife who is overly generous with money, and her emotions, but who, for him, knows the value of nothing and must be controlled. It is far more judgemental, and more accusatory, than her evaluation of herself. The imagery used by Ibsen throughout the play is that of a woman reduced to nothing more than an add-on to her husband. Her decision is portrayed as brave and unavoidable.

In the final scene of the play Nora says to Torvald that 'for eight years [she has] been living here with a complete stranger'; it is a damning conclusion. Ibsen shows us how society traps people into loveless marriages: they gradually drift apart until they become unrecognisable from the people they once were. By exposing this situation Ibsen not only reveals a deep truth at the heart of 19th century European culture, but, through Nora's actions, he also challenges its right to continue.

And this is Katja's opening paragraph:

No, I don't think that Nora's decision to leave her husband and children was the right thing to do. In fact, Ibsen himself, when under pressure from his audience in Germany, decided to change the ending of the play, allowing the couple to continue to live together, but perhaps to make up for their mistakes. I think this is a better and more hopeful ending, and I also think that it is more believable: Nora clearly loves her children, and although it is understandable that she would want to leave her husband, it is much more difficult for a woman to leave her children. By this I mean that both sociologically, and biologically, a woman finds it more difficult to leave her children than a man does. Ibsen realised this, of course, and in the version that we read in class – which sees Nora leave them – he was aware that it would cause a huge outcry. Torvald, although an unpleasant character, does not deserve to be rejected in this way: yes, he does control Nora, but he does so in a way which is perfectly in keeping with male behaviour at the time. In this he is not unusual.

Now look at their conclusions. Don't forget to refer to the prompts given by the teacher.

This is Alex's conclusion:

Ibsen's play, although outwardly bleak, does have hope. Nora's transformation, from a 'squanderbird' and a 'doll' to a woman who is not 'bound' to her husband in any way, but is free from 'any such obligations', is a truly radical, liberated change, and one which a modern audience would respond to more favourably than those who originally saw it. Importantly, she also releases Torvald from their loveless marriage which is, in itself, a selfless act, and one which is often overlooked by those critics who seek to condemn Nora's actions as being totally self-motivated. Ibsen seems to be saying that if women become free in a society men also become free.

And this is Katja's conclusion:

A Doll's House is not an optimistic play. Nora not only leaves her husband, but she also leaves her innocent children. As I have said earlier, this is an unnatural and unforgivable act. She goes further, though, and tells Torvald that they are now strangers, and that she never wants to see her children again. I don't agree that this marriage is typical of the time: there were many people who were happily married at the time, and so Ibsen does misrepresent marriage, or, rather, makes it too black and white. If there is hope it lies with Torvald who is now left to protect his children and who might recover to be a better man. In fact, at the end, he says he wants to believe in miracles, and perhaps Ibsen is saying that the miracle he will soon experience is a world free from his manipulative, selfish wife.

Activity 1.7

1   Like his reflective statement, Alex's opening paragraph appears stronger than Katja's, but can you be specific: where would Alex pick up marks, and where would Katja lose them? Although these supervised pieces are not assessed they are kept on file for reference as part of your course. It may help you to think about assessing both pieces using some of the criteria. Mark both students' work according to the criteria below. Don't just look at the marks available; consider also the questions in the second column.

Criterion B	How well does the student understand and interpret the texts? Does he/she have a secure grasp of the context, and does he/she analyse Ibsen's meaning convincingly?	6 marks
Criterion C	To what extent does the student show an appreciation of the way in which Ibsen's choices have shaped the meaning of the play?	6 marks

Criterion D	How effectively organised is the student's response? Do the arguments link? Are they coherent and objectively developed?	5 marks
Criterion E	How effective is the student's use of language? Is it appropriately formal? Are literary terms used effectively?	5 marks
Total		**22 marks**

2   Now imagine that you are Alex's and Katja's teacher. You are going to give
them feedback on their introductions and conclusions which will help them
improve on their next supervised essay. What advice would you give them? You
should aim to write five points for each student but two of those points should
be encouraging and positive: find the strengths of the pieces and make them
both aware of these. You also have to point out where they have lost marks, and
suggest strategies for building on their work so that they can write a stronger
essay next time. You may wish to encourage them to consider the following areas:
   • literary terms to pin down meaning
   • using quotations to support arguments
   • linking and developing their points
   • ensuring the prompts are effectively covered.

Stage 4: Production of the essay

What is the final essay for the written assignment?
• The final essay is the fourth and final stage of Part 1: Works in translation.
• It is a 1200–1500 word essay on a literary aspect of one work, developed from one of
  the pieces of supervised writing.
• Your teacher will guide you in choosing the aspect you wish to focus on; your teacher
  is allowed to look at a single draft of the assignment before evaluating its potential.
  This evaluation process could take the form of a conversation and/or a written
  response separate from the draft assignment. After this feedback from your teacher,
  your will complete the final essay and then submit it for external assessment.
• The final essay will be accompanied by the appropriate reflective statement. The
  required length of the whole assignment is 300–400 words for the reflective
  statement and 1200–1500 words for the essay.

What is meant by the 'aspect'?

By 'aspect' we mean the subject area you are going to concentrate on in your final
essay: it should be focused, rather than general, but have enough depth to support an
essay of this length. The aspect should lead the analysis, and your treatment of this
aspect is what you are assessed on (rather than the aspect itself). It is very important
that you get this right, and that you spend time thinking about it and the essay
question you are going to research. Remember that your teacher should not give you an
aspect to explore: it should come from you. Remember too that the essay title, although
worked on with your teacher, should be essentially your ideas and your wording.

   A typical example of this process might begin with a student interested in writing
on Ibsen's representation of women in *A Doll's House* (this is an example of the aspect,
although it isn't clearly defined yet). The teacher thinks this sounds promising and asks
the student to write an essay title for it (in doing so the teacher hopes that the student

Key terms

Contrastive pair Two words, phrases or images that work in contrast to each other for effect.

Matriarchy A society dominated by women.

Patriarchy A society dominated by men.

Exposition A device in which a writer gives essential information about what has happened leading up to the action about to unfold.

tip

You will notice that the final essay title is not phrased as a question, and is structured in two parts: an opening statement followed by an **exposition** which expands on the statement. The two parts of the title are separated by a colon, and this sort of essay structure is quite commonly found in undergraduate and postgraduate assignments. You could also replace the opening statement with a particularly apposite quotation from the text.

will clarify the aspect). The student then begins to think about a suitable title for the final essay. The ideas for the title may develop through several stages. For example:

Draft one: The representation of women in *A Doll's House*.

Draft two: To what extent is the behaviour of women in *A Doll's House* shaped by social pressures?

Draft three: To what extent is Nora's behaviour in *A Doll's House* controlled by the male characters?

Draft four: To what extent is Nora's development a rejection of a patriarchal society?

Draft five: From 'squanderbird' to freebird: an analysis of the female rejection of a patriarchal society in Ibsen's *A Doll's House*.

Draft six: From 'squanderbird' to freebird: an analysis of the relationship between femininity and patriarchy in Ibsen's *A Doll's House*.

As you can see, this process can take time and it could be argued that the title in draft three is a perfectly acceptable one for the final essay; however, by draft six the student has arrived at a title that has many strengths. Let's deconstruct each element to see why it might work so well.

From 'squanderbird'[1] to freebird:[2] an analysis[3] of the relationship[4] between femininity and patriarchy[5] in Ibsen's *A Doll's House*.[6]

1 'Squanderbird' referencees Torvald's derogatory name for Nora; this shows an immediate awareness of the text.

2 Although this isn't a direct quotation it does act as an effective contrastive pair: the juxtaposition shows the journey that Nora symbolically makes.

3 It is important to show that this is something more than an overview (the first four draft titles were vague in this area).

4 This is the key difference between drafts five and six. In draft five the use of the word 'rejection' is too direct and allows for little subtlety of approach: it characterises Nora as rejecting all men throughout the play, when of course she doesn't do this (and it could be argued that she is rejecting the male behaviour personified by her husband, rather than men per se).

5 Strictly speaking the contrastive pair should be 'matriarchy' and 'patriarchy' but the former is not appropriate to either Ibsen or Nora: the play explores what it means to be female in a male-dominated (or patriarchal) society, rather than the differences between a female-dominated (matriarchal) society and one dominated by men.

6 Only a minor point, but it is good to have the author's name and the title of the work included in the title.

After further reflection the student felt that the following title more clearly clarified the aspect under analysis:

Draft seven: From 'squanderbird' to freebird: an analysis of the symbols of repression in Ibsen's *A Doll's House*.

You are interested in an aspect of the text (for example, the representation of female characters in Ibsen's *A Doll's House*).

You take your idea for the essay to your teacher who says that although it is an interesting area it is too broad and needs to be more focused. Your teacher tells you to try to write an essay title on this aspect.

After several drafts you eventually get the essay title which you are happy with: it is focused but it allows you the scope to explore the main themes of the text.

You write the first draft of the essay and submit it to your teacher.

Your teacher gives you feedback on your essay and discusses where you might re-draft it. You make the changes and submit your second draft. It includes references and a bibliography, which you have drawn up carefully.

Your teacher is happy with this new draft and it is submitted, together with the appropriate reflective statement, to the IB.

Figure 1.6 A typical process for a final essay.

Key term

Bibliography The list of sources used by an author in an essay or other piece of writing; these usually appear at the end of the work

Further advice on the final essay for the written assignment

- As we have seen, the aspect is very important, so take a lot of care getting its focus just right; it should be open to detailed analysis and developed argument.
- Try to avoid questions on very general themes, or basic analyses of key characters. Instead, identify more particular, even quirky, topics to investigate. For example, which final essays would you prefer to read?

  o An analysis of the character of Meursault in *The Outsider*
    Or
  o The suicidal impulse: an analysis of self-alienation and destruction in Camus' *The Outsider*

  o A study of imprisonment in *One Day in the Life of Ivan Denisovitch*
    Or
  o 'Art isn't a matter of what, but of how': an analysis of individualism and captivity in Aleksandr Solzhenitsyn's *One Day in the Life of Ivan Denisovitch*

  o Female characters in *Woman at Point Zero*
    Or
  o The flight from the self: escape and imprisonment in Nawal El Saadawi's *Woman at Point Zero*

tip

Too many students choose vague topics such as 'jealousy', 'loneliness' or 'hatred', and they fail to be specific about the author's aims. Do not get the subject and the theme confused: 'hatred' is a subject, while 'the idea that all-consuming hatred is psychologically disturbing' is a theme.

Motif A recurring structural device that reminds the audience of an important theme.

Connote/connotation To imply something in a word or phrase other than its literal definition; an association evoked by a particular word.

- Emphasise how an author develops the characters rather than relating how characters simply develop by themselves.
- Don't simply retell the plot; concentrate instead on analysing how the author has used certain plot devices to move the narrative along.
- Look closely at the author's style, and how this style develops key themes.
- Some authors repeat the same – or similar – symbols to explore and represent themes they are especially interested in (colour is a very common one). These repeated symbols are referred to as **motifs**. Find them, and as you begin to link them you may see an argument developing. Sometimes they are obvious (for example, the repeated use of the colour red in a text can **connote** passion, sex, love, or even death); others are less obvious, but these can be even more appropriate for the final Part 1 essay. For example it would be possible to write an assignment on 'An analysis of class in Chekhov's *Three Sisters*' on Chekhov but it might be more focused, and different, to consider writing on 'The representation and importance of inanimate objects in Chekhov's *Three Sisters*'. These aspects don't immediately sound related, but there are two points to take from such a change in title and focus:
  1 Class in Chekhov is a very familiar theme, and it's a good idea to avoid very obvious aspects.
  2 Chekhov explores class in many different ways, and one way it is represented is through inanimate objects (or motifs) – a samovar, a book, a picture frame – and the characters' different attitudes to these objects illuminates subtle differences within society. In other words, you're exploring the same subject, but from a different angle.
- Be specific: don't write too generally, and don't try to force too much diverse material into one essay (or indeed into one paragraph).
- Paragraph regularly and correctly, and make sure you link your paragraphs.
- Use key quotations to support your points.
- Don't be afraid to give a personal view of the question, although it is often advisable to avoid using 'I' in these formal, assessed essays. Instead, write 'the reader' or 'we', or, if it is a play, 'the audience'.
- Consult critical texts but be very careful to record where you take every quotation or reference from: you gain marks by doing such research. If you fail to state your sources you could be guilty of plagiarism. If you take a quotation from a website, record its complete URL (for example, not just www.gutenberg.org but http://www.gutenberg.org/files/7986/7986-h/7986-h.htm) and the date you accessed it.
- Within your group ensure – with your teacher's cooperation – that nobody else uses the same title or analyses the same key passage.

Activity 1.8

Below are twelve titles from six children's folk tales. It is not important to know their plots, although many of you will have read them. What is important is that you think about why some titles are interesting and others less so. This might not appear to be a very serious exercise, but some insight might develop from it: which title not only appears more intriguing but offers greater scope for meaningful analysis? Some might sound odd, but that may be because nobody has ever thought of them before, and if you can capture that originality of approach then your essay could really stand out as distinctive.

Titles	Which is the stronger title and why?
Journeying in *Little Red Riding Hood* The use of the colour red as a motif of experience in *Little Red Riding Hood*	Both titles are interesting, but 'journeying' is rather vague: physical journeying (through the woods)? Or spiritual journeying? The use of red (in her name, in her clothing, with blood) has many connotations, and they are linked through the colour motif.
Aggression in *The Three Billy Goats Gruff* 'The grass is always greener': an analysis of utopianism and hierarchy in *The Three Billy Goats Gruff*	
In *One Thousand and One Nights*, would you agree that Bulukiya's quest is as much about an internal search for fulfilment as it is a physical searching? Is Bulukiya deluded?	
Imprisonment in *Rapunzel* The unreachable woman: an analysis of the idealised woman in *Rapunzel*	
Materialism in *Goldilocks and the Three Bears* The threat of the unknown: race and the threatened familiar in *Goldilocks and the Three Bears*	
Snow White as a mother figure in *Snow White and the Seven Dwarfs* The fragmented self: multiple personality disorder in *Snow White and the Seven Dwarfs*	

Developing the essay: sample student work

Look at the following essay written by a student studying Patrick Süskind's novel *Perfume*. This novel was first published in German in 1985. It is set in 18th century France, and tells the story of Jean-Baptiste Grenouille, a perfumer (born with no personal scent, but with a very pronounced sense of smell) who murders 25 girls. As you would expect, this novel is a dark, surreal narrative which is also preoccupied with the sense of smell, and so the teacher was intrigued when the student suggested writing on the 'visual elements' in the novel as her aspect for the final essay.

This was the first draft of her opening paragraph:

For Grenouille, darkness provides enlightenment, comfort and the ability to travel as desired; however, it also hits Grenouille like a bolt out of the blue that he has no scent. Grenouille's journey to the cave is packed with events using darkness as a period to find his own scent. Sleeping in the daytime in 'the most inaccessible spots' and eventually 'he travelled only by night' suggests animalistic qualities.

He seemed to evolve into a nocturnal animal (by choice) because of his long-lived separation from society. Grenouille 'did not need light to see by', he had a gifted sense of smell, allowing him to sense, pursue and avoid both people and places. This illustrates Grenouille's use of darkness as an advantage and a friend. The seclusion and dimness of the cave was one of the only places in which Grenouille 'enjoyed himself' for darkness was 'the only world that he accepted, for it was much like the world of his soul'. Grenouille is aware of his unique sense of smell, which makes the dark surroundings in the cave (and elsewhere) hospitable, in fact he would not have liked the cave if 'at the end of the tunnel it was' not 'pitch black night, even during the day'. In the darkness 'he was safe at last'. At its peak, the cave became the trigger that enlightened Grenouille with the need for a journey to find his odour. The cave made Grenouille face up to himself and realise that 'He could not flee' the fact he had no odour, and 'had to move towards it'.

There are lots of interesting ideas here but the student's teacher felt that further work was needed on it. He talked to her about where he thought she could improve it, and provided her with some written feedback, and after several re-drafts she submitted it for the second time to her teacher. These are the opening paragraphs of the essay which was finally submitted to the IB examiner for assessment:

For Grenouille darkness, ironically, provides enlightenment. He is at ease in his cave, and he 'travelled only by night', giving him animalistic qualities. He seems to evolve into a nocturnal creature; to some extent this is done by choice, but it is also as a result of being rejected by society. Süskind writes that Grenouille 'did not need light to see by', which emphasises both his powerful sense of smell, and also his mystical persona. Darkness becomes his friend, his ally, and the cave becomes the only place where he 'enjoyed himself' because darkness was 'the only world that he accepted, for it was much like the world of his soul'. This last statement is telling: here Süskind clearly links his main protagonist to evil, and so his habitat becomes more understandable, and, in one sense, natural (at least for Grenouille).

The setting is, then, an extension of the character: Grenouille would not have liked the cave if 'at the end of the tunnel it was [not] pitch black night, even during the day.' And it is the cave which forces him to face himself, to realise he could no longer 'flee' from his fate, and that instead of denying he 'had no odour' to himself he 'had to move towards it' instead. This acceptance – of himself and his own personal darkness – is pivotal in both plot and character.

Key terms

Irony Language that is intended to mean the opposite of what is expressed; a humorous reversal of what was expected or intended; a situation in which one is mocked by fate.

Persona A role or character adopted by someone in a text.

Protagonist The main character in a work of literature.

Activity 1.9

Spend some time reading both drafts. Why is the second one better than the first? You may want to think about how much the student has understood and interpreted the text (Criterion B), her appreciation of the ways in which the writer's choices shape meaning (Criterion C), how well organised the second draft is (Criterion D), and her use of language (Criterion E).

The final draft is stronger than the first, although they are both recognisably by the same student writing about something she is interested in. The assignment has evolved. The teacher's input has been crucial here, as, undoubtedly, have the several re-drafts the student did herself.

Criterion E is important, so let's look at how she has improved things between the first and final draft. One obvious difference is that by the second draft she has included the following literary terms:

ironically persona protagonist setting character plot

Because she has written about their effect (rather than just listing them) each literary term extends the student's argument, and pins down her meaning; you can also clearly see here how Criterion E informs Criterion B. She has also erased the clichés which can be rather lazy methods of expression (bolt out of the blue, packed with events, at its peak, face up to himself). Add to this the tighter use of punctuation and paragraphing, and the consistent use of the present tense, as well as various other improvements, and it is clear that this student will have moved from a 2 or a 3 for Criterion E to a 4 or a 5. Such gains make a critical difference.

Applying the criteria: what do they mean?

			How are these relevant to the final essay for the written assignment?
Criterion B	Knowledge and understanding	6 marks	It is easier to show you know your text than it is to show you understand it. One of the best ways to show that you know your text is to give detailed references and quotations to support your arguments; an *effective* and skilful use of appropriate examples from your texts shows that you understand the author's meaning. An awareness of the cultural background is also important here, and an *implicit* use of that awareness can show knowledge and interpretative understanding of the work.
Criterion C	Appreciation of the writer's choices	6 marks	You need to show that you are aware of the craft of the writer: understanding his or her technique is a critical part of interpreting the text's meaning. You should also show that you understand how such choices are influenced by the conventions of the genre you are studying.
Criterion D	Organisation and development	5 marks	A common weakness is that the introduction to the essay can be too long and too vague. You should state the focus of your essay and explain why it deserves analysis; you should not spend any time writing about why this work is relevant to your own personal experiences in life. Make sure your essay is clearly structured: a short, clear introduction , followed by an unambiguous development of your points and a suitably strong conclusion, is vital for scoring highly here.

Key terms

Cliché An overused or unoriginal phrase.

Punctuation The marks in language (such as commas, full stops and question marks) used to separate clauses, sentences and paragraphs, and which aid meaning.

Present tense A grammatical tense that fixes the action in the present.

tip

We all use clichés: they are those 'ready-made' phrases that slip off the tongue with much less thought and preparation time – than original statements. We use them because they quickly convey shared meaning, and we know that they work. However, in the written assignment you should guard against them: to an examiner they appear lazy and often vague; they can also introduce an unwanted informality into your writing. Some of the most common clichés are: 'thinking outside the box', 'at the end of the day', 'what goes around comes around', 'live and learn', 'hit the ground running'.

Key term

Introduction The opening part of a text or argument.

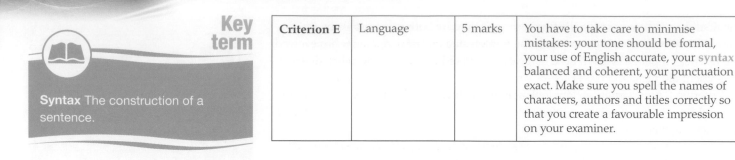

Criterion E	Language	5 marks	You have to take care to minimise mistakes: your tone should be formal, your use of English accurate, your syntax balanced and coherent, your punctuation exact. Make sure you spell the names of characters, authors and titles correctly so that you create a favourable impression on your examiner.

Unit 1.4 How should you structure and present your final Part 1 essay?

All successful essays are clearly organised and show a very secure knowledge of the text. Furthermore, there is a very strong focus on the effects of the writer's choice of language, structure and form. A good final essay also shows a very confident understanding of the conventions of the genre being analysed. If you have followed the four steps, then the aspect you want to explore in your final essay for the written assignment may well have suggested itself to you by the time you have to write it: you will have discussed the texts in class, you will have talked to your teacher about important themes, and you will have completed several written tasks in advance of the main assignment. As we said earlier in this chapter, preparation is vital: think ahead and the final essay will be both easier and more enjoyable.

1   Firstly, remember to:
    - write the title of the essay at the top of the page
    - use italics, inverted commas or underlining to indicate the title of the text
    - use the author's full name or surname
    - write about literature in the present tense
    - use formal, precise language: aim to say something very clever very simply
    - use the correct terminology for the text you are writing about (is it a novel, a play, a poem?).

2   Include an introduction which:
    - is one, concise paragraph
    - shows that you understand the essay title
    - focuses on the specific text (or extract) you are writing about
    - sets out a clear argument.

3   In the main body of the essay:
    - structure paragraphs: **P** (point) – **E** (evidence) – **A** (analysis) (the evidence should be a quotation)

P: signpost where each paragraph is going in the first sentence
E: use short, embedded quotations
A: analyse the effects of the language you quote; you might use the word 'suggests' or a similar word

---

    - always consider how the author is shaping meaning
    - refer to literary techniques but always give examples and analyse their effects
    - always refer back to the main 'thread' of the argument so that you answer the question
    - use linking words in your writing
    - show awareness of different possible interpretations and contexts.

4   Write a concise conclusion that pulls together the threads of your arguments. Try to avoid beginning your conclusion with empty phrases such as 'As I have shown', or 'In my conclusion I am going to show'; instead, make your final paragraph clear and balanced, re-stating your analysis but without repeating what you have spent the previous pages explaining.

The final essay: some examiners' feedback

Here are some common issues cited by examiners about Part 1 essays. They are taken from subject reports over a number of years and are issued as feedback to schools after the grades have been awarded. Some will apply to you, others will not, but remember an earlier tip: start to think like a teacher or an examiner and you will begin to make fewer mistakes.

The aspect

Examiners feel that students should choose an aspect that is:
- clearly literary in its focus
- very specific
- clearly expressed
- sophisticated
- shows independent learning by the student
- of real interest to the student.

The treatment

Examiners favour assignments that:
- are led by the aspect, not the knowledge of the whole text
- are aware of how the context shapes the aspect
- have clearly defined arguments
- have a clear personal response.

The aspect has to drive the essay: this is your opportunity to show how strong your grasp is of a particularly significant part of a writer's technique.

The presentation and language

Presentation and language are of course very important, and examiners are very keen that students' assignments:
- stay within the word limit
- have introductions that are succinct and are not heavily biographical
- have fresh and memorable conclusions that do not simply provide an overview of the essay
- are carefully proofread so that simple mistakes are spotted and corrected
- contain quotations that are clearly supportive of the point being made and are accurately copied and shaped to purpose
- have bibliographies and footnotes.

The format

- Your essay should be word-processed.
- Use double spacing for your first draft so that you can write your own changes between lines as you re-draft; for the final draft use single spacing.
- When you submit your essay make sure you include your name, your candidate number, and the title of the essay.

tip

Writing about windows as a motif in an author's work could be more effective than writing about the writer's treatment of fate, or life and death: the former is focused whereas the latter are too broad. Windows may be symbolic of life or death, but you need to use the aspect as a way of pushing your argument ahead forcefully. Drilling down into symbols and similes can often be very rewarding and allow you to concentrate on the text itself.

Key term

Footnotes The use of references which are expanded upon at the foot of the page (as opposed to endnotes).

- Remember that quotations are included in your word count, but bibliography and footnotes are not.
- Begin a separate page for your bibliography.
- Have a 'header' on every page with your name and candidate number on it.
- Number all pages.
- Approach the upper end of the word limit (1500 words) but be careful not to exceed it.
- Make sure you keep a copy of your final essay.
- Do a spell check, but do not rely on that as your only method of checking the English: do that yourself, taking your time.
- Give the word count at the end.

Using quotations and 'close references' effectively

Why use quotations and close references to the text?

Examiners expect you to have a good knowledge of the texts you are writing about, both for coursework and in the exams. Using regular – and appropriate – references to the text can show the examiner that you do know that text very well; however, you have to show that as well as *knowing* the text you also *understand* it, and one very obvious means of conveying this deeper appreciation of the text is to quote effectively. By interpreting the text – and by using quotations to support your analysis – you will invariably push your argument forward. And remember that it is the *text* that you are being assessed on, rather than the context it was written in: making short, telling references to specific parts of the text is fundamental to your work.

When is it appropriate to use a quotation?

This depends on your argument. For example, if you want to make reference to Macbeth's growing alienation then you could refer to key episodes in the play. Should you wish to make a point about how his wife's death makes his disillusionment with life profoundly bleak then you may wish to quote his description of life as 'a tale told by an idiot full of sound and fury signifying nothing'. This articulates very well how, by Act V, existence had become meaningless for him, and in turn explains his actions from this point onwards until his death. Here, you will see that the point is quite specific, that it is supported very well by a key quotation, that this quotation is embedded, and that the point is expanded upon after the quotation. As noted above, the pattern you should follow throughout your essay is:

P (point) – **E** (evidence) – **A** (analysis)

Think objectively about what you are arguing: if a point is relatively simple then you may only need to use one quotation or even a reference to where we can see this point in the text, but a major theme (such as alienation in *Macbeth*) will require several quotations to support your argument.

How should you use a quotation?

1 Remember to give some context to begin with: help the reader so that he or she knows where the quotation is coming from. It is important to know that the above quotation from *Macbeth* comes towards the end of the play rather than the beginning. Complex characters develop over the course of a work and you should show the examiner and your teacher that you are aware of this.

2 You should embed your quotation. This means that it should be integrated smoothly into your sentence; one test of this is to see if, when the quotation marks are taken away, the sentence still flows. Consider these two examples:
   - Macbeth's growing disillusionment with life can be found in Act V: 'it is a tale told by an idiot … signifying nothing'. This shows that Macbeth sees life like an idiot.
   - Macbeth's belief that life is 'a tale told by an idiot' emphasises how disillusioned he has become by Act V.

   The first example is less 'smooth' than the second, and if you take the speech marks away its sense will be impaired still further; the second example has an embedded quotation and you can take the speech marks away and it still makes grammatical sense.

3 Expand your point after the quotation so that you make explicit what the quotation shows. In the first example above the second sentence repeats the point of the quotation, whereas the second quotation moves the argument along, deepening the point and expanding on the quotation.

4 Choose quotations carefully: they must support your arguments and be rich enough to expand upon. Don't just drop a quotation into a sentence in the hope that it will be self-explanatory.

How long should a quotation be?

Students often include quotations that are too long in their essays. This can cause problems because long quotations can break up the flow of the sentence, and this, in turn, dilutes the strength of the argument. For example, consider the argument this student is trying to make about Macbeth's growing sense of nihilism:

Key term

Nihilism A philosophy that promotes an active destruction of conventional rules and conventional societal structures.

> When Macbeth hears of his wife's death in Act V he articulates his growing disillusionment with life:
>> Tomorrow, and tomorrow, and tomorrow
>> Creeps in this petty pace from day to day
>> To the last syllable of recorded time;
>> And all our yesterdays have lighted fools
>> The way to dusty death. Out, out, brief candle,
>> Life's but a walking shadow, a poor player
>> That struts and frets his hour upon the stage
>> And then is heard no more. It is a tale
>> Told by an idiot, full of sound and fury
>> Signifying nothing.
>
> This shows just how alienated he has become – from his wife, his friends, and even himself.

As you can see, there is too much in this long quotation to be contained within the point the student is trying to make. This overloading of ideas has to be guarded against or it will unbalance not just key parts of the point you are making, but even the whole

Figure 1.7 A still from the James Roose-Evans production of *Macbeth*, at Ludlow Castle/Ludlow Festival, 2007.

essay itself. Be selective: you can omit words if you feel they are not crucial to what you want to say, but remember to indicate where these cuts have been made. For example:

By Act V Macbeth increasingly sees life as a 'tale told by an idiot [which means] nothing' and this nihilism partly explains his actions on the battlefield in the final scene.

The square brackets here show that words have been omitted, but the quotation remains embedded and the point is well made.

You can also use ellipses to indicate where words have been taken out. To use an example from another of Shakespeare's (1564–1616) plays:

Hamlet uses an extended metaphor when he articulates 'how weary, stale, flat and unprofitable / Seem to me all the uses of this world! / [...] 'tis an unweeded garden / That grows to seed', and this imagery of dying nature clearly describes his own barren view of life.

You can also break quotations down into the key parts. For example:

In Act I, disgusted by his mother's swift remarriage, Hamlet describes the world as 'an unweeded garden' full of 'things rank and gross', which in turn vividly describes how empty his view of the world has become since his father's untimely death.

Longer quotations – of three or four lines – should be indented and set off from the rest of your text, and they should be used sparingly; they should almost always be introduced by a colon.

What else should you remember about using quotations? Don't introduce quotations with rather empty introductions such as 'The following quotation is important:' or 'An example of this can be seen in this quotation:'. It's difficult to embed a quotation when you revert to such introductions. Always try to avoid writing 'this shows' immediately after your quotation because it should be very obvious what the quotation shows without you having to write it. Be more imaginative in your writing. Embedding a quotation effectively can be a challenge for some students, and, perhaps understandably, they decide to avoid using quotations from the texts they are studying because they feel that in doing so they will lose marks because they are not fully integrated into their own writing.

Provided that the evidence you are using from the text is appropriate and focused there is a simple rule: it is always better to quote than not quote. The more you practise using embedded quotations the more comfortable you will be in using them.

Is there anything else you should know about using quotations? If you are quoting from poetry or verse drama you should indicate the ends of lines with slash (/) marks (you can see one of these used above in the example from *Hamlet*), and follow the punctuation of the poetry as well (if the first letter of each line is capitalised then you should show that as well). Also, follow all spacing and indentations.

Finally, do remember to record where you take each quotation from and include it in your footnotes.

Chapter 1 summary

In the course of this chapter, we hope that you have:

- understood what you will study in Part 1 of the course and how it is assessed
- understood not only the different requirements for each part of the course, but also how they interlink
- developed a clear understanding of some of the factors involved in contextualising a translated work
- looked at a number of extracts and responded to them analytically
- developed a range of strategies to plan, prepare and deliver a successful final essay.

This part of the course is varied, both in structure and assessment, but we hope that you can now approach each task with confidence. Remember to be well organised and open-minded, and to take notes throughout. Challenging though it undoubtedly is, Part 1 is also a hugely rewarding course in itself; we hope that it acts as an introduction to writers whose work you will continue to read once you have finished your Diploma, and that it will also open up new world views.

2 Detailed study

Objectives

In this chapter you will:
- learn what studying Part 2 involves and how it is assessed through an oral commentary and, at HL only, a discussion of a second text
- explore strategies for preparing, planning and practising your commentary
- engage with a number of text extracts from a variety of different genres and practise analysing how particular effects are achieved through writers' choices of language, structure and form
- consider sample student responses and be encouraged to practise delivering your own commentaries.

Key terms

Canon A body of writing by a particular writer (for example the Shakespeare canon); it can also refer to texts of established value (for example the Western canon).

Genre A type or form of writing with clear characteristics (for example the Gothic novel).

Novel A sustained piece of fictional writing which uses character, plot and action to explore various themes.

TOK

This chapter looks at several texts which are very famous but might also be considered too traditional. Do you think we should still study the English 'canon'? Some critics argue that the study of English Literature too often means the study of long-established, 'classic' **novels**. How far do you think a literature course should be a study of famous writers from the past? Do you think we should just study contemporary writers?

How is this chapter structured?

This chapter follows the shape of Part 2: Detailed study and is organised into four units. In the first, Unit 2.1, we set out what you have to do in Part 2: Detailed study, and how you will be assessed.

1. In Unit 2.2 you will look in detail at the requirements of the individual oral commentary and the HL discussion; this section suggests ways in which you might prepare for, structure and present these oral assessments.

2. In Unit 2.3 you will look at a number of different texts you might study; here you will find examples of how you might respond to specific passages. The texts are largely taken from the canon in keeping with the IB's aim that in Part 2 you will 'study some of the most important works' in English literature. Texts from the canon of English literature are those which have, over a period of time, been consistently highly rated by readers and writers. They are taken from a number of different genres because each of the texts you study in Part 2 will be from a different genre. In this section you will also read a number of student sample responses to show you how you might go about presenting an effective and convincing commentary on passages from a number of different genres and, for HL students, to give you a sense of what you might expect in the discussion.

3. In Unit 2.4 you will have the opportunity to practise writing your own commentaries based on sample extracts from the same texts used in Unit 2.3 and building on what you have learned from the sample student commentaries.

Unit 2.1 What is Part 2: Detailed study?

Part 2 of the English Literature course is called the detailed study; in this part you will develop an in-depth knowledge of a number of texts and demonstrate your knowledge by responding in the form of an oral commentary to an extract from one of those texts. The assessment – the individual oral commentary (which is abbreviated by many IB students and teachers to IOC) – is a unique part of the Diploma Programme; it is both challenging and rewarding. In Part 2, you will be assessed on your ability to talk convincingly about the texts you have studied. Both SL and HL students complete a commentary on one of the texts they have studied. The SL commentary could be on either of the two texts studied; the HL commentary will be on poetry. HL students will also take part in a short discussion about one of their other two texts.

Whilst skills such as understanding and analysis transfer smoothly from other sections of the course, the oral component to this assessment presents you with exciting challenges, building on your interactive oral from Part 1 and the presentation from Part 4.

This chapter gives you hints and advice on how best to prepare, present and perfect your oral commentary; however, if you want to become skilled at delivering a commentary, you will need to practise regularly. Your literature lessons are the perfect place to do this. By participating fully in each task you will be training yourself to perform well in the commentary.

Figure 2.1 Should we still study writers like Shakespeare?

How and what will you study for Part 2?

Part 2 is the section of the course where you will study some of the most important works from the English literary heritage. Whilst the information in this chapter is relevant to any work on the prescribed list of authors (PLA), the examples we have suggested are mostly from the canon of English literature. Whilst you can choose any works from the PLA, for many teachers and students Part 2 is the area of the course where you can study works that are famous in the history of English literature and which continue to influence writers today.

In Part 2 SL students study two works; HL students study three works.
- All the works studied must be taken from the PLA.
- Each must be from a different literary genre.
- At HL one genre must be poetry as this is the genre on which the HL commentary will be based.

In terms of approach, in Part 2 the focus is on the detailed analysis of a work; this means that you will need to be able to analyse both the content of the extract and the techniques the writer uses. In order to help you to focus in this way, in this chapter we suggest strategies that will help you to practise your close reading and improve your in-depth analysis.

Your final commentary will be on a passage of about 20–30 lines from one of the texts. In order to help you to prepare for this and to develop your close reading skills, we strongly advise that you spend a significant amount of class time practising reading and responding to passages of this length.

What will you have to do in your final individual oral commentary and HL discussion?

After completing your study of all of the Part 2 works, both SL and HL students will complete a formal individual oral commentary which will last for 10 minutes, including time for your teacher's questions. The commentary is a literary analysis of an **extract** from one of your texts. The HL commentary is on poetry; the SL commentary could be on either of the two texts studied for this part. The extracts will be accompanied by guiding questions set by your teacher. You won't know which extract you've been set until you are handed it immediately prior to the exam, but once you are given the passage you will then have 20 minutes to prepare before your commentary starts. All individual oral commentaries and discussions are recorded.

tip

Treat every English lesson as an opportunity to talk analytically and convincingly about literature. This way you will be constantly practising and preparing for the commentary and (for HL students) the discussion.

Key term

Extract A short piece taken from a longer text.

For HL students the IOC is followed by a 10-minute discussion based on one of the other works studied in Part 2.

- The discussion is conducted by the teacher and follows immediately after the IOC without stopping the recording.
- The work on which the discussion is based will be one of the Part 2 works that was not used for the commentary.
- You will not know which work you will discuss until the time of the discussion (i.e. after the commentary).
- You won't be able to refer to your text.

How is Part 2 assessed?

For both SL and HL the assessment of Part 2 counts for 15% of your total marks for English Literature.

There are four assessment criteria for the SL commentary:

Criterion A	Knowledge and understanding of the extract	10 marks
Criterion B	Appreciation of the writer's choices	10 marks
Criterion C	Organisation and presentation	5 marks
Criterion D	Language	5 marks
Total		**30 marks**

There are six assessment criteria for the HL commentary and discussion:

Criterion A	Knowledge and understanding of the poem	5 marks
Criterion B	Appreciation of the writer's choices	5 marks
Criterion C	Organisation and presentation of the commentary	5 marks
Criterion D	Knowledge and understanding of the work used in the discussion	5 marks
Criterion E	Response to the discussion questions	5 marks
Criterion F	Language	5 marks
Total		**30 marks**

Unit 2.2 How should you approach the individual oral commentary?

Key term

Audience In the theatre the audience means the spectators; in literature it refers to the readers.

All successful commentaries are organised clearly; they demonstrate an excellent knowledge of the text and are rigorously focused on the effects of the writer's choices of language, structure and form. Good commentaries also demonstrate an often impressive grasp of the importance of the particular genre of the text under discussion. Having said this, successful commentaries can be organised in a number of different ways. There is no right or wrong way to organise your commentary.

Your commentary will definitely need very clear signposts, or phrases that explicitly remind your audience of how you are structuring your commentary. It is difficult to exaggerate the importance of making sure that the person listening to you knows exactly where you are in your commentary and exactly what point you are making at each stage. In this chapter, we suggest some clear strategies to assist you with these signposts and with the structure in general. If you tell your audience exactly where you will be going on the journey that is your commentary, they will find it much easier to follow. The more you practise, the easier you will find it to use signposts to help structure your commentary. This coursebook suggests a structure that you might find useful. It does not claim to be the 'right' or only effective way of structuring a commentary; nevertheless, it should provide you with some clear guidance about how you might helpfully approach this assessment.

It is worth remembering that although Part 2 is assessed on a speaking task, the skills involved in constructing an oral commentary are very similar to those involved in constructing a written commentary. Indeed, much of the advice in Chapter 5 on structuring your written commentary for Paper 1: Commentary is directly relevant to the oral commentary for Part 2. You should aim to read the relevant sections of Chapter 5 alongside this chapter.

> **tip**
>
> This chapter suggests helpful ways in which you might structure your commentary. To see this structure working in practice, turn to the sample commentary transcripts. All of the student sample material in this chapter uses the commentary structure suggested here.

> **tip**
>
> You should use 'signposts' throughout your commentary to help the examiner know exactly where you are. You might use phrases like: 'The first thing I want to look at is the writer's use of metaphor ... If we look at line 3, for example, you can see how ...' Your commentary should be easy to follow.

Figure 2.2 'Signposts' help show the examiner exactly where your commentary is going.

How should you plan your commentary?

Always start with the end in mind: you will want to deliver a commentary that is awarded as many marks as possible. Therefore, start by thinking about how you are being assessed. Indeed, if you can use the structure of the commentary to show the examiner how you are addressing each of the criteria, then you will make it easier for him or her to give you as much credit as possible.

As for many good speeches and essays, the structuring principle for your commentary might well be:

1. Tell the examiner what you are going to say.
2. Say it analytically, convincingly and in detail.
3. If there is time briefly remind the examiner how you made your commentary convincing and effective.

This threefold structure will serve you well. Remember that you will always be asked guiding questions; often, answering these in turn will provide you with an excellent foundation or structure for your commentary. However, you should also remember that you are not compelled to answer the guiding questions: they are there to provide you with help if you want it.

In your commentary you have to demonstrate:
1   a knowledge and understanding of the extract
2   an appreciation of the ways in which the writer's choices shape meanings.

Because you are assessed using these criteria you should structure your commentary in such a way that the examiner is in no doubt that you will fulfil these requirements completely. Good guiding questions ought to lead you to talk about your knowledge and understanding of the text and the writer's choices. Indeed, very often the guiding questions will direct you to cover exactly these two areas. In this case, you can be explicit about using the questions for two of you structuring themes.

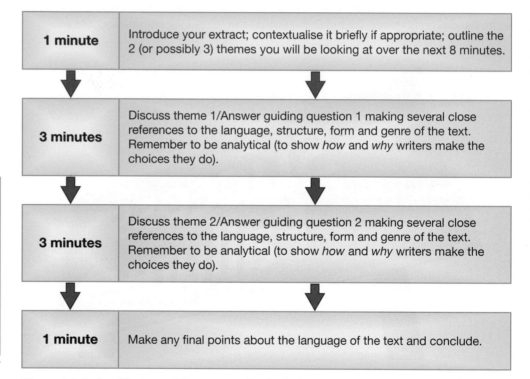

1 minute	Introduce your extract; contextualise it briefly if appropriate; outline the 2 (or possibly 3) themes you will be looking at over the next 8 minutes.
3 minutes	Discuss theme 1/Answer guiding question 1 making several close references to the language, structure, form and genre of the text. Remember to be analytical (to show *how* and *why* writers make the choices they do).
3 minutes	Discuss theme 2/Answer guiding question 2 making several close references to the language, structure, form and genre of the text. Remember to be analytical (to show *how* and *why* writers make the choices they do).
1 minute	Make any final points about the language of the text and conclude.

Figure 2.3 A simplified possible structure for the individual oral commentary.

The total time for this assessment is 10 minutes; so aiming for about 8 minutes leaves your teacher time to ask you the compulsory questions as 2 minutes at the end of the IOC.

How should you use the preparation time?

Once you have been given your extract you will have 20 minutes to prepare for your commentary. You should be left to prepare in a quiet room. During this time you will be able to read, mark up and plan. It is vital that you use this time as effectively as possible. You can mark up the passage with whatever notes you want during the preparation time. However, you should remember that writing too many notes may confuse you. Some students find it helpful to write out the first and last couple of sentences of their commentary in order to make themselves feel confident about how they will start and end. We would strongly discourage you, though, from writing out in full any more than one or two key lines that you intend to use in

tip

Use a watch to time your commentary. You may even find it helpful to work out how long you should be spending on each section of your commentary and mark up your planning notes accordingly so that you stick to your intended timings.

tip

Practise this timed preparation as often as possible. To prepare for this assessment, you should practise reading, marking up and planning in 20 minutes as often as you practise actually delivering the commentary itself.

your commentary. You will need to work from notes, key words and phrases you have written in the margins. Practise talking in detail and at length about texts so that you don't have to read from a script or from overly detailed notes.

We recommend marking up the extract so that the structure of your presentation is absolutely clear to you. If it's not clear to you, it won't be to the examiner either! Later on in this chapter you will find examples of marked up extracts that will help you to understand what you should be aiming to achieve.

During the preparation time, we would advise you to work through the following six stages:

1 **Read the text and the guiding questions** carefully and underline the key words and phrases and the aspects of the extract you think are most interesting or about which you think you can talk most convincingly. At this stage it may well be appropriate to identify a range of literary features in the passage – as long as you intend to analyse them in your commentary. If it's an extract, rather than a single poem, make sure you've worked out where it has been taken from the original text.

2 **Identify your two or three big themes** (you might use the guiding questions to help you to do this) and write a brief summary of each of them at the top of the extract.

3 **Mark up the points that you will use to develop and analyse your themes.** You may wish to use a different colour pen for each of these themes. You may find that you add a brief third point at the end in order to cover any final points that you think are important to make but which don't fit into your big themes.

4 **Sequence your points so that you are clear about the order in which you will talk about them.** Make sure that whatever system you use is absolutely clear and is one that you have used in many practice run-throughs. You won't necessarily want to make the points in the order in which they appear in the extract. For instance, you might want to talk about a poet's use of metaphor at the start of your commentary even though the best examples of these come at the end of the poem.

5 **Make sure that you have clear notes.** In particular, make sure your notes for what you will say in the introduction and conclusion to your commentary are very clear.

6 **Practise**: spend any remaining time working through each of the points, rehearsing your commentary and adding brief marginal mark-ups (usually just one or two words) to remind you of what you want to say.

Clearly there is a lot to fit into your 20-minute preparation time. Do remember, though, that if you have revised effectively, you should know the extract that you have to talk about in detail and you will already have a clear idea about many of the points you want to make. You will need to practise using this preparation time regularly so that you know what it feels like to work for 20 minutes; you want to be confident that you can fit all of the stages of planning and preparation into the time available.

What tone of voice should you use in your commentary?

It is important to recognise that the individual oral commentary is a formal assessment. Therefore, your language should be formal and as technically accurate as you can make it, and you should adopt a register appropriate to a thoughtful discussion of literature. You should model yourself on anyone you have heard who speaks seriously and effectively. Ask yourself: what is it that makes them a powerful or effective speaker?

tip

Be aware of your audience. It is not just the teacher sitting in the room with you. It is also the examiner who will be listening to a recording. You cannot rely on any gestures, eye contact or body language to help communicate your ideas; you will need to convey everything you want to say through the words you choose and how you say them.

Having said this, it is equally important that you speak in your own voice. Don't try to put on a voice for the commentary; it simply won't seem natural and will lack the clear sense of personal engagement with the text which characterises effective commentaries. Above all it is important that you speak clearly and relatively slowly. You need to make sure that the examiner can follow every word of your commentary. Listening back to your practice recordings and your teacher's feedback will be important in helping you to improve the ways in which you control your register and tone of voice in your commentary.

In your commentary you are assessed on your use of language. Clearly, this will involve you using technical vocabulary wherever appropriate. Throughout this coursebook we suggest effective ways for you to use technical literary terms to support your analysis; however, as ever, you are reminded that the use of such terms for their own sake will rarely be rewarded. In your commentary you should aim to show how the writer's choices of particular words and literary devices help shape the meaning of the passage. Remember that the Glossary contains a list of all the technical vocabulary and literary terms we have used in this coursebook.

Finally, you should give the examiner a clear sense that you are enjoying both the text and the process of analysing it. A real sense of engagement with and enjoyment of the task will make a very positive impression.

How should you start your commentary?

- Make sure you remember the obvious: state your name, centre number and candidate number at the start of the recording. This will also give you an opportunity to gauge the level and speed of your voice.
- Having done that, it is vital that you make a very good impression in the first few sentences to set the tone for the commentary as a whole. First, identify the extract and the author, and briefly set it in context. This might be as simple as saying what happens immediately before and after the passage. For a poem, you might mention any relevant contextual details, although these should be brief and focused.
- Your next stage should be to outline the main themes you will examine in your commentary. If it helps you to feel more confident about the opening section of your commentary, you might wish to write the first couple of sentences at the top of the extract so that you are absolutely clear about the way you will introduce these important themes. In many cases you will be signalling your intention to answer the guiding questions that have been set. Try to introduce an argument at this stage too which will show the examiner how you intend to engage personally with the extract throughout your commentary.
- This introductory section of your commentary should take no more than about 1 minute.

How should you structure the main body of your commentary?

If you have used the preparation time effectively, you should know which points you want to make and the order in which you want to make them. Ideally, all the points you want to make are covered by the two or three main themes you have used to help structure your commentary.

As you will see when you look at the student sample responses later on in this chapter, effective commentaries are rigorously and consistently analytical and avoid being overly descriptive. These qualities should be true of every literature assessment

Try to relax. Before you start marking up the text take a few seconds to compose yourself: breathe regularly and deeply or simply close your eyes and empty your mind of anything other than the work you have to do. Now look at the extract you have to work on. Visualise it: where does it come from? Who is involved? Now think of the literary features involved in this text ... and start thinking and making notes.

You will need to practise recording commentaries as often as possible. Most computers or mobile phones have the capacity to record your voice so that you can listen back to it and work out how to improve. Some students are able to send these recordings to their teachers for feedback. If you don't have access to this technology, ask your teacher for a tape recorder, or practise in front of a friend.

you undertake; nevertheless, it is always worth reminding yourself that the focus of your commentary should not be *what* happens in the extract but *how* and *why* it happens. In the main body of your commentary it will always be appropriate to comment on the writer's choices of particular literary features. Remember that, whilst it is important to identify the literary features correctly and accurately, the real credit comes from analysing *how* and *why* you think the writer uses them in this particular text.

For each of the points you make about the writer's choice of certain words or particular forms, you should aim to follow the structure **P** (point) – **E** (evidence) – **A** (analysis). In doing this, you should:

1 identify a technique, device or interesting feature
2 draw the examiner's attention to where the writer uses this technique (and perhaps quote the key words)
3 analyse how this technique works – the key questions you need to answer here are *how* and *why* the writer makes the choices he or she does.

You might include three or four of these smaller analytical points in your answer to one of the guiding questions.

In the main body of your commentary you might want to draw attention to key literary and historical contexts that will help you to appreciate and analyse the extract. Referring to contexts can be important and helpful. However, you need to note that merely mentioning a context won't gain any credit in itself. You might know some interesting facts about the life of the writer of the passage; however, you should only include these if they directly support a point you are making about the passage. Too many students fill too much of their commentary with regurgitated information about the writer or related events. Try to avoid making this mistake. Remember, the main focus for your commentary should be your analysis of the writer's choices of language, structure and form in the extract in front of you.

How should you conclude your commentary?

You will need only a brief conclusion but it is a good idea to draw your commentary to a recognisable end and to finish off as effectively as you started. It is worth remembering that the last thing the examiner hears might have an important bearing on the final decision about how many marks you are awarded. You might choose to conclude by looking at the way the extract ends and the writer's choice of language here; however, any number of different strategies could be effective. The key is that you are clear, focused and assured. Anyone listening to your commentary should have a very clear sense that it has finished. The student sample material later on in this chapter will provide you with some helpful and effective strategies to conclude your commentary.

How long should your commentary be?

The oral commentary lasts 10 minutes in total and you need to include time for your teacher to ask you questions. We would therefore advise that you aim to talk for about 8 minutes. If you practise regularly enough, you will be amazed at how accurately you can get the timing spot-on. Using the structure suggested in this chapter, you might aim for an introduction which lasts about a minute, two or three substantial points each of about 2–3 minutes, and a conclusion that lasts between 30 seconds and 1 minute.

Figure 2.4 Always talk about *how* and *why* things happen in a text.

Think like the writer. Imagine what the writer was thinking when he or she wrote the words in front of you. Every word was selected carefully and for particular effect. Your job is to explain to your audience *how* and *why* you think the writer made those particular choices.

When you are practising for the commentary you don't need to complete a full 8-minute commentary every time. Often it will be a good idea to practise one of the main points and to speak for 2–3 minutes. If you can break down the commentary into several shorter sections then you will find it a more manageable process.

How should you approach the questions at the end of the commentary?

At the end of your commentary your teacher will ask you a series of questions. However, if you have managed to fill 8 minutes, there may well be time for only one or two. Your teacher will aim to ask questions to help you to talk about any important aspects of the extract you have missed in your commentary; equally, your teacher may prompt you to address aspects of the assessment criteria you did not cover. You should see these questions as an excellent opportunity to expand on the points you've already made and to satisfy the criteria as successfully as you can in order to give you the best possible mark.

Remember to be specific and to remain analytical. In other words, don't just answer the questions in general terms; refer back to the extract in your answers and show they are informed by your understanding and analysis of the passage in front of you. It will often be appropriate to quote from the extract in answering your teacher's questions.

How should you approach the discussion at HL?

Both SL and HL students will complete the individual oral commentary; however, HL students will also undertake a discussion about one of the other texts you have studied. The discussion will follow immediately after the commentary (the recording will continue without a pause). Here are some examples of the sort of discussion questions you might be asked:

- Which character from the novel do you find most interesting?
- How does the writer make him or her an interesting character?
- How does the writer use settings in the novel?
- Can you give an example of how settings are important in terms of the narrative?
- Could you give examples of how a writer creates tension between characters in the play you have studied?
- How important are contextual considerations in affecting your appreciation of a particular work?

When answering the questions during the discussion it is important to be as specific as possible. You won't have the book in front of you so it is particularly important that you know your texts as well as you can so that you can make reference to particular scenes and episodes and even, in response to certain questions, quote from memory.

Our general advice for the discussion is to apply the same standards to your answers as you will to your commentary. You will need to:

- talk about the writer's choices
- be rigorous and analytical (the point-evidence-analysis structure will prove helpful)
- be specific and refer to the events and language of the text in answer to every question
- make sure that you demonstrate personal engagement with the text and, wherever possible, show how you enjoyed reading and studying it.

In Unit 2.3 you will find sample extracts from discussions on Charles Dickens's (1812–70) *Great Expectations* and William Shakespeare's *Macbeth*. Looking at these transcripts will help you to think about how these students tackled the questions and you will be able to judge how successfully you thought these candidates performed.

What do the examiners say?

Examiners frequently tell teachers that only a minority of students sound as if they are actually enjoying their IOC. Everyone accepts that, because it is an exam, you may be less relaxed than normal, but if you practise feeling at ease and engaging with the task, then this will be conveyed to the examiner and can make a difference. Examiners

One of the most common mistakes students make is to 'tell the story' of the extract in their own words. Examiners will give little credit to such a **narrative** or descriptive account. They will have read the texts themselves so will already know what happens in them: they don't need a summary. What they do want to hear – and what they will reward – is an informed personal analysis of the writer's choices.

Key term

Narrative A connected series of events which form the basic plot (or story).

also feel that too few students have a structured, planned response to the extract and, as a result, their commentaries can seem rather loose. Again, be prepared: plan and sequence your thoughts, and stick to your plan: you will find this helps a great deal when you are talking. Lastly, examiners would prefer students not to go through an extract or a poem line by line: again, plan for a less rigid response because it can interrupt the flow of your commentary.

If you follow the advice in this chapter carefully you should feel better prepared – and more relaxed – for the IOC, and in doing so you will avoid making the errors that examiners so frequently encounter. And the better prepared you are, the more you will enjoy your commentary and discussion.

Unit 2.3 **Assessment: Sample student responses**

In this unit you will look at a number of different text extracts and a variety of sample student responses. The texts are mostly by writers who appear on the prescribed list of authors, and all are famous works from English literature. The extracts are organised under three headings:

1   Poetry
2   Novels
3   Drama

The drama extracts in this chapter are all taken from Shakespeare. We've chosen Shakespeare in this chapter because we're focusing on the English canon in this part and Shakespeare has arguably been more influential than any other writer in the history of English literature. In Chapter 3 you will look at several examples of modern drama in preparation for Paper 2. If you prefer to practise your oral commentaries and discussions on modern drama, you should still follow the advice in this chapter.

In each section of this unit you will find carefully chosen extracts each with an introduction and guiding questions (some of which have been annotated to help you), transcripts of sample student commentaries, questions and answer sessions and HL discussions. This unit gives you the opportunity to read extracts from some great literary works (which might inspire you to go away and read them in their entirety), to practise preparing commentaries and to read student sample material.

The unit also provides you with a model for studying texts. The assessment will always be on an extract or a poem, so you have the chance here to look at a series of extracts or poems which will provide you with an effective way to prepare for the commentary. Clearly you will need to read the whole text or selection of poems first, but this detailed approach here will give you the chance to be constantly preparing and refining your skills in advance of the commentary.

Poetry

We've started with poetry because HL students must do their commentary on poetry and many SL students will talk about poetry as well. In this section you will work through the process of reading and marking up a poem; you will then look at planning and delivering sections of an individual oral commentary. We have broken down the process and have tried to explain exactly what you might do at each stage. In the later stages of this chapter you will be encouraged to have a go at completing this process on your own and practising commentaries for real.

But to start with, let's work through an example. We've chosen a poem here, 'I wish I could remember that first day' by Christina Rossetti (Text 2.1), which you won't be able to use in your real commentary (she's not an author selected by the IB for this part of the course), but we want to show you the *process* we think you should go through. You should then be able to apply this process to the poems you will be studying in class.

Starting the commentary: what should you do first?

We would advise you to follow the six-stage process outlined on page 39. Here it is again:

1. Read the text and the guiding questions.
2. Identify your two or three big themes.
3. Mark up the points that you will use to develop and analyse your themes.
4. Sequence your points so that you are clear about the order in which you will talk about them.
5. Make sure that you have clear notes.
6. Practise.

So the first thing you need to do is read the poem, carefully, a couple of times.

Figure 2.5 Christina Rossetti (1830–94).

Text 2.1 *I wish I could remember that first day*, Christina Rossetti

Christina Rossetti (1830–94) was an English poet and the sister of the famous artist and poet Dante Gabriel Rossetti. She was born in London and began writing as a very young girl. Many readers have identified feminist themes in her poetry.

> I wish I could remember that first day,
>   First hour, first moment of your meeting me,
>   If bright or dim the season, it might be
> Summer or Winter for aught I can say;
> 5 So unrecorded did it slip away,
>   So blind was I to see and to foresee,
>   So dull to mark the budding of my tree
> That would not blossom yet for many a May.
> If only I could recollect it, such
> 10 A day of days! I let it come and go
>   As traceless as a thaw of bygone snow;
> It seemed to mean so little, meant so much;
> If only now I could recall that touch,
>   First touch of hand in hand – Did one but know!

Guiding questions

1. What are Rossetti's main thematic concerns in this poem?
2. How does Rossetti use language and structure in interesting ways?

The first question asks about 'thematic concerns'; it's basically saying: what are the big themes? You might start thinking about starting points and memory and history. When you look at a poem in the real commentary, you should remember having discussed things like this when you studied the poem in class.

The second question asks about language and structure. It is likely that if you had looked at the poem previously in class you would have noticed that it was a **sonnet** (it has 14 lines and a particular **rhyme scheme**); in terms of language, you might have looked particularly at metaphorical language and at repetition.

So, in very broad terms, your themes might be:
- The relationship between memory and history and the way the poem explores starting points.
- The use of the sonnet form, metaphor and repetition.

Having reminded yourself of these thoughts, you should now go back to the poem and mark up some of the aspects you will want to discuss in your commentary. Here is an example of how you could mark up the poem:

I wish I**1** could remember**2** that first day,
    First hour, first**3** moment of your**4** meeting me,
    If bright or dim the season, it might be
Summer or Winter for aught I can say;**5**
So unrecorded**6** did it slip away,
    So blind was I to see and to foresee,
    So**7** dull to mark the budding of my tree**8**
That would not blossom**9** yet for many a May.
If**10** only I could recollect it, such
    A day of days!**11** I let it come and go
    As traceless as**12** a thaw of bygone snow;
It seemed to mean so little,**13** meant so much;
If only now I could recall that touch,
    First touch of hand in hand**14** – Did one but know!**15**

Key terms

First person pronoun The pronoun 'I' or 'we'.

Narrator The person (character) telling the story.

Quatrain Four lines of poetry.

Caesura A break or pause in a line of poetry.

1   Repetition of the first person pronoun in the first three words – makes the reader think about the narrator.
2   Introduces theme of memory and history.
3   Another interesting repetition.
4   Introduces a second character.

5   Note the rhyme scheme in the first quatrain (4 lines).
6   Interesting word?
7   Repeated three times.
8   Is this a metaphor?
9   Continuation of the metaphor? Why?
10 Repetition of 'if' throughout the poem. Why?

11 Further repetition for effect?
12 An interesting simile?
13 Is this an important caesura (break in the line)?
14 Double repetition.
15 Interesting conclusion to the poem.

The next thing you need to do is sequence your ideas. This might take the form of brief notes. Look, for instance, at how you might sequence the second big thematic point (structure and language):
- Sonnet form
  o Normal expectations of sonnet form
  o Division of this poem into two quatrains and six lines with the rhyme scheme cddccd
  o What happens in each of these sections and how that is important
- Metaphor
  o Use of the metaphor of a tree on line 7
  o The metaphor extended into line 7
  o The effect of the simile in line 11

- Repetition
    - o Repetition of the first person pronoun at the start
    - o Repetition of 'so' in the second quatrain
    - o Double repetition in the last two lines

This gives you a clear plan and a structure for your commentary in the form of brief notes which you might write by the side of the text in your planning time. In the last few minutes of your preparation time, you will need to make sure that you can use your notes effectively. You will need to work through each point and think about how you are going to be analytical and talk about *how* and *why* the poet makes the decisions she does.

If you have any time left, you should use it to run through some of the points you are going to make. For instance, you might be keen to make sure you are particularly analytical when talking about metaphor under your second big theme. Think about how you might do this; here is an extract from a student sample commentary. This is the section on the use of metaphor in this poem.

One of the techniques Rossetti uses in this poem is metaphorical language. In lines 7 and 8 she uses a metaphor to describe her experience as being like a tree beginning to grow. She tells us that she failed to notice its original 'budding' (the very beginning of the relationship) because it 'would not blossom yet for many a May'. This metaphor from nature suggests that she sees her relationship as something natural and beautiful; however, it also reinforces her point about small beginnings. She contrasts the bud (small and almost unnoticeable) with the 'blossom' (which is visible to everyone). She underlines this point by using a simile in line 11 when she describes the day of the first meeting as if it were 'As traceless as a thaw of bygone snow'. The simile is drawing attention to how the meeting is 'traceless' in her memory. It does this effectively by asking us to think of a landscape where snow has melted and to try to find the snow there. Like her memory, it is lost.

You might also want to think carefully about exactly how you will start your commentary. It might be helpful to write a few notes so that you are confident about the first words you will say. Here is an example of how one student started her commentary on this poem:

This poem by Christina Rossetti is a sonnet. In it she explores how difficult it is to remember exactly when something – in this case a relationship – actually starts. In my commentary, I want to answer the guiding questions and in doing so want to look at two themes. In the first instance I will talk about the way Rossetti presents the relationship between memory and history and look at how the poem explores starting points. My second point will look at structure and language. I will explore Rossetti's use of the sonnet form and how she uses metaphor and repetition effectively in this poem.

You should now see how the process of reading, marking up, planning and delivering a commentary might work. As you work through the rest of this chapter, you should keep this process very clearly in mind. The next text is a very different type of sonnet, *Anne Hathaway* by Carol Ann Duffy. It has been annotated for you.

Text 2.2 *Anne Hathaway*, Carol Ann Duffy

Carol Ann Duffy (1955–) is a Scottish poet and the British Poet Laureate. Her poems are much loved and read in schools. This poem is a response to the famous line in Shakespeare's will which gave his wife, Anne Hathaway, his 'second best bed'. Duffy writes the poem as if she is Anne Hathaway, reflecting on her husband.

'Item I gyve unto my wife my second best bed ...'
(from Shakespeare's will)

The bed we loved in was a spinning world
of forests, castles, torchlight, clifftops, seas[1]
where he would dive for pearls.[2] My lover's[3] words
were shooting stars[4] which fell to earth as kisses
5 on these lips; my body now a softer rhyme[5]
to his, now echo, assonance;[6] his touch
a verb[7] dancing in the centre of a noun.[8]
[9]Some nights, I dreamed he'd written me, the bed
a page beneath his writer's hands. Romance
10 and drama played by touch, by scent, by taste.[10]
In the other bed, the best, our guests dozed on,
dribbling[11] their prose.[12] My living laughing love –[13]
I hold him in the casket[14] of my widow's head
as he held me upon that next best bed.[15]

1	This is an interesting list.
2	Metaphorical language is being used here.
3	Is she referring to Shakespeare here?
4	Another interesting metaphor – why are the words like shooting stars?
5	Why does she use language from poetry here?
6	More poetic/linguistic language.
7	More poetic/linguistic language.
8	More poetic/linguistic language.
9	The poem changes direction here.
10	A reference to all of the senses.
11	This is an interesting (and dismissive) word.
12	How does prose compare to poetry?
13	Interesting use of alliteration here?
14	Why do you think she uses this word?
15	The last two lines are a rhyming couplet.

Guiding questions

1 How does Duffy present the character of Anne Hathaway in this poem?
2 How and why does Duffy use the language of writing (prose, poetry and technical linguistic terms) in this poem?

Activity 2.1

You have looked at how you might work through the Christina Rossetti poem. Now you should have a go at working through the Carol Ann Duffy poem in the same way. The poem has been annotated to give you some clues as to what you might begin to say. You should follow the six-point structure and aim to finish by having a first go at delivering a commentary. Don't worry if first time out you don't manage to speak for 8 minutes – most students don't! Remember that the structure you should follow is:

1 Read the poem and the guiding questions.
2 Identify your two or three big themes.
3 Mark up the points that you will use to develop and analyse your themes.
4 Sequence your points so that you are clear about the order in which you will talk about them.
5 Make sure that you have clear notes.
6 Practise.

Then deliver your commentary. Why not record it so that you can hear what it sounds like?

Key terms

Alliteration A literary device in which consonants are repeated at the beginning of words.

Rhyming couplet Two successive lines in poetry which rhyme.

Long poems

One option for the poetry text for Part 2 is to choose a longer poem. The IB syllabus describes this as a poem that has at least 600 lines. An excellent, if challenging, choice of poem which fulfils this brief is any of the 12 books of John Milton's 1667 epic *Paradise Lost*. We have chosen extracts from Book One, which would qualify as a text in its own right.

Activity 2.2

Over the next few pages, you will find several examples of sample student commentaries in response to the extracts. You should have a go at the following activities:

- Read the transcripts of the commentaries out loud and time them. How long do they take? Is this about right for the IOC?
- Have a go at assessing the commentaries yourself. Get hold of the assessment criteria and see what mark you would give these students for each of the criteria. Compare your marks with those of other students in the class and discuss how you could make them better, or use some of the good ideas in your own commentaries.

John Milton (1608–74) is one of the most famous poets to have written in the English language. He was a puritan and a republican who lived during the English Civil War and under the rule of Oliver Cromwell. He is most famous for his long, religious epic poem *Paradise Lost*. When he wrote it he was blind and had to dictate the whole poem (all 12 books of it) to a scribe.

Text 2.3 *Paradise Lost: Book One* (lines 192–224), John Milton

This extract, which comes from near the start of Book One, describes the enormous bulk of Satan chained to a burning lake in hell and then him rising from the lake. The extract is followed by guiding questions, a transcript of a sample student commentary, answers to the teacher's questions and questions for discussion in response to reading the passage and the commentary.

Figure 2.6 Gustave Doré's illustration of Satan chained to the burning lake in hell.

> Thus Satan talking to his nearest mate
> With head uplift above the wave, and eyes
> That sparkling blazed, his other parts besides
> 195 Prone on the flood, extended long and large
> Lay floating many a rood, in bulk as huge
> As whom the fables name of monstrous size,
> Titanian, or Earth-born, that warred on Jove,
> Briareos or Typhon, whom the den
> 200 By ancient Tarsus held, or that sea-beast
> Leviathan, which God of all his works
> Created hugest that swim the ocean stream:
> Him haply slumbering on the Norway foam
> The pilot of some small night-foundered skiff,
> 205 Deeming some island, oft, as seamen tell,

With fixèd anchor in his scaly rind
Moors by his side under the lee, while night
Invests the sea, and wishèd morn delays:
So stretched out huge in length the arch-fiend lay
210 Chained on the burning lake, nor ever thence
Had risen or heaved his head, but that the will
And high permission of all-ruling heaven
Left him at large to his own dark designs,
That with reiterated crimes he might
215 Heap on himself damnation, while he sought
Evil to others, and enraged might see
How all his malice served but to bring forth
Infinite goodness, grace and mercy shown
On man by him seduced, but on himself
220 Treble confusion, wrath and vengeance poured.
Forthwith upright he rears from off the pool
His mighty stature; on each hand the flames
Driven backward slope their pointing spires, and rolled
In billows, leave i' the midst a horrid vale.

Guiding questions

1   How does Milton depict the landscape of hell in this extract?
2   How does Milton portray conflict in this extract?

Sample student response: transcript of sample student commentary

This passage is from *Paradise Lost* by John Milton. It comes towards the beginning of Book One. The passage is describing Satan, who is chained to the burning lake in hell. At the end of the passage he rises off of that lake for the first time. Immediately prior to this extract Satan is responding to Beelzebub, one of his archangels, and reminds him that for the devils in hell 'ever to do ill' is their 'sole delight'. I am going to answer both of the guiding questions; the first is 'How does Milton create a sense of the landscape of hell?' The second, 'How does Milton present conflict in this extract?' And then I am also going to go on to look at some of Milton's interesting uses of language in this poem.

The first question asks about how Milton creates a sense of the landscape of hell and the first point I want to make is about the idea of size and in some ways this anticipates the scene later on in this poem when the devils fly into Pandemonium and Milton creates a sense of their vastness. That sense of vastness is introduced at the start of the passage when Milton describes in line 195 how Satan 'extended long and large' and he 'lay floating many a rood in bulk as huge as whom the fables name of monstrous size' and he goes on to list from fables or from stories or myths of the past characters such as Titanian, Briareos or Typhon but then he goes on to use a very interesting technique, in essence an heroic simile, and what he does here is he invites the reader to make an extended comparison between Satan in hell and another scene which he describes for us.

That simile starts in line 196–197 when Milton is describing Satan as being 'as huge as' but then continues in line 200–201: 'or that sea-beast Leviathan'. Leviathan is a whale and Milton reminds us that God 'of all his works' created the whale as the 'hugest' so he is taking a figure from the natural world which is massive but then he actually tells us a little story. He describes a pilot of a little boat and he gives a sense of the fragility, the smallness of that boat by the use of the word 'skiff' and 'slumbering'; he gives us a sense of the potential danger that it might find itself in. Anyway this is a story as seen and told and the pilot, the captain of the little boat, sees what he thinks is an island and he fixes his anchor in the 'scaly rind' which is an incredibly powerful description of the island – 'scaly rind' is obviously a whale, not an island – it is describing the whale – but it is also anticipating Satan's transformation into the serpent in the key part in Book Nine when of course he tempts Adam and Eve and therefore creates the fall. The simile finishes in line 209: 'So stretched out huge in length the arch-fiend lay' so Milton uses that literary feature in order to convey a sense of just how massive Satan is within the landscape of hell. That sense of his enormous impact on the landscape is also drawn attention to in the last couple of lines of the extract where Satan for the first time comes up from the lake and in the final line of the passage leaves 'in the midst a horrid vale' as if when he rises from the lake he leaves in his place a huge gap as if he is affecting the landscape; he is almost a part of that landscape.

Having looked at how Milton conveys the landscape of hell I now want to have a look at how he portrays conflict and I think that conflict starts at the very beginning of the passage where Satan is described as talking to his 'nearest mate'. Now his mate is obviously Beelzebub, but there is a sense of humanity conveyed in the language here and I think that humanity is continued in the way in which his eyes are described as 'sparkling blazed' almost as if the other parts of his body which lay 'prone on the flood' are the evil parts, they are like the serpent, but the eyes have that aspect of humanity. There is a conflict here within Satan himself but the more important conflict is the conflict between good and evil, and we see that in lines 212 and 213, where we note the contrast between 'all-ruling heaven' and Satan's 'dark designs' and that alliterative coupling – the repetition of the 'd' sound in 'dark' and 'designs' – gives us a very powerful sense of Satan's manipulative nature in contrast with heaven. This is stressed again in lines 217 and 218 when Milton describes how all Satan's malice is serving 'but to bring forth infinite goodness, grace and mercy' and obviously those are the qualities that Milton is applying to God and to heaven. It is interesting that this threefold repetition, a tricolon, anticipates a similar tricolon 'treble confusion, raft and vengeance' describing Satan so the poem creates a conflict of equally powerful forces between God and Satan although it does constantly remind us, for example in line 212, that nothing happens without the go-ahead of 'all-ruling heaven'.

Finally, I want to look at a couple of points about the language. In lines 195–196, a sense of the ongoing length, the vastness, of Satan in hell is suggested by the alliteration of 'long', 'large' and 'lay', suggesting the extent of his size.

Key term

Tricolon A sentence that is made up of three parts, often each with ever-growing rhetorical power.

The alliterative coupling in 'dark designs' has that same effect. Finally, at the end of the passage, we have these powerful verbs 'poured', 'driven', 'rolled' and 'reared' to give a sense of the enormity of Satan moving off of that lake in the concluding passage.

After you've given your commentary, your teacher will ask you further questions. Here is an example of the sort of question your teacher might ask you following your commentary and the sort of answer you might give.

Teacher: Do you think Milton wants us to feel sympathetic towards the character of Satan in this extract?

Student: I would say both yes and no. As I said in my commentary, he gives him certain human characteristics which do make us more sympathetic towards him. However, Milton is doing this so that we can understand that he is making moral decisions (which humans do). It is important to remember that even when Satan appears at his most sympathetic, he is still making morally bad decisions. Even in this passage, however, Milton keeps reminding us of the constant presence and goodness of God. We see this in the epic simile when the leviathan is described as: 'which God of all his works/ Created hugest'. Milton wants to remind us who's in charge. Similarly, he makes continual reference to 'all-ruling heaven'. Milton makes Satan sympathetic to the extent that he doesn't want the reader to think of him as a sort of pantomime devil – we have to believe in him as someone who is making moral choices. However, Milton also keeps reminding us that he is the rebel angel and the cause of all the problems in the first place.

Text 2.4 *Paradise Lost: Book One* (lines 242–70), John Milton

This next passage comes from a few lines further on in Book One. Having raised himself off the lake, Satan is now in a position to speak to his fellow rebel angels and to persuade them to back him in his plans. Satan is speaking throughout this extract. The passage is followed by guiding questions and a transcript of a sample student commentary.

> Is this the region, this the soil, the clime,
> Said then the lost archangel, this the seat
> That we must change for heaven, this mournful gloom
> 245 For that celestial light? Be it so, since he
> Who now is sovereign can dispose and bid
> What shall be right: furthest from him is best
> Whom reason hath equalled, force hath made supreme
> Above his equals. Farewell, happy fields
> 250 Where joy forever dwells: hail horrors, hail
> Infernal world, and thou profoundest hell
> Receive thy new possessor: one who brings
> A mind not to be changed by place or time.
> The mind is its own place, and in itself
> 255 Can make a heaven of hell, a hell of heaven.

What matter where, if I be still the same,
And what I should be, all but less than he
Whom thunder hath made greater? Here at least
We shall be free; the almighty hath not built
260   Here for his envy, will not drive us hence:
Here we may reign secure, and in my choice
To reign is worth ambition though in hell:
Better to reign in hell, than serve in heaven.
But wherefore let we then our faithful friends,
265   The associates and copartners of our loss
Lie thus astonished on the oblivious pool,
And call them not to share with us their part
In this unhappy mansion, or once more
With rallied arms to try what may be yet
270   Regained in heaven, or what more lost in hell?

Guiding questions

1   How does Milton present the contrast between heaven and hell, and God and Satan in this extract?

2   How does Milton present Satan's character in this extract?

Sample student response: transcript of sample student commentary
This commentary has been marked up to show you how the student addresses some of the assessment criteria.

This passage comes from Book One of John Milton's epic poem *Paradise Lost*. Immediately prior to this extract Satan, who had been chained to the burning lake, has risen off of that lake and this is his first speech without his shackles on.[1] This is Satan speaking to the cast of devils in hell as a slightly freer individual and it marks the start of his capacity to plot which eventually reaches its manifestation in Book Nine with the temptation of Adam and Eve. In answer to the two guiding questions, I am going to look at[2] how Milton creates a very powerful contrast between heaven and hell and between God and Satan. I am then going to go on and look at the presentation of Satan's character and I am going to argue that Milton gives him a strangely human presence as well as making him a rhetorically confident orator and therefore creating a sense that he is almost like a man who will be a leader and who will be able to manipulate the other devils to get his own way.

I want to start by looking at the contrast between heaven and hell, between God and Satan, and that contrast starts in lines 245 and 246 of the extract. Indeed, hell is described as having a 'mournful gloom' in comparison with heaven's 'celestial light' and it is interesting the way in which the consecutive lines include these two-word phrases, a noun with a qualifying adjective,[3] the qualifying adjective drawing attention to either the amount of or lack of light to give a very powerful sense of light as being representative of goodness, and darkness as being representative of evil. This fits in very powerfully with the

1   Knowledge and understanding (Criterion A) are immediately in evidence as the extract is placed in context.

2   Criterion C (Organisation and presentation) is addressed because the opening section makes very clear what the focus of this commentary will be.

3   The focus on the writer's choice of individual words means that this commentary successfully addresses Criterion B (Appreciation of writer's choices).

idea, mentioned elsewhere in Book One, of hell being full of 'darkness visible'. It is a conflict, a contrast. That conflict or contrast is continued in lines 244, 250 and 251 where a strangely human phrase, 'farewell happy fields (249)', is then followed by the use of alliteration[4] to introduce the new world: 'hail horrors, hail infernal world'. This expresses the realities of the hell in which he has found himself so the language shifts from almost colloquial comfort to harsh biting reality and indeed the adjective that Milton uses in line 251 to describe hell as 'profoundest' has both a literal sense of depth and therefore distance from heaven which accentuates that sense of a contrast, and also picks up on the ambiguity of 'profound' which can also mean 'deeply' in terms of thinking. One of the things we are going to go on and look at is how Satan is presented as a deep thinker, almost as a human character. The final point about the contrast is at the end of the passage where the 'faithful friends,/ The associates and copartners' are lying in an astonishing 'oblivious pool' and Satan says no, let's not live in this 'unhappy mansion' any longer, let us try to regain where we have come from, and he issues a clear rallying call to his troops to reject the environment in which they find themselves.

I want to move on now and look at the presentation of Satan's character.[5] Firstly I want to look at his humanity. Now clearly Satan is not a human character but one of the ways in which Milton makes him sympathetic is to present him as having human characteristics and we see some of those in terms of his thoughts on philosophy. We find that in line 253, for instance, when Satan talks about one who brings in minds 'not to be changed by place or time' and he says 'the mind is its own place, and in itself/ Can make a heaven of hell, a hell of heaven', and what he is putting his finger on there is an idea that Shakespeare explores in *Hamlet* when he says 'for there is nothing either good or bad but thinking makes it so'; however, the way in which the pattern of the words is mirrored – 'heaven of hell, hell of heaven' – shows Satan's internal conflict and how he is conflicted and troubled by the various pressures on him and his various desires. That sense of humanity is also demonstrated when he talks about the almighty in line 259 as having not built here for his 'envy'. He recognises, I think, that God hasn't created hell and put the devils into hell motivated by the sort of emotion that Satan is implicitly acknowledging that he has himself, which is envy. Again this is his philosophical musing. It's almost as if he is convincing himself that 'to reign is worth ambition thought in hell:/ Better to reign in hell than serve in heaven.' It's a contestable view but the poetic power of the lines and the sheer rhetorical weight of Satan's assertion make it almost undeniable and that rhetoric which comes up throughout the passage also marks Satan out as being a leader and a powerfully convincing figure. Indeed, the passage starts 'this region, this soil, the clime'; he speaks naturally in the rhetorical patterns of great orators, he is using tricolon here, or the repetition of three.[6] He uses rhetorical questions in line 245 and in line 258, asking or demanding of the audience to consider for themselves

4 The use of accurate technical vocabulary secures credit in both Criteria B and F (Language).
5 The fact that the student really does follow the helpful structure announced at the start means good marks for Criterion C (Organisation and presentation).
6 The student gains credit here for the use of accurate technical language and clear appreciation of the craft of the writer (Criteria F and B).
7 The organisation of the commentary is underlined as the student returns to the key point about the presentation of Satan and, in doing so, directly answers the second guiding question.

Extended essay

Milton would make an excellent subject for an extended essay in English, especially if you are considering studying Literature at university. Talking about *Paradise Lost*, the English poet William Blake famously said that Milton 'was of the devil's party without knowing it'. This might make an interesting starting point for a discussion that could easily be pursued in an extended essay.

Figure 2.7 A Marcus Stone illustration from the 1862 edition of *Great Expectations*.

what the situation is like and this finds its ultimate manifestation in the final lines of the poem where he asks questions of what are two audiences really: firstly, the crew of demons in hell but, secondly, us as the reader. He calls us with 'rallied arms to try what may be yet? Regained in heaven, or what more lost in hell', finishing the speech with the powerful rhetoric of an orator. Indeed, that rhetorical insistence on his humanity, his 'faithful friends' and the repetition of 'associates and copartners' and 'our loss' sees Satan using emotive language and this again stresses the dual quality that Milton presents him as having, of both a great rhetorical orator and a character that is infused with humanity.[7]

Novels

When analysing novels you will be talking about aspects such as narrative, characterisation and setting. In this section, you will look at a number of extracts from two of the most famous novels in the canon of English literature: *Great Expectations* by Charles Dickens and *Pride and Prejudice* by Jane Austen.

Text 2.5 *Great Expectations*, Charles Dickens

Charles Dickens was born in England in 1812. He wrote many successful novels, often commenting on the social difficulties of the age he lived in. *Great Expectations* tells the story of an orphan, Pip, who starts his life as an apprentice to a blacksmith in a small village. However, a chance encounter with an escaped prisoner changes his life forever.

This extract comes from Chapter 21 of the novel. It is the start of Part 2 of Pip's 'great expectations' and he has just moved to London. In this extract he first visits his new home in London.

'Do you know where Mr Matthew Pocket lives?' I asked Mr Wemmick.
'Yes,' said he, nodding in the direction. 'At Hammersmith, west of London.'
'Is that far?'
'Well! Say five miles.'
5   'Do you know him?'
'Why, you're a regular cross-examiner!' said Mr Wemmick, looking at me with an approving air. 'Yes, I know him. *I* know him!'
There was an air of toleration or depreciation about his utterance of these words that rather depressed me; and I was still looking sideways
10   at his block of a face in search of any encouraging note to the text, when he said here we were at Barnard's Inn. My depression was not alleviated by the announcement, for I had supposed that establishment to be a hotel kept by Mr Barnard, to which the Blue Boar in our town was a mere public-house. Whereas I now found Barnard to be a disembodied spirit,
15   or a fiction, and his inn the dingiest collection of shabby buildings ever squeezed together in a rank corner as a club for Tom-cats.
We entered this haven through a wicket-gate, and were disgorged by an introductory passage into a melancholy little square that looked to me like a flat burying-ground. I thought it had the most dismal trees in it, and
20   the most dismal sparrows, and the most dismal cats, and the most dismal houses (in number half a dozen or so), that I had ever seen. I thought the

windows of the sets of chambers into which those houses were divided, were in every stage of dilapidated blind and curtain, crippled flower-pot, cracked glass, dusty decay, and miserable makeshift; while To Let, To

25 Let, To Let, glared at me from empty rooms, as if no new wretches ever came there, and the vengeance of the soul of Barnard were being slowly appeased by the gradual suicide of the present occupants and their unholy interment under the gravel. A frouzy mourning of soot and smoke attired this forlorn creation of Barnard, and it had strewn ashes on its

30 head, and was undergoing penance and humiliation as a mere dust-hole. Thus far my sense of sight; while dry-rot and wet-rot and all the silent rots that rot in neglected roof and cellar – rot of rat and mouse and bug and coaching-stables near at hand besides – addressed themselves faintly to my sense of smell, and moaned, 'Try Barnard's Mixture.'

35   So imperfect was this realisation of the first of my great expectations, that I looked in dismay at Mr Wemmick. 'Ah!' said he, mistaking me; 'the retirement reminds you of the country. So it does me.'

He led me into a corner and conducted me up a flight of stairs – which appeared to me to be slowly collapsing into sawdust, so that one of those

40 days the upper lodgers would look out at their doors and find themselves without the means of coming down – to a set of chambers on the top floor. Mr Pocket, Jun., was painted on the door, and there was a label on the letter-box, 'Return shortly.'

Guiding questions

1 How does Dickens present the environment of Barnard's Inn in this extract?
2 What do we learn about the character of Pip from this extract?

Sample student response: transcript of sample student commentary

This is an SL commentary (you will remember that an HL commentary will always be on poetry). It was awarded very good marks by the teacher who was assessing it. The commentary has been marked up to show you how the student addresses some of the assessment criteria.

This passage from *Great Expectations* by Charles Dickens is taken from Chapter 21. It comes at the start of the second section of the novel. Pip has arrived in London, has met Mr Jaggers in his office and then is taken by Mr Wemmick, Jaggers' clerk, to visit the place where he is going to stay, the home of Mr Matthew Pocket.[1] In this extract I want to look at the two areas suggested by the guiding questions; firstly to look at how the character of Pip is presented by Charles Dickens, and secondly to look at the way he presents the environment at Barnard's Inn.[2]

The first focus is the character of Pip. It is important to point out that this is a first person narrative. Pip is telling us his story and Charles Dickens makes it very obvious to the reader how Pip is feeling at particular points. In line 9, for instance, he describes himself as being rather depressed. The opening dialogue suggests that Pip is inquisitive, lively, interested and, indeed, he draws the comment from Mr Wemmick 'you are a regular cross-examiner', which Dickens describes as being said with 'an approving air'; coming from a legal background, Wemmick approves of

Key term

Dialogue The direct speech of characters engaged in conversation.

1 From the outset, the student's knowledge of the text is made very obvious by placing the extract in context. This successfully addresses Criterion A.
2 Criterion C (Organisation and presentation) is going to be a strength of this commentary. The student sets out a very clear structure from the start.

3   Excellent knowledge of the text (Criterion A) is evident when the student makes passing reference to other sections of the book.

4   By talking about the writer's narrative choices the student makes sure he addresses Criterion B.

5   The student's focus on the writer's word choices underlines how the commentary will be very successful in terms of Criterion B.

6   Accurate use of technical language gains credit for both Criteria B and D.

7   This is another example of how the careful and accurate use of language can address both Criteria B and D.

8   The commentary reaches an obvious conclusion. This will gain further credit for Criterion C.

cutting to the chase, approves of speaking your mind and approves of being to the point. Pip also shows his naivety when he uses the phrase in line 10, 'I had supposed that establishment to be a hotel kept by Mr Barnard', and he makes the link back to the Blue Boar from his village back in Kent,[3] showing that his frame of reference for making judgements about the environment he finds himself in is rather limited. By drawing our attention to that through Pip's narrative, Dickens is showing how Pip is both naive and innocently lacking in experience. We also learn that this is an important staging process in terms of the narrative.[4] The first part of Pip's great expectations ends with his journey to London.

The arrival in London is the second part of his great expectations. He makes it very clear in line 35 that the realisation of the first of 'my great expectations' was – and the phrase he uses is, in this instance – 'so imperfect'. His dream of living in a pleasant environment has been rather shattered by his first impression of Barnard's Inn. Indeed, the narrative tension is suggested by the very last couple of words of the extract, 'Return shortly'.[5] We anticipate and await the arrival of Mr Pocket. However, perhaps the passage's most interesting concern is with the presentation of Barnard's Inn; Barnard's Inn which so disappoints Pip's great expectations. After admitting that he had anticipated some sort of hotel like the Boar, what Pip describes is a 'disembodied spirit, or a fiction, and his inn' (Mr Barnard's), was the 'dingiest collection of small buildings every squeezed together in a rank corner at a club for Tom-cats'. The fact that Barnard is seen to be a 'disembodied spirit' starts the process of personification[6] which continues throughout this passage. In order to create a sense of the nastiness of Barnard's Inn, its lack of dignity and its lack of propriety, Dickens makes it out to have the qualities of a rather unappealing or unattractive human being, a 'disembodied spirit', a spirit that has been taken away from its body and therefore does not have a sense of being grounded. It's a 'fiction'; indeed, the fact that he uses the word 'fiction' suggests that it is so removed from what he might expect something to be in reality that it has the qualities of being made up.

The third paragraph starts: 'We entered this haven through a wicker gate,' and we can see Dickens's use of irony here; clearly 'haven' is the opposite of what the Barnard's Inn building is actually like so he is using that to signpost just how out of sync his expectations are with what he actually discovers. This idea of Barnard's Inn being an actively nasty influence is encouraged by Dickens's use of verbs[7] like we were 'disgorged' by the introductory passage, almost as if they are being spat out; they – Wemmick and Pip – feel as if they are the victims of this building and this establishment. Dickens uses repetition: 'most dismal trees, most dismal sparrows, most dismal cats and most dismal houses' to draw attention to his constant surprise that the buildings are even worse that he had imagined they might be; but the fact that 'most dismal' is used to qualify not only manmade buildings but also nature seems to suggest that this establishment has had an influence beyond the constructed environment and into the natural world. Indeed, the sign 'to let, to let, to let' – the repetition drawing attention to just how unpopular this place is as a residence – is described as if it 'glared at me', again giving the sense that Barnard's Inn has this personal quality; Dickens is using personification in order to convey how disappointed Pip feels on encountering these rooms. Techniques like alliteration

Key term

Personification The attribution of certain human qualities to inanimate objects.

in line 28, the 'soot and smoke' which are described as a 'frowzy mourning of soot and smoke', again cast Barnard's Inn in a rather unappealing light.

Finally,[8] the last use of repetition is the ongoing repetition of rot: 'dry rot, wet rot, silent rots that rot, rot of rat and mouse and bug and coaching stables'. The way in which Dickens conveys the horror that Pip feels on discovering what Barnard's Inn is actually like results in his realisation that the first of his great expectations was 'so imperfect'.

After you've given your commentary, your teacher will ask you further questions. Here is an example of the sort of question your teacher might ask you following your commentary and the sort of answer you might give.

Teacher: Why do you think Dickens includes this passage at the start of the second section of Pip's 'great expectations'?

Student: Dickens uses the structure of the novel very carefully. In the first section, Pip begins to dream of a world beyond the one he knows. However, Dickens wants to show us that what Pip thinks will be automatically better won't necessarily be. When Pip arrives in London he is surrounded by death and punishment (just like in the first section, with the gibbets, Miss Havisham, the Hulks and the convict). That difficult first impression is extended in this passage where the rot and decay and destruction are used by Dickens to suggest that all is not as it seems.

HL discussion questions

If you are an HL student and have been studying *Great Expectations* for Part 2, you might discuss this text after you have given your IOC on poetry. Here is an example of the sort of question you might be asked with a sample student response

Teacher: Why do you think Dickens calls his main character Pip?

Student: Pip tells us the story of *Great Expectations*. Indeed, it is *his* story. We learn his name at the very start of the novel, so it is obviously very important. Dickens tells us that it came about literally because, as a child, Pip was incapable of saying anything else. However, it also has an important symbolic value. A pip is something from which something grows. In other words, it contains the potential for further growth. *Great Expectations* is, of course, the story of Pip's life and of his *growth* – physically, mentally and morally. The novel has sometimes been called a bildungsroman. This term means a novel which is about someone's growth and development. In this case, Pip is the main character who grows and develops so it is entirely appropriate that he should be called Pip, a name that he is given at the start of this story about his life.

Figure 2.8 A still from the film adaptation of *Great Expectations*, directed by David Lean, 1946.

Key term

Bildungsroman A German word meaning 'formation novel'; usually a novel that describes a central character's process of growing up.

Activity 2.3

Look again at the criteria that are used to assess the discussion, particularly:
- Criterion D: Knowledge and understanding of the work used in the discussion
- Criterion E: Response to the discussion questions.

Then consider and discuss the following:
- How successful is this student in answering the teacher's question?
- What does the response do well?
- If there were more time, how could the student take this discussion even further?

Figure 2.9 A still from the film adaptation of *Pride and Prejudice*, directed by Joe Wright, 2005.

Figure 2.10 Jane Austen, (1775–1817).

Text 2.6 *Pride and Prejudice,* Jane Austen, 1813

Jane Austen (1775–1817) is considered one of the most subtle and sophisticated observers of personal relationships and of the English class system. *Pride and Prejudice* is perhaps her most famous novel; it tells the story of the Bennet family, and a mother's determination to see that her five daughters find suitable husbands.

In this extract, from Chapter 2 of the novel, Jane Austen describes the Bennet family. At the beginning of the extract the narrator tells us that Mr Bennet has already visited a new arrival in the neighbourhood, Mr Bingley; however, he keeps this information secret from his wife and daughters.

Mr Bennet was among the earliest of those who waited on Mr Bingley. He had always intended to visit him, though to the last always assuring his wife that he should not go; and till the evening after the visit was paid, she had no knowledge of it. It was then disclosed in the following manner.

5 Observing his second daughter employed in trimming a hat, he suddenly addressed her with,

'I hope Mr Bingley will like it, Lizzy.'

'We are not in a way to know *what* Mr Bingley likes,' said her mother resentfully, 'since we are not to visit.'

10 'But you forget, mama,' said Elizabeth, 'that we shall meet him at the assemblies, and that Mrs Long has promised to introduce him.'

'I do not believe Mrs Long will do any such thing. She has two nieces of her own. She is a selfish, hypocritical woman, and I have no opinion of her.'

'No more have I,' said Mr Bennet; 'and I am glad to find that you do not

15 depend on her serving you.'

Mrs Bennet deigned not to make any reply; but unable to contain herself, began scolding one of her daughters.

'Don't keep coughing so, Kitty, for heaven's sake! Have a little compassion on my nerves. You tear them to pieces.'

'Kitty has no discretion in her coughs,' said her father; 'she times them ill.'

20 'I do not cough for my own amusement,' replied Kitty fretfully.

'When is your next ball to be, Lizzy?'

'To-morrow fortnight.'

'Aye, so it is,' cried her mother, 'and Mrs Long does not come back till the day before; so, it will be impossible for her to introduce him, for she will

25 not know him herself.'

'Then, my dear, you may have the advantage of your friend, and introduce Mr Bingley to *her*.'

'Impossible, Mr Bennet, impossible, when I am not acquainted with him myself; how can you be so teazing?'

30 'I honour your circumspection. A fortnight's acquaintance is certainly very little. One cannot know what a man really is by the end of a fortnight. But if *we* do not venture somebody else will; and after all, Mrs Long and her nieces must stand their chance; and therefore, as she will think it an act of kindness, if you decline the office, I will take it on myself.'

35 The girls stared at their father. Mrs Bennet said only, 'Nonsense, nonsense!'

'What can be the meaning of that emphatic exclamation?' cried he. 'Do you consider the forms of introduction, and the stress that is laid on them, as nonsense? I cannot quite agree with you *there*. What say you, Mary? for you are a young lady of deep reflection I know, and read great books, and
40   make extracts.'

Mary wished to say something very sensible, but knew not how.

'While Mary is adjusting her ideas,' he continued, 'let us return to Mr Bingley.'

'I am sick of Mr Bingley,' cried his wife.

'I am sorry to hear *that*; but why did not you tell me that before? If I had
45   known as much this morning, I certainly would not have called on him. It is very unlucky; but as I have actually paid the visit, we cannot escape the acquaintance now.'

Guiding questions

1   How does Jane Austen present the various characters in this extract?
2   How does Austen make her story ironic?

Sample student response: transcript of sample student commentary

This extract from *Pride and Prejudice* by Jane Austen comes very early in the novel. A new arrival in the neighbourhood, Mr Bingley, has been visited by Mr Bennet. What this means is that, in terms of the social conventions of the time, Mrs Bennet and, perhaps even more importantly, her daughters will now be able to visit Mr Bingley and clearly Mrs Bennet has it in mind that one of her daughters might be an appropriate match in marriage for Mr Bingley. However, Mr Bennet, although he has made this visit, has told neither his wife nor his daughters and so has great fun at their expense disguising the truth of the situation.

In terms of the guiding questions, I am going to look at Jane Austen's presentation of character and her use throughout the passage of a playfully ironic tone. But before we come to those things it is worth just saying a couple of things about the narrative structure because this is an incredibly carefully constructed piece of writing. In the very first sentence of the extract we discover that 'Mr Bennet was among the earliest of those who visited on Mr Bingley.' It tells us in very clear terms what had happened. We are also told that he had always intended to visit him but we are then rather importantly informed that he has no intention of telling his wife or daughters at this point. Therefore, when he suddenly addresses his daughter Lizzy with a mention of Mr Bingley, he knows exactly what effect this will have on the female members of his household and, indeed, the structure of this passage is a building crescendo towards the moment at which Mrs Bennet, in infuriation, says, 'I am sick of Mr Bingley' and gives Mr Bennet the opportunity to reveal the fact that he has indeed already visited him.

So the structure is very important. Within that structure Jane Austen is able to give us very clear pointers as to how we might read the various characters. Elizabeth is presented in contrast to her mother, who we see from line 9 is described as speaking 'resentfully' and one might almost describe her language – 'we are not in a way to know what Mr Bingley likes' – as sarcastic: she is aiming her barbs at her husband who hasn't done, or she thinks he hasn't done, what she would have liked him to have done in visiting Mr Bingley. Elizabeth is, however, conciliatory: 'but you forget, mama', Elizabeth says, 'that we shall meet him at the assemblies', so she tries to make things better.

Mrs Bennet has a very clear view of the world. She is in competition with people like Mrs Long and her nieces of her own in order to get her daughters married off and we know from the rest of the novel that Mrs Bennet's sole concern in life is the marriage of her daughters. She is rudely dismissive of Mrs Long, describing her as a 'selfish, hypocritical woman' of whom she has no opinion and when we look at irony in a couple of minutes we will come back and talk about that. Mr Bennet keeps the conversation ticking on and again Jane Austen is using an ironic tone because we know as a reader that he has a piece of information that he has kept from the immediate audience.

Kitty is presented as lightweight and uncertain; she replies 'fretfully' in line 20 and is rather sarcastically dismissed by her father as having 'no discretion in her coughs'. Mrs Bennet is infuriated: 'Impossible, Mr Bennet,' she says in line 28, 'impossible, when I am not acquainted with him myself. How can you be so teasing?' And this is another example of Austen's irony because although she realises Mr Bennet is teasing her, Mrs Bennet does not know the half of it because she is yet to find out that he has actually visited Mr Bingley. Mary is represented and is rather cruelly dismissed by her father Mr Bennet as rather stupid. Mr Bennet says to her, 'you are a young lady of deep reflection' and the narrative voice then interrupts with, 'Mary wished to say something sensible, but knew not how.' It is worth pointing out that the narrative interjection draws the humour out of the situation here. You might argue that it is rather cruel here because Mr Bennet is being very rude at his daughter's expense.

Having looked at the presentation of the various characters it is worth saying something about the ironic and playful tone. That playful tone, which is Jane Austen's trademark style, is obvious from the very beginning of the passage. The narrator says, 'It was then disclosed in the following manner.' There is here a very matter-of-fact introduction to this game and when Mr Bennet suddenly addresses the female members of his household with the line, 'I hope Mr Bingley will like it, Lizzy' he is dropping that name 'Mr Bingley' in on purpose. Mrs Bennet's fantastic line about Mrs Long – 'She is a selfish, hypocritical woman, and I have no opinion of her' – is doubly clever; on the one hand she is contradicting herself – if she has no opinion of her then she can't also think her to be a 'selfish, hypocritical woman' – but Jane Austen is also cleverly and ironically demonstrating Mrs Bennet's bad qualities in that she is, in criticising someone else, identifying the worse aspects of her own character.

In terms of the continued irony, Mr Bennet's line to Mary, 'For you are a young lady of deep reflection, I know, and read great books and make extracts,' is a classic example of the ironic voice in its very literal manifestation of being the opposite of its intended meaning. Mr Bennet, and by association the reader, knows

Key term

Interjection A sudden interruption, often used to express a single response or emotion.

very well that Mary is not a young lady of deep reflection and Jane Austen is using the irony here, as she does throughout the passage, as a strategy to tease and playfully undermine her characters. The passage ends with a big narrative moment, Mrs Bennet crying, 'I am sick of Mr Bingley,' which gives Mr Bennet the opportunity to bring the story back to the withheld piece of information: 'It is very unlucky; but as I have actually paid the visit, we cannot escape the acquaintance now.'

After you've given your commentary, your teacher will ask you further questions. Here is an example of the sort of question your teacher might ask you following your commentary and the sort of answer you might give.

Teacher: Do you think Mr Bennet is presented as a sympathetic character by Jane Austen?

Student: Mr Bennet is presented as alright really; he has been to see Mr Bingley, after all, and has therefore done exactly what his wife and daughters wanted him to do. However, you could argue that he is a bit cruel by playing a game with them. You might also argue that he considers himself superior to his wife and most of his daughters and so is actually being presented as rather arrogant and not really very nice at all. However, the fact that Lizzy has a very good relationship with her father, and that she is the character the reader feels closest to and most sympathetic towards, might suggest that Jane Austen does really want us to be sympathetic towards Mr Bennet.

Activity 2.4

Look again at the various criteria which are used to assess this SL commentary. Read the transcript again and note down every time in the commentary you think you could reward this student for addressing:

- Criterion A: Knowledge and understanding of extract
- Criterion B: Appreciation of the writer's choices
- Criterion C: Organisation and presentation
- Criterion D: Language.

Extended essay

EE

Are you thinking of writing your extended essay on a novel or a series of novels? The novel has been the dominant literary form over the last couple of centuries and there is an enormous wealth of material out there to write on. If you have particularly enjoyed the novels of one writer, you should consider writing about them. There has been critical writing about narrative and this could be a very good starting place for an extended essay on novels.

Shakespeare's plays

William Shakespeare (1564–1616) is considered by many people to be the finest playwright – if not writer – to have written in English. His output is astonishingly prodigious, in terms of both the sheer number of plays and poems that he produced and their unrivalled quality: to have written *Hamlet*, *Othello*, *King Lear* and *Macbeth* alone was enough to have marked him out as a writer of genius. Unlike many writers, his reputation was established in his lifetime. His influence remains undiminished and reaches far beyond his home country. Although it is not compulsory to study Shakespeare in this course, many students will come across his plays and poems in this part of the course.

Shakespeare famously wrote a number of different types of play, including tragedies and comedies. The extracts here are from very well-known example of both: *Macbeth* and *A Midsummer Night's Dream*. They are both plays that you might very well study.

Figure 2.11 A scene from Act 3 Scene 4 of *Macbeth*, Royal Shakespeare Company, Barbican Theatre, London, 1993.

Text 2.7 From Act 3 Scene 4 *Macbeth*, William Shakespeare

This extract comes from the 'banquet scene' in Act 3. Macbeth has invited many of the noblemen of Scotland to dine with him. One of the expected guests at the banquet is Macbeth's erstwhile friend Banquo. Unbeknown to the other guests, including Lady Macbeth, Macbeth has had Banquo murdered that same day. Macbeth is shocked and horrified to see the ghost of Banquo sitting down to the banquet; however, none of the other guests can see the ghost. Lady Macbeth tries to reassure the guests and challenges her husband to act more like a man.

Lady Macbeth	Sit, worthy friends. My lord is often thus,
	And hath been from his youth. Pray you, keep seat.
	The fit is momentary; upon a thought
	He will again be well. If much you note him **55**
	You shall offend him and extend his passion.
	Feed, and regard him not. [*To Macbeth*] Are you a man?
Macbeth	Ay, and a bold one, that dare look on that
	Which might appal the devil.
Lady Macbeth	O proper stuff! **60**
	This is the very painting of your fear:
	This is the air-drawn dagger which you said
	Led you to Duncan. O, these flaws and starts,
	Impostors to true fear, would well become
	A woman's story at a winter's fire **65**
	Authorised by her grandam. Shame itself!
	Why do you make such faces? When all's done
	You look but on a stool.
Macbeth	Prithee, see there! Behold, look, lo! How say you?
	[*To Ghost*] Why, what care I? If thou canst nod, speak too. **70**
	If charnel-houses and our graves must send
	Those that we bury back, our monuments
	Shall be the maws of kites.
	[*Exit Ghost of Banquo*]
Lady Macbeth	What, quite unmanned in folly?
Macbeth	If I stand here, I saw him.

Lady Macbeth	Fie, for shame.	
Macbeth	Blood hath been shed ere now, i' th' olden time,	75
	Ere humane statute purged the gentle weal;	
	Ay, and since too, murders have been performed	
	Too terrible for the ear. The time has been	
	That when the brains were out, the man would die,	
	And there an end. But now they rise again	80
	With twenty mortal murders on their crowns	
	And push us from our stools. This is more strange	
	Than such a murder is.	
Lady Macbeth	My worthy lord,	
	Your noble friends do lack you.	
Macbeth	I do forget —	
	Do not muse at me, my most worthy friends.	85
	I have a strange infirmity which is nothing	
	To those that know me.	

Guiding questions

1 How does Shakespeare make this extract dramatically interesting?
2 How does Shakespeare's choice of language affect the audience's response to this extract?

Sample student response: transcript of sample student commentary

This SL commentary was awarded a very good mark by the teacher who assessed it. The transcript has been marked up with the teacher's comments to help you to see why it achieved good marks.

This extract from William Shakespeare's play *Macbeth* is taken from Act 3 Scene 4, an amazing scene commonly referred to as 'the banquet scene'. Prior to this scene Macbeth has arranged for the two murderers to kill Banquo, his friend, and importantly Fleance, Banquo's son, although of course Fleance escapes. At the banquet Macbeth is not expecting Banquo although everybody else is, but Banquo's ghost turns up. In this scene, despite the fact that this is a very public occasion and that there are lots of Lords and Scottish noblemen present, the only two characters who speak in the extract in front of us are Lady Macbeth and Macbeth and there is quite an extraordinary level of dramatic control being exercised by Shakespeare here.[1]

In answering the guiding questions, what I am firstly going to do is look at how the scene is rendered dramatically interesting by looking at the interplay between Macbeth and Lady Macbeth and then I am going to have a look at some of the language patterns and look particularly at the language of death, the language of mourning and the language of blood, patterns which reappear throughout the play.[2]

The murder of Banquo is distinguished from the earlier deeds that Lady Macbeth and Macbeth commit in that Macbeth does it independently. Indeed he says, just before this scene, to his wife 'be innocent of the knowledge, dearest chuck', and so he is taking on his own shoulders part of the burden. And yet at the beginning of the scene it is Lady Macbeth's job to keep propriety. She encourages

Key term

Language patterns A general term used to denote repeated structures, and literary devices and techniques employed regularly by an author throughout a text.

Chapter 2 – Detailed study

1. The student immediately demonstrates an excellent knowledge and understanding of the extract by helpfully placing it in context and thus addressing Criterion A.

2. The student reveals what the structure of the IOC is going to be. This clearly addresses Criterion C (Organisation and presentation) and can be suitably rewarded.

3. This paragraph includes a number of points which are rewarded in terms of Criterion B (Appreciation of the writer's choices). The student's discussion of the language choices made here is, at times, really quite sophisticated.

4. The focus on language choices can be rewarded under Criterion B.

5. Almost as an aside, the student reveals excellent knowledge (Criterion A).

6. This is good, clear evidence of appreciation of the writer's choices (Criterion B).

7. The overall accuracy and quality of the language used means that the student is highly impressive in terms of Criterion D (Language).

the worthy friends, the noblemen, to 'keep seat', which is in stark contrast to the end of the scene when she says 'stand not upon the order of your leaving'. Keeping seat means that they are seated and they would have been seated in a formal order so she is insisting that they continue to observe the social niceties and the conventional expectations of behaviour. Despite the fact that Macbeth is having a fit she puts a spin on his behaviour, saying that it is a momentary thing and that he will again be well, and she tells them simply to eat and not to look at him, but then in line 57 the dialogue shifts from Lady Macbeth addressing the nobles to her addressing Macbeth, and look at the way in which that line finishes halfway through; it pauses in the middle – 'Feed, and regard him not.' – and then turns and asks the pointed question, just four monosyllabic words: 'Are you a man?'[3]

Remember that earlier on in the play Macbeth has told us that he dare do all that 'may become a man who dares do more is none', and Lady Macbeth is returning to her challenge of, his masculinity, to challenge his manhood, and Macbeth answers that he is 'a bold one, that dare look on that/Which might appal the devil.'. Maybe there is an acknowledgement in the language that he is in fact becoming himself a devil. Lady Macbeth's language is dismissive and patronising:[4] 'O proper stuff!/ This is the very painting of your fear:', she says. The fact that she uses the word 'painting' draws attention to the fact that she sees his fear as a representation of actual fear, that he is not truly experiencing the emotions he says he is and she makes a comparison to the air-drawn dagger (we remember the famous speech: 'Is this a dagger I see before me?')[5] and Lady Macbeth's dismissive 'you said' suggests that this is simply Macbeth's argument and one which she does not necessarily agree with. Indeed, these flaws and starts and the dismissive monosyllabic words draw attention again to her disapproving nature, to her mind comparable to a 'woman's story at a winter's fire/Authorised by her grandam'. What she is saying here is that this is a story that would be most appropriate told in a very safe setting by a woman and her grandmother, in specific contrast to the idea of manliness which she has been challenging earlier and she comes back to that, saying: 'What, quite unmanned in folly?' It's a constant challenge to Macbeth's sense of himself as a man and, in answering that question, he is left simply to state facts: 'If I stand here, I saw him'. And, again, the fact that it is simple monosyllabic language shows that he is desperately trying just to be clear in his thoughts.[6]

In terms of moving from that interplay between Lady Macbeth and Macbeth and the dramatically interesting nature of the fact that they are having a personal discussion in a very public arena, we will move from that and look at how the language that is used also highlights some of Shakespeare's ongoing concerns in the play. We have just heard that Macbeth's response to Lady Macbeth's question is clear, simple and monosyllabic and yet his longer speech, beginning: 'Blood hath been shed ere now', develops a more wistful, melancholic, even nostalgic tone. Phrases like 'I' th' olden time' or 'the time has been' suggest that Macbeth is already seeing himself as having gone beyond the point of no return in 'blood steeped so far' as he says elsewhere in the play. Indeed, the references to blood at the beginning of that speech, the 'mortal murders', the repetition of the word 'murder' at the end of the speech – it comes three times within eight lines – it is a reminder of the imagery of death, the imagery of blood that pervades the play. The idea of death and of death exceeding the bounds that one might normally expect of it is referred to when Macbeth says, 'If charnel-houses our graves must send/ Those that we bury back, our monuments/Shall be the maws of kites', saying, if you like, that dead bodies should be in our graveyards and yet those graveyards are rejecting them to be eaten by birds of prey.[7]

At the end of the scene Macbeth tries to adopt the tone of his wife: 'Do not muse at me, my most worthy friends./I have a strange infirmity which is nothing/To those that know me.', and this very personal public scene draws to an end.[8]

> **8** The commentary is concluded effectively, providing the examiner with more evidence that the student has achieved very highly in Criterion C.

After you've given your commentary, your teacher will ask you further questions. Here is an example of the sort of question your teacher might ask you following your commentary and the sort of answer you might give.

Teacher: Could you say anything about the way in which Shakespeare uses verse form – the rhythm and structure of the lines – in this extract?

Student: Shakespeare normally writes in iambic pentameters. This means that each line has a regular pattern of five beats. However, very regular rhythm makes the characters sound in control and happy. Here they are neither of those two things. Therefore, Shakespeare breaks up his normal structure. If we look, for instance, at lines 69–70, Macbeth says: 'Prithee, see there! Behold, look, lo!/ How say you?/Why, what care I?' The first line makes Macbeth sound tense and uncertain. 'How say you?' sounds very strange and suggests that perhaps Shakespeare is indicating to the actor playing Macbeth that he should leave a big pause here. The second line containing the question 'Why, what care I?' adds to the sense of uncertainty in this passage.

Activity 2.5

The student's commentary has been annotated to show where it did well in terms of the four criteria on which it is assessed. You should now do the same for the answer to the teacher's question.
- Point out where the student manages to hit the various criteria.
- Are there any criteria the student doesn't hit?
- How could the student extend this answer even further?

HL discussion questions

If you are an HL student and have been studying *Macbeth* for Part 2 you might discuss this text after you have given your IOC on poetry. Here is an example of the sort of question you might be asked with a sample student response.

Teacher: How would you describe the role of the soliloquies in *Macbeth*?

Student: Shakespeare uses soliloquies for very specific purposes. A soliloquy is when the actor talks directly to the audience and is alone on stage. In this way

Key term

Soliloquy A speech in which a character articulates his innermost thoughts alone on stage.

Chapter 2 – Detailed study

we can learn things about what they are thinking; it is almost as if the character is sharing their thoughts with us. In Macbeth's first soliloquy he concludes that the only thing making him think about killing Duncan is his 'vaulting ambition'. The audience learns that he is determined not to go ahead with the murder because he realises that his motives are not very good. This makes the fact that Lady Macbeth manages to persuade him to do it anyway very powerful. We also see in the soliloquies that he's not sure whether he's seeing things or not when he asks himself whether he can see a real dagger or if it's just an illusion. Shakespeare uses the soliloquies to show us what Macbeth is actually thinking.

Figure 2.12 A still from Act 2 Scene 1 of *A Midsummer Night's Dream*, Royal Shakespeare Company, Barbican Theatre, London, 1995.

Text 2.8 From Act 2 Scene 1 *A Midsummer Night's Dream*, William Shakespeare

In this extract Puck, a mischievous fairy, is talking to another fairy about the fairy king, Oberon, and the fairy queen, Titania. Shakespeare uses this conversation to prepare us for the arrival and introduction of the fairy king and queen.

Puck	The King doth keep his revels here tonight.	
	Take heed the Queen come not within his sight,	
	For Oberon is passing fell and wrath,	20
	Because that she as her attendant hath	
	A lovely boy stol'n from an Indian king;	
	She never had so sweet a changeling,	
	And jealous Oberon would have the child	
	Knight of his train, to trace the forests wild.	25
	But she perforce withholds the lovèd boy,	
	Crowns him with flowers, and makes him all her joy.	
	And now they never meet in grove or green,	
	By fountain clear or spangled starlight sheen,	
	But they do square, that all their elves for fear	30
	Creep into acorn cups and hide them there.	
Fairy	Either I mistake your shape and making quite,	
	Or else you are that shrewd and knavish sprite	
	Called Robin Goodfellow. Are not you he	
	That frights the maidens of the villagery,	35
	Skim milk, and sometimes labour in the quern,	
	And bootless make the breathless housewife churn,	
	And sometime make the drink to bear no barm,	
	Mislead night-wanderers, laughing at their harm?	
	Those that 'Hobgoblin' call you, and 'Sweet Puck',	40
	You do their work, and they shall have good luck.	
	Are not you he?	
Puck	Thou speak'st aright;	
	I am that merry wanderer of the night.	
	I jest to Oberon, and make him smile	
	When I a fat and bean-fed horse beguile,	45
	Neighing in likeness of a filly foal;	
	And sometime lurk I in a gossip's bowl	

> In very likeness of a roasted crab,
> And when she drinks, against her lips I bob,
> And on her withered dewlap pour the ale.　　　**50**
> The wisest aunt, telling the saddest tale,
> Sometime for threefoot stool mistaketh me;
> Then slip I from her bum, down topples she,
> And 'Tailor' cries, and falls into a cough;
> And then the whole choir hold their hips and loffe,　　　**55**
> And waxen in their mirth, and neeze, and swear
> A merrier hour was never wasted there.
> But room, Fairy: here comes Oberon.
> **Fairy**　And here my mistress. Would that he were gone!

Guiding questions

1　How does Shakespeare prepare the audience for the arrival of Oberon and Titania?
2　How does Shakespeare present the character of Puck in this extract?

Sample student response: transcript of sample student commentary

This extract from William Shakespeare's comedy *A Midsummer's Night's Dream* comes at the beginning of Act 2. In Act 1, we have been introduced to the human characters and to the mechanicals. At the beginning of Act 2 we are, for the first time, introduced to the world of the fairies and, before we meet the fairy king and queen, Oberon and Titania, we are prepared for their introduction through this dialogue between Puck and one of Titania's fairies. This passage comes immediately before the entrance of Titania and Oberon and the very famous lines of dialogue: 'Ill met by moonlight, proud Titania!/ What, jealous Oberon?' and in answer to the first of the guiding questions I am going to look at the way in which this passage prepares us for the fairy king and queen's arrival. Secondly, I am going to go on and look specifically at how Shakespeare presents the character of the 'knavish' Puck in this extract.

Let's first look at how this scene serves as a preparation for the arrival of the king and queen; in many ways the interplay between Puck and the fairy anticipates the interplay between Oberon and Titania. They are the servants of the king and queen and in many ways take on similar roles. It is worth mentioning that this passage is written in rhyming couplets, so the first couplet: 'The King doth keep his revels here tonight./Take heed the Queen come not within his sight' gives the passage as a whole a tripping lightness of tone which is appropriate to comedy and makes it stand out from the much more serious and more grave aspects of Shakespeare's tragedies.

In that very famous exchange which is anticipated in this passage, Oberon is reported as 'jealous', and Titania 'proud' and in his first speech Puck prepares us for that as he refers to Oberon using the same adjective – 'jealous' – in line 24 and then goes on to describe Titania's behaviour towards the little boy, the changeling, that she has stolen from an Indian king, and describes how she crowns him with flowers and makes him 'all her joy', again anticipating the way in which she is going to be seen as 'proud' in the next scene. Clearly if 'all her joy' is dedicated to this boy

Key term

Comedy A work of art characterised by its humorous or satirical nature; in comedy characters usually triumph in adversity.

then there is none left for Oberon, the king. The anticipation of this friction is rather wonderfully characterised at the end of Puck's first speech where he describes how all the elves, the train, the followers, the servants of Oberon and Titania, 'for fear/ Creep into acorn cups and hide them there'. They want to get out of the way and he uses the natural world, in this instance the acorn, which not only gives us a sense of protection but also gives us a lovely sense of the size of these creatures that Shakespeare wants to portray, convinces us that they wanted to be protected from the fallout that will inevitably result from the meeting of Oberon and Titania.

Although the hint of seriousness is never quite realised because of the lightness, the comedy of the piece is underlined by the introduction of some of Puck's characteristics and Shakespeare does this in two ways. One, he has the fairy ask him 'Are not you he?' and 'you are that shrewd and knavish sprite/ Called Robin Goodfellow' – Puck's other name – and adjectives like 'shrewd' and 'knavish' give a very clear indication of the sort of character that Puck is; Shakespeare wants to show his audience just what a playful and, indeed, naughty character Puck actually is. This is added to by Puck agreeing with the fairy 'Thou speak'st aright;/ I am that merry wanderer of the night', characterising himself in slightly ironic terms – as a 'merry wanderer' – having a sort of joviality which is undercut in reality by Puck's quite nasty behaviour at times. Indeed Shakespeare presents specific incidences of his behaviour, for instance getting an old woman to mistake him for a three-foot stool and making her fall down at which the whole choir – everybody who is watching – 'hold their hips and loffe/ And waxen in their mirth, and neeze, and swear/ A merrier hour was never wasted there.' Puck is a troublemaker; he likes causing other people discomfort, pain and annoyance in order to make people laugh.

Indeed, if we go back to the fairy's introduction, the fairy asks whether indeed he is 'Robin Goodfellow' and one of the things he is described as doing is misleading 'night-wanderers' and then laughing at their harm so that the vindictiveness that Puck admits to is demonstrated by the fairy as well. Clearly, Puck's reputation precedes him and Shakespeare wants us, as the audience, to appreciate the level of esteem in which he is held or certainly the level to which his reputation has been sealed. There is a nice anticipation of some of the mistakes and mismatches that will happen later on in the play – we think particularly of Bottom and Titania, with Bottom wearing the ass's head – when the fairy begins the speech by saying: 'Either I mistake your shape and making quite,/Or else you are that shrewd and knavish sprite'; we are not quite sure whether Puck is who the fairy thinks he is and this again anticipates one of the themes that Shakespeare will come back to.

And so this extract ends with the arrival of Oberon; Puck says: 'here comes Oberon' and the fairy completes the couplet and so, therefore, uses the line that rhymes: 'And here my mistress. Would that he were gone!' There is a sense that there is about to be fireworks and Shakespeare has used the interplay between these two characters very cleverly to set up the audience's anticipation of the meeting. The very next lines are: 'Ill met by moonlight, proud Titania!/What, jealous Oberon?'

After you've given your commentary, your teacher will ask you further questions. Here is an example of the sort of question your teacher might ask you following your commentary and the sort of answer you might give.

Teacher: Thank you for this. What can you say about the way in which Shakespeare uses language to describe nature and the natural world?

Student: Well, if you look at line 27, for example, we can see how Puck describes Titania as using the natural world (in this case flowers) to 'crown' the little boy and, perhaps, to make him even more beautiful. He then tells us how Oberon and Titania no longer meet in the beautiful natural places they once did. Shakespeare uses alliteration to create a vividly memorable depiction of the natural world, almost to suggest that it has been forgotten by the fairy king and queen because of their dispute. He is almost being nostalgic when he remembers the 'grove or green' where they used to meet. And in the following line the beauty is stressed by the alliterative phrase 'spangled starlight sheen'.

Activity 2.6

Look at the assessment criteria and then read the sample commentary and answer again. Making careful reference to the four SL criteria, discuss how you would mark this commentary. Decide what marks you would award for each of the criteria.

Unit 2.4 Practise writing a commentary: Sample extracts

The following extracts are all from the same texts as those on which the student sample material in Unit 2.3 is based, the idea being that you can practise on a similar extract and use some of the ideas and structures from the sample material to help you.

Activity 2.7

You should now use the extracts which follow to practise commentaries of your own. Make sure you spend as much time practising the timed preparation as delivering the commentary itself. Both are vital if you are to deliver a successful final commentary. Remember to follow the six planning and preparation stages:

1   Read the text and the guiding questions.
2   Identify your two or three big themes.
3   Mark up the points that you will use to develop and analyse your themes.
4   Sequence your points so that you are clear about the order in which you will talk about them.
5   Make sure that you have clear notes.
6   Practise.

Remember to look back at the sample commentaries in Unit 2.3 on extracts from the same texts. These will help you with your ideas.

Text 2.9 *Paradise Lost: Book One* (lines 622–63), John Milton

This extract comes from slightly later on in *Paradise Lost,* Book One than Texts 2.3 and 2.4. Once again Satan is addressing his fellow rebel angels. The passage has been annotated to help you but there is no sample commentary on this extract. Your task is to prepare and perform a commentary of your own based on what you have learned in this chapter and from the sample commentaries on Texts 2.3 and 2.4.

```
      O myriads of immortal spirits, O powers
      Matchless, but with almighty, and that strife
      Was not inglorious, though the event was dire,
625   As this place testifies, and this dire change
      Hateful to utter: but what power of mind
      Foreseeing or presaging, from the depth
      Of knowledge past or present, could have feared,
      How such united force of gods, how such
630   As stood like these, could ever know repulse?
      For who can yet believe, though after loss,
      That all these puissant legions, whose exile
      Hath emptied heaven, shall fail to reascend
      Self-raised, and repossess their native seat?
635   For me be witness all the host of heaven,
      If counsels different, or danger shunned
      By me, have lost our hopes. But he who reigns
      Monarch in heaven, till then as one secure
      Sat on his throne, upheld by old repute,
640   Consent or custom, and his regal state
      Put forth at full, but still his strength concealed,
      Which tempted our attempt, and wrought our fall.
      Henceforth his might we know, and know our own
      So as not either to provoke, or dread
645   New war, provoked; our better part remains
      To work in close design, by fraud or guile
      What force effected not: that he no less
      At length from us may find, who overcomes
      By force, hath overcome but half his foe.
650   Space may produce new worlds; whereof so rife
      There went a fame in heaven that he ere long
      Intended to create, and therein plant
      A generation, whom his choice regard
      Should favour equal to the sons of heaven:
655   Thither, if but to pry, shall be perhaps
      Our first eruption, thither or elsewhere:
      For this infernal pit shall never hold
      Celestial spirits in bondage, nor the abyss
      Long under darkness cover. But these thoughts
660   Full counsel must mature: peace is despaired,
      For who can think submission? War then, war
      Open or understood must be resolved.
```

Guiding questions

1 How does Milton present the character of Satan in this extract?

2 How does the language used in this extract contribute to its effectiveness?

Text 2.10 *Great Expectations*, Charles Dickens

In this extract, from Chapter 8 of the novel, Dickens describes a character called Mr Pumblechook and his seed shop, and gives us a snapshot of the various shopkeepers' lives. Pip meets Mr Pumblechook for breakfast (he is to accompany him to meet Miss Havisham for the first time) and is subjected to a series of rather unwelcome mental arithmetic questions.

Mr Pumblechook's premises in the High Street of the market town, were of a peppercorny and farinaceous character, as the premises of a corn-chandler and seedsman should be. It appeared to me that he must be a very happy man indeed, to have so many little drawers in his shop; and I wondered
5 when I peeped into one or two on the lower tiers, and saw the tied-up brown paper packets inside, whether the flower-seeds and bulbs ever wanted of a fine day to break out of those jails, and bloom.
   It was in the early morning after my arrival that I entertained this speculation. On the previous night, I had been sent straight to bed in an attic with a
10 sloping roof which was so low in the corner where the bedstead was, that I calculated the tiles as being within a foot of my eyebrows. In the same early morning, I discovered a singular affinity between seeds and corduroys. Mr Pumblechook wore corduroys, and so did his shopman; and somehow, there was a general air and flavour about the corduroys, so much in the
15 nature of seeds, and a general air and flavour about the seeds, so much in the nature of corduroys, that I hardly knew which was which. The same opportunity served me for noticing that Mr Pumblechook appeared to conduct his business by looking across the street at the saddler, who appeared to transact *his* business by keeping his eye on the coachmaker,
20 who appeared to get on in life by putting his hands in his pockets and contemplating the baker, who in his turn folded his arms and stared at the grocer, who stood at his door and yawned at the chemist. The watchmaker, always poring over a little desk with a magnifying glass at his eye, and always inspected by a group in smock-frocks poring over him through the
25 glass of his shop-window, seemed to be about the only person in the High Street whose trade engaged his attention.
   Mr Pumblechook and I breakfasted at eight o'clock in the parlour behind the shop, while the shopman took his mug of tea and hunch of bread-and-butter on a sack of peas in the front premises. I considered
30 Mr Pumblechook wretched company. Besides being possessed by my sister's idea that a mortifying and penitential character ought to be imparted to my diet – besides giving me as much crumb as possible in combination with as little butter, and putting such a quantity of warm water into my milk that it would have been more candid to have left the milk out altogether – his
35 conversation consisted of nothing but arithmetic. On my politely bidding him Good-morning, he said pompously, 'Seven times nine, boy!' And how should *I* be able to answer, dodged in that way, in a strange place, on an

empty stomach! I was hungry, but before I had swallowed a morsel, he began a running sum that lasted all through the breakfast. 'Seven?' 'And
40 four?' 'And eight?' 'And six?' 'And two?' 'And ten?' And so on. And after each figure was disposed of, it was as much as I could do to get a bite or a sup, before the next came; while he sat at his ease guessing nothing, and eating bacon and hot roll, in (if I may be allowed the expression) a gorging and gormandising manner.

Guiding questions

1 How does Dickens create a sense of the character of Mr Pumblechook in this extract?
2 How does Dickens use language in interesting ways in this extract?

Text 2.11 *Pride and Prejudice*, Jane Austen, 1813

This extract is the opening to the novel. The first sentence is very famous as an excellent example of Jane Austen's ironic style. We are introduced to Mr and Mrs Bennet who are talking together about a new arrival in the neighbourhood, Mr Bingley.

It is a truth universally acknowledged, that a single man in possession of a good fortune, must be in want of a wife.

However little known the feelings or views of such a man may be on his first entering a neighbourhood, this truth is so well fixed in the minds of the
5 surrounding families, that he is considered the rightful property of some one or other of their daughters.

'My dear Mr Bennet,' said his lady to him one day, 'have you heard that Netherfield Park is let at last?'

Mr Bennet replied that he had not.
10 'But it is,' returned she; 'for Mrs Long has just been here, and she told me all about it.'

Mr Bennet made no answer.

'Do you not want to know who has taken it?' cried his wife impatiently.

'*You* want to tell me, and I have no objection to hearing it.'
15 This was invitation enough.

'Why, my dear, you must know, Mrs Long says that Netherfield is taken by a young man of large fortune from the north of England; that he came down on Monday in a chaise and four to see the place, and was so much delighted with it, that he agreed with Mr Morris immediately; that he is to
20 take possession before Michaelmas, and some of his servants are to be in the house by the end of next week.'

'What is his name?'

'Bingley.'

'Is he married or single?'
25 'Oh! Single, my dear, to be sure! A single man of large fortune; four or five thousand a year. What a fine thing for our girls!'

'How so? How can it affect them?'

'My dear Mr Bennet,' replied his wife, 'how can you be so tiresome! You must know that I am thinking of his marrying one of them.'

30 'Is that his design in settling here?'

'Design! Nonsense, how can you talk so! But it is very likely that he *may* fall in love with one of them, and therefore you must visit him as soon as he comes.'

'I see no occasion for that. You and the girls may go, or you may send 35 them by themselves, which perhaps will be still better, for as you are as handsome as any of them, Mr Bingley may like you the best of the party.'

Guiding questions

1 What do we learn about the characters of Mr and Mrs Bennet from this extract?

2 In what ways might you describe this extract as ironic?

Text 2.12 From Act 1 Scene 7 *Macbeth*, William Shakespeare

This scene immediately follows Macbeth's famous soliloquy which ends with his realisation that it is just his ambition that is making him think about killing the king, Duncan. He therefore resolves, not to go ahead with his murderous plans. Yet he doesn't take into account the resolve of his wife, Lady Macbeth, who encounters him at this point and persuades him to change his mind and proceed with the plan to kill Duncan after all.

Figure 2.13 A still from Act 1 Scene 7 of *Macbeth*, Almeida Theatre production 2005.

Macbeth	How now! What news?	
Lady Macbeth	He has almost supped. Why have you left the chamber?	
Macbeth	Hath he asked for me?	
Lady Macbeth	Know you not, he has?	30
Macbeth	We will proceed no further in this business.	
	He hath honoured me of late, and I have bought	
	Golden opinions from all sorts of people,	
	Which would be worn now in their newest gloss,	
	Not cast aside so soon.	
Lady Macbeth	Was the hope drunk	35
	Wherein you dressed yourself? Hath it slept since?	
	And wakes it now, to look so green and pale	
	At what it did so freely? From this time,	
	Such I account thy love. Art thou afeard	
	To be the same in thine own act and valour,	40
	As thou art in desire? Wouldst thou have that	
	Which thou esteem'st the ornament of life,	
	And live a coward in thine own esteem,	
	Letting I dare not wait upon I would,	
	Like the poor cat i' th'adage?	
Macbeth	Prithee, peace:	45
	I dare do all that may become a man;	
	Who dares do more is none.	
Lady Macbeth	What beast was't, then	
	That made you break this enterprise to me?	
	When you durst do it, then you were a man.	
	And to be more than what you were, you would	50
	Be so much more the man. Nor time, nor place	

Did then adhere, and yet you would make both.
They have made themselves and that their fitness now
Does unmake you. I have given suck and know
How tender 'tis to love the babe that milks me: 55
I would, while it was smiling in my face,
Have plucked my nipple from his boneless gums
And dashed the brains out, had I so sworn
As you have done to this.

Macbeth   If we should fail?
Lady Macbeth   We fail?
But screw your courage to the sticking-place,   60
And we'll not fail.

Guiding questions

1   How does Shakespeare create tension in this extract?
2   How does Shakespeare use language in interesting ways in this extract?

Text 2.13 From Act 2 Scene 1 *A Midsummer Night's Dream*, William Shakespeare

This extract sees the introduction of the fairy king, Oberon, and the fairy queen, Titania. They are angry with each other because they are arguing about a boy whom they both think should belong to them. They accuse each other of being jealous and proud.

Oberon   Ill met by moonlight, proud Titania!   60
Titania   What, jealous Oberon? Fairies, skip hence.
I have forsworn his bed and company.
Oberon   Tarry, rash wanton! Am not I thy lord?
Titania   Then I must be thy lady. But I know
When thou hast stol'n away from Fairyland,   65
And in the shape of Corin sat all day
Playing on pipes of corn, and versing love
To amorous Phillida. Why art thou here
Come from the farthest step of India? –
But that, forsooth, the bouncing Amazon,   70
Your buskined mistress and your warrior love,
To Theseus must be wedded; and you come
To give their bed joy and prosperity.
Oberon   How canst thou thus, for shame, Titania,
Glance at my credit with Hippolyta,   75
Knowing I know thy love to Theseus?
Didst not thou not lead him through the glimmering night
From Perigenia, whom he ravishèd,
And make him with fair Aegles break his faith,
With Ariadne, and Antiopa?   80
Titania   These are the forgeries of jealousy:
And never since the middle summer's spring

Met we on hill, in dale, forest, or mead,
By pavèd fountain or by rushy brook,
Or in the beachèd margent of the sea   **85**
To dance our ringlets to the whistling wind,
But with thy brawls thou hast disturbed our sport.
Therefore the winds, piping to us in vain,
As in revenge have sucked up from the sea
Contagious fogs; which, falling in the land,   **90**
Hath every pelting river made so proud
That they have overborne their continents.
The ox hath therefore stretched his yoke in vain,
The ploughman lost his sweat, and the green corn
Hath rotted ere his youth attained a beard.   **95**
The fold stands empty in the drownèd field,
And crows are fatted with the murrion flock;
The nine-men's-morris is filled up with mud,
And the quaint mazes in the wanton green
For lack of tread are undistinguishable.   **100**

Guiding questions

1   How does Shakespeare create tension between Oberon and Titania in this extract?
2   How does Shakespeare use language in interesting ways in this extract?

Chapter 2 summary

In the course of this chapter, we hope that you have:
- understood what you will study in Part 2 and how it is assessed
- reminded yourself of some of the key ways in which you can analyse writers' choices of language, structure and form
- looked at a number of extracts and responded to them analytically
- found out about the individual oral commentary and the HL discussion
- developed a range of strategies to plan, prepare and deliver a successful commentary.

By now you should feel prepared and confident about tackling this part of the course, the individual oral commentary and, for HL students, the discussion.

3 Literary genres

How is this chapter structured?

This chapter follows the shape of Part 3: Literary genres and is organised into four units. In the first unit, Unit 3.1, you will find out what studying Part 3 involves and look at how it is assessed. In Unit 3.2 you will consider some of the features and conventions of the different genres available for study in Part 3. In Unit 3.3 you will find support and guidance to help you to write an effective comparative essay in preparation for the examination. The final unit, Unit 3.4, contains student sample material which has been marked up to show where the students have gained marks using the assessment criteria.

Unit 3.1 **What is Part 3: Literary genres?**

In this part of the course you will study three texts at SL and four texts at HL. All of the texts will be from the same literary genre. This means that you will study texts that are all either poetry, or drama, or prose (novels and short stories or other forms of prose). Your teacher will choose your texts carefully to ensure that there are plenty of points of comparison between them and that they are all taken from the prescribed list of authors (PLA).

You will study each of these works in depth. As part of your course you will be expected to learn to identify and analyse particular literary conventions and features which are common to texts of the genre you are studying. Because all the works are from the same genre you should find that there are plenty of ways to compare them in your final essay in the exam. When studying Part 3 you will be aiming to:
- understand the conventions of your chosen genre
- develop your skills of analysis in your chosen genre
- develop your ability to write an effective comparative essay.

How is Part 3 assessed?

Part 3 is assessed by an exam, Paper 2, at the end of the course. At SL you have 1 hour 30 minutes to complete the question; at HL you have 2 hours. At both levels you will need to write about at least two texts and make detailed comparisons between them. The exam is closed text; this means that you won't be able to take copies of your text into the exam room. You will therefore need to learn a number of quotations by heart in order to be able to refer closely to the text in your answer. In the exam you will write a formal, comparative literary essay; you can find advice on how to do this in Unit 3.3 and some sample student responses in Unit 3.4.

There are five assessment criteria for Paper 2 at both SL and HL:

Criterion A	Knowledge and understanding	5 marks
Criterion B	Response to the question	5 marks
Criterion C	Appreciation of the literary conventions of the genre	5 marks
Criterion D	Organisation and development	5 marks
Criterion E	Language	5 marks
Total		25 marks

You should consider what each of these criteria means and what you'll need to do in Paper 2 to score as highly as possible on each.

Criterion A: Knowledge and understanding

You will be expected to demonstrate your knowledge by quoting from your texts in your essay. Therefore, from as early as possible in the course, note down key quotations and commit them to memory. In the exam you will demonstrate your understanding of the ways these texts work by writing analytically about the choices the writers make. If all this sounds rather a lot to cope with, don't worry: Unit 3.3 gives you plenty of help and advice on how to write analytically, especially in the context of a comparative literary essay, which is what you will have to write in Paper 2.

Criterion B: Response to the question

A rigorous focus on answering the question is often the hallmark of a successful exam script. If you have worked effectively throughout the course you will find that, by the time the exam comes, your knowledge of the texts will be excellent. You will need to avoid the temptation of writing down everything you have learned and can remember! You'll have to accept that you will leave out far more of what you know about the texts than you include. This is because your final essay will need to be very carefully focused. A key element to writing an effective comparative essay, as we will explore in Unit 3.3, is to learn how to include a thesis and a tightly structured argument to ensure that you really do answer the question!

Criterion C: Appreciation of the literary conventions of the genre

One of the keys to a successful Part 3 essay is a detailed understanding and appreciation of what makes a particular genre work. You will be studying texts from the same genre, so you will need to become an expert in the conventions of that genre, whether drama, poetry or prose. This chapter should help you to use vocabulary and terminology appropriate to your chosen genre. It is a good idea, as early as possible in your Part 3 course, to make a list of all the various terms and devices which are specifically relevant

tip

In the exam you will be expected to quote from memory. Learning quotations throughout the course is much easier than trying to learn them all at the last minute. As you study each text you should note down key quotations and try to learn them as you go: why not keep a notebook with an ongoing list of key quotations? You should aim to return to these several times throughout your course to help you to remember them accurately.

to the genre you are studying. Unit 3.2 helps you to do exactly that. It takes you through the genres and looks at the various features you will need to comment on and the various terms you will need to use, and it gives you examples of how you should write in a genre-specific manner. We suggest a series of questions to ask of any of the texts you are studying in order to help you think about them in terms of their genre and see how the writers comply with the conventions of that genre. Key terms are highlighted and defined for you throughout the coursebook, and the Glossary at the end will help you to become better acquainted with the various literary conventions and terms you are advised to use.

Criterion D: Organisation and development

The way you structure your essay will be the key to how successfully your response is organised. To help you to become skilled in writing this type of essay, Unit 3.3 looks in detail at how you might structure such a response for Paper 2. The more you practise writing essays the easier you will find it to organise them successfully. In Unit 3.4 you will find student sample responses; you will also find further advice on what a successful exam response looks like in the form of examiners' comments on the student work.

Criterion E: Language

The same advice about the way you use language applies in Part 3 as for all other parts of the course. You should use accurate, appropriately formal English and make careful use of literary terminology wherever possible. Although you should be ambitious in your writing it is still worth bearing in mind the following piece of good advice for all of your writing about literature: say something sophisticated but say it as simply and as clearly as possible.

What will you be asked to do in your final exam?

The exam is called Paper 2 and, apart from the amount of time you will have to complete your answer, the details for SL and HL are identical. The paper counts for 25% of the marks at both SL and HL.

- In Paper 2 there will be three essay questions for each literary genre represented on the PLA. You have to answer **one** essay question only.
- The questions will guide you to discuss how the content of the texts is informed by the conventions of the particular genre you have studied. You will be expected to compare at least two of the texts you have studied.

Unit 3.2 What are the features of the different literary genres?

Part 3 is all about genre. You will study texts from one of the following genres: prose (novels and short stories or other prose), poetry or drama. Regardless of which genre you are studying, you should make sure that you always use the most appropriate vocabulary, terminology and approach for that genre. In this unit you will look at the key features and conventions for each genre and we suggest a series of questions to ask about the texts you are studying. There is no right or wrong approach to comparing the texts in Part 3 but you will be expected to focus on the ways in which writers use the aspects of the genre in which they are writing. As you work through this unit you should be aiming to ask the questions suggested about the books you are studying; this should provide you with a helpful structure for studying these texts and for comparing them effectively in the exam at the end of the course.

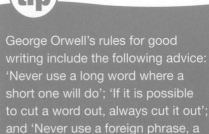

tip

George Orwell's rules for good writing include the following advice: 'Never use a long word where a short one will do'; 'If it is possible to cut a word out, always cut it out'; and 'Never use a foreign phrase, a scientific word or a jargon word if you can think of an everyday English equivalent'. We would advise you to follow this advice. However, you might be interested to know that he also said: 'Break any of these rules sooner than say anything outright barbarous'!

What are the key features of prose texts?

There are many advantages of studying prose texts as your chosen genre for Part 3.

- They are rich in ideas, characters and narratives.
- You study some of the best and most loved of all literary works.
- There is a wealth of critical material to support your study.

Prose is the dominant genre for the majority of written texts; many of the conventions of this genre are common to all varieties of prose. This section deals with novels and short stories first and then considers some additional features of other types of prose texts such as essays, memoirs and travel writing. Novels and short stories, and many other varieties of prose, are in the business of telling stories about people and places. Perhaps the most useful starting point for your study of this genre is therefore to think about how writers use narrative, setting and characterisation. This unit suggests ways you can think about all three of these key aspects of the novel and the short story. The approaches suggested here are not exhaustive but aim to encourage you to start asking the right questions about this genre.

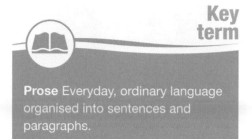

Key term

Prose Everyday, ordinary language organised into sentences and paragraphs.

How do writers construct narratives?

Narrative is perhaps the single key feature of novels and short stories. Novels tell stories and narrative is the process the writers use to tell these stories. The choices writers make in constructing narratives include the order in which they include events and the characters they choose to tell their stories.

Many novels and short stories work within the traditional conventions of the genre. Some of these stories, for instance, start at a particular point in time and take the reader chronologically through a series of events, describing the actions, characters and settings along the way. These stories might follow a surprising route – we might not always be able to predict what will happen next – but we can rely on the writer to tell us about the events in the order in which they happen. In contrast, some writers consciously play around with the conventions of the genre. They surprise the reader by making unconventional and sometimes surprising decisions – not just about what happens in their stories but also about when it happens and who tells us. These narratives are often fertile ground for comment on and analysis of the process of constructing narrative.

In Part 3 of the course your focus will be on how the writer works within a particular genre, therefore, if the writer is subverting it, or playing around with narrative and the way in which the story is told, you will have plenty to say. Some of the extracts in this section are taken from novels where the writers deliberately challenge the traditional assumptions about how the genre works but others offer more conventional approaches so that you can see the different ways in which writers work and learn to ask the right questions about narrative.

Who is telling the story?

The first thing you should ask of any novel is: 'Who is telling this story?' Sometimes this question will be very easy to answer. At other times it will present more of a challenge because writers sometimes construct deliberately multi-layered and complex narratives. In order to support your study of this genre, it will help if you have a secure understanding of the choices writers can make about who will tell the story. The most common options are a first person or a third person narrator.

- A first person narrative has an identifiable narrator telling the story in the first person (in other words, he or she will use 'I' or sometimes 'We'). If one specific character tells the story it can mean that we don't always see the whole picture; it is only

tip

Study smartly. You know that the specific focus of your study is the way in which the writer works within a particular genre, so you should focus your note-taking on the key features and conventions of the genre you are studying as outlined in this chapter. You should do this from the moment you start studying the texts for Part 3.

Figure 3.1 George Eliot, author of *Middlemarch*. Despite the name, she was a woman. Her real name was Mary Anne Evans.

one person's story after all, and sometimes, as we will see, narrators are not always entirely reliable.

- In a third person narrative the narrator is usually unidentified. This can give the writer the ability to describe events at will, almost as if the writer has the power to see everything and understand what every character is thinking. We call a narrator who is all-knowing 'omniscient'.

The first extracts you will look at are the openings of two classic novels by 19th century English female writers. In *Middlemarch* by George Eliot (she adopted a pseudonym: her real name was Mary Anne Evans) the writer uses a third person narrator. Read the opening couple of sentences of the novel in the following extract.

Text 3.1 *Middlemarch*, George Eliot, 1874

Miss Brooke had that kind of beauty which seems to be thrown into relief by poor dress. Her hand and wrist were so finely formed that she could wear sleeves not less bare of style than those in which the Blessed Virgin appeared to Italian painters; and her profile as well as her stature and bearing seemed to gain the more dignity from her plain garments, which by the side of provincial fashion gave her the impressiveness of a fine quotation from the Bible, or from one of our elder poets, in a paragraph of to-day's newspaper.

The first sentence is short and clear, in contrast to the second which is long and complex. Someone is telling the reader about a character called Miss Brooke. The narrator describes Miss Brooke's beauty and, although any judgements about beauty might be considered to be subjective, the authoritative tone of this third person narrator encourages the reader to accept this judgement as objective. The narrator is leading us, the readers, by the hand and telling us what to think: although Miss Brooke doesn't dress very well she is nevertheless still beautiful. Indeed, she appears more beautiful because of her simple, plain clothes. When writers choose not to use a first person narrator the most common response by the reader is to immediately trust what the unnamed storyteller says. The narrator is omniscient – he knows everything that is going on – so why shouldn't we trust him?

Text 3.2 *Jane Eyre*, Charlotte Brontë, 1847

There was no possibility of taking a walk that day. We had been wandering, indeed, in the leafless shrubbery an hour in the morning; but since dinner (Mrs Reed, when there was no company, dined early) the cold winter wind had brought with it clouds so sombre, and a rain so penetrating, that further outdoor exercise was now out of the question.

I was glad of it: I never liked long walks, especially on chilly afternoons: dreadful to me was the coming home in the raw twilight, with nipped fingers and toes, and a heart saddened by the chidings of Bessie, the nurse, and humbled by the consciousness of my physical inferiority to Eliza, John, and Georgiana Reed.

The first paragraph of *Jane Eyre* gives the reader an obvious clue that this story will be told in the first person: 'We' is the first person plural pronoun. The second paragraph confirms that this is going to be Jane's story. The reader hears her opinion – 'I was glad of it: I never liked long walks' – and we realise that this story is going to be told through her eyes. Even in the first two paragraphs Charlotte Brontë manages to establish a degree of sympathy for her narrator when she highlights her 'physical inferiority'.

The narrative choice Brontë makes – to have an identifiable narrator telling us the story – changes the way we read. Rather than accepting that things simply are the way they are (as we might do when reading the Eliot extract above) the reader starts thinking about the characteristics of the person telling us the story. We are encouraged to ask questions such as:

- Who is this person?
- Why are they telling us this story?
- What do they think about the situation?
- Can we trust them?

Activity 3.1

Read the opening sections of *Middlemarch* (Text 3.1) and *Jane Eyre* (Text 3.2) again and think carefully about the narrative decisions the writer has made in each. What distinguishes the two approaches? How do they affect the reader differently? In your notes you should make a list of the reasons why a writer might use either a first person narrator or a third person narrator.

If you can work out straight away who is telling the story in any novel or short story you come across then you can start thinking about the writer's narrative choices and *how* and *why* they are telling their story rather than simply what they are telling the reader. By using an identifiable narrator – with whom we can empathise – to tell her story, Charlotte Brontë is employing a very similar narrative strategy to Alice Walker in *The Color Purple* (Text 3.3).

Is the person who is telling the story reliable?

Alice Walker's Pulitzer Prize winning novel *The Color Purple* uses a range of interesting narrative techniques to establish the reader's sympathy for her narrator. You will look at the opening section of the novel to see how some of these are apparent even in the first few lines.

Activity 3.2

Read Text 3.3 and note down all the interesting narrative decisions Walker makes before comparing your notes with the commentary that follows.

Text 3.3 *The Color Purple*, Alice Walker, 1982

Dear God,
I am fourteen years old. ~~I am~~ I have always been a good girl. Maybe you can give me a sign letting me know what is happening to me.

Last spring after little Lucious come I heard them fussing. He was pulling on her arm. She say It too soon, Fonso, I ain't well. Finally he leave her alone. A week go by, he pulling on her arm again. She say Naw, I ain't gonna. Can't you see I'm already half dead, an all these children.

Did you manage to identify some of the narrative choices Walker makes? Firstly, she uses a first person narrator: the third word is 'I'. The girl telling the story is only 14 years old; this makes the reader both sympathetic and suspicious: a child narrator is more likely to be a victim but might also prove a less reliable storyteller. Perhaps the reader is being asked to consider whether the narrator can be trusted. Alice Walker is well aware of the narrative tensions she is setting up here and underlines these in the second sentence by employing the unusual technique of including a correction in the text. 'I am' is crossed out and replaced by 'I have always been'. This writer wants the reader to be aware of the narrator's weaknesses and to recognise that her character might be altered by the story she is telling.

The young narrator in Alice Walker's novel writes letters (this first one is addressed simply 'Dear God'). Writing a novel made up of letters is a traditional narrative technique. We call this an epistolary novel (you could compare, for instance, Mary Shelley's *Frankenstein* or Samuel Richardson's *Clarissa*, in which the stories are also told through a series of letters). The epistolary form of *The Color Purple* gives us the sense that we are being granted a privileged glimpse into the narrator's private world. Within a few sentences we have begun to trust this narrator; we want to hear her story despite the various hints that she might be unreliable.

We can see a similar technique, but used for very different effect, at the beginning of F. Scott Fitzgerald's classic *The Great Gatsby*. This is another first person narrative. The story in this case is being told by a character called Nick Carraway. He introduces himself to us at the beginning of the novel and readers often feel they start to trust Nick at this point in the novel. However, Fitzgerald hints that his narrator might not be entirely reliable.

Text 3.4 *The Great Gatsby*, F. Scott Fitzgerald, 1925

In my younger and more vulnerable years my father gave me some advice that I've been turning over in my mind ever since.

'Whenever you feel like criticizing anyone,' he told me, 'just remember that all the people in this world haven't had the advantages that you've had.'

He didn't say any more, but we've always been unusually communicative in a reserved way, and I understood that he meant a great deal more than that. In consequence, I'm inclined to reserve all judgements, a habit that has opened up many curious natures to me and also made me the victim of not a few veteran bores. The abnormal mind is quick to detect and attach itself to this quality when it appears in a normal person, and so it came about that in college I was unjustly accused of being a politician, because I was privy to the secret griefs of wild, unknown men. Most of the confidences were unsought – frequently I have feigned sleep, preoccupation, or a hostile levity when I realized by some unmistakable sign that an intimate revelation was quivering on the horizon; for the intimate revelations of young men, or at least the terms in which they express them, are usually plagiaristic and marred by obvious suppressions. Reserving judgements is a matter of infinite hope. I am still a little afraid of missing something if I forget that, as my father snobbishly suggested, and I snobbishly repeat, a sense of the fundamental decencies is parcelled out unequally at birth.

The opening sections of novels often give us important clues as to how reliable the narrator will be. First impressions are very important and are sometimes deliberately misleading: writers of crime novels, for instance, often try to throw their readers off the scent while at the same time leaving clues as to what has really happened. In *The Great Gatsby* Carraway describes himself, in the first sentence, as 'vulnerable', which could make us sympathetic towards him; however, the description is actually applied to his 'younger … years' so the reader could equally see him as rather arrogant. In a similar vein, he tells us that he is 'inclined to reserve all judgments' but in the same sentence includes a crushing judgement, describing some former acquaintances as 'veteran bores'. If the reader is in any doubt about Nick Carraway's character, Fitzgerald gives him the following line: 'as my father snobbishly suggested, and I snobbishly repeat'. The repetition of 'snobbishly' is a good clue that the narrator of this novel is a snob; indeed, he tells us as much. And yet many readers come to trust his judgement absolutely. Fitzgerald is a master craftsman at manipulating his reader and his tools are the various narrative devices at his disposal.

Is it always the same person telling the story?

Nick Carraway is the sole narrator of *The Great* Gatsby. However, writers sometimes use multiple narrators to present the events of the story from different perspectives. When a writer shifts narrator this important decision affects the reader's experience of the story. You will now look at two extracts from Jean Rhys's 1966 novel *Wide Sargasso Sea*. In this book Rhys returns to the story of Charlotte Brontë's famous 1847 novel *Jane Eyre*. Brontë's narrator, Jane, whom we met briefly in Text 3.2, falls in love with and eventually marries a character called Mr Rochester, but he has a murky past and Jane discovers that his mad wife, Bertha Mason, has for several years been locked up in an upstairs room. Rhys decides to tell Bertha's story. She renames her Antoinette and imagines that she grew up on the Caribbean island of Martinique. Part One of the novel tells Antoinette's story; Part Two is written from the perspective of Mr Rochester whom Rhys presents as a far nastier character than the man we meet in *Jane Eyre*. You will now read the openings to these contrasting sections.

> **tip**
>
> Narrative is about telling stories but examiners don't want to read about *what* happens in the story – they already know because they've read the books! They want you to write about *how* the writer tells the story in a particular way and *why* they make the narrative choices they do.

Text 3.5 *Wide Sargasso Sea*, **Jean Rhys, 1966**

Part One

They say when trouble comes close ranks, and so the white people did. But we were not in their ranks. The Jamaican ladies had never approved of my mother, 'because she pretty like pretty self' Christophine said.

She was my father's second wife, far too young for him they thought, and, worse still, a Martinique girl. When I asked her why so few people came to see us, she told me that the road from Spanish Town to Coulibri Estate where we lived was very bad and that road repairing was now a thing of the past. (My father, visitors, horses, feeling safe in bed – all belonged to the past.)

Another day I heard her talking to Mr Luttrell, our neighbour and her only friend. 'Of course they have their own misfortunes. Still waiting for this compensation the English promised when the Emancipation Act was passed. Some will wait for a long time.'

Figure 3.2 Antoinette, the first narrator in *Wide Sargasso Sea*, grew up on Martinique in the Caribbean.

Part Two

So it was all over, the advance and retreat, the doubts and hesitations. Everything finished, for better or for worse. There we were, sheltering from the heavy rain under a large mango tree, myself, my wife Antoinette and a little half-caste servant who was called Amelie. Under a neighbouring tree I could see our luggage covered with sacking, the two porters and a boy holding fresh horses, hired to carry us up 2,000 feet to the waiting honeymoon house.

The girl Amelie said this morning, 'I hope you will be very happy, sir, in your sweet honeymoon house.' She was laughing at me I could see. A lovely little creature but sly, spiteful, malignant perhaps, like much else in this place.

tip

Think and study comparatively. You should begin your study of each new text with the final exam in mind. When you start a new text you should immediately start comparing it with others you have studied and asking questions like: Who is telling the story? How does this writer start their story? How is this different from the previous book we studied?

Activity 3.3

Read Texts 3.5 and 3.6 carefully. They have very different effects because the story is being told by two contrasting narrators. Before you read the commentaries, make a list of all of the narrative differences. How would you describe each narrator?

The first account is Antoinette's. Her narrative is signalled through the use of the first person pronouns ('we' and 'I') and her storytelling exudes a gossipy hastiness. She quotes the Jamaican ladies and cites other conversational opinions: her father's second wife, for instance, was 'far too young for him they thought'. She refers to as yet unknown characters such as Christophine and she invites the reader to share her nostalgia and melancholy: '(My father, visitors, horses, feeling safe in bed – all belonged to the past.)'. Her narrative invites the reader into her confidence.

In contrast, Part Two is narrated by the (unnamed) Mr Rochester. His narrative voice is more detached in tone: 'Everything finished, for better or for worse.' Rochester objectifies female characters, referring to 'my wife Antoinette' and 'the girl Amelie'. He is suspicious: 'She was laughing at me I could see'; the reader is left to ask whether that suspicion is justified. He is also presented as judgemental and malicious: 'A lovely little creature but sly, spiteful, malignant perhaps, like much else in this place.'

How do writers start narratives effectively?

Some traditional narratives start at the obvious beginning of a story and end where you might expect: perhaps with a marriage or a death. A Bildungsroman is a novel that tells the story of the narrator's life (*Great Expectations* by Charles Dickens is a good example). Pip, the first person narrator, tells the story of his life and the growth of his personality. There is a tradition of such novels in English literature stretching from classics like *Tom Jones* by Henry Fielding to more modern examples such as *Oranges are not the Only Fruit* by Jeanette Winterson.

Figure 3.3 A traditional narrator? Phiz (Hablot Knight Browne) drew this original sketch for the serialisation of Dickens's *David Copperfield*, 1849–50.

Dickens's novel *David Copperfield* starts: 'Whether I shall turn out to be the hero of my own life, or whether that station will be held by anybody else, these pages must show. To begin my life with the beginning of my life, I record that I was born (as I have been informed and believe) on a Friday, at twelve o'clock at night. It was remarked that the clock began to strike, and I began to cry, simultaneously.' This is a fairly traditional opening as the narrative starts at the beginning of the eponymous hero's life (many biographies open with a line such as: The subject was born on whatever particular date in whatever particular place ...). However, there is an element of doubt even here: the simple 'I was born' is qualified by the parenthesis: '(as I have been informed and believe)'. Dickens knows that all stories are shaped by their tellers and starts his narrative by foregrounding his narrator's reliance on re-telling the stories that he's heard others tell.

Ian McEwan's 1997 novel *Enduring Love* starts with the line: 'The beginning is simple to mark.' His point is ironic: the beginning is never simple to locate. At the start of this novel the central character, Joe, rushes towards a hot-air balloon which has become unsecured from its anchor ropes in order to assist a man struggling to control the balloon. Joe is racing into his narrative and the reader is being dragged into the story in the same unsuspecting and innocent manner. The opening of a novel is, on one level, very simple to locate: it is the first word of Chapter One. (Or is it the title? The dedication? The quotation on the title page?) Stories are rarely simple. The writer will often tell us a 'back story': as a reader we will need to know about important things that have happened in the characters' lives before the time covered by any particular narrative.

In Arundhati Roy's Booker prize winning novel *The God of Small Things* of 1997, almost all of the things that happen in the book take place before the day that is being described in the opening chapter. The Nobel Prize winning Colombian writer Gabriel García Márquez opens his famous 1967 novel *One Hundred Years of Solitude* with the lines: 'Many years later, as he faced the firing squad, Colonel Aureliano Buendía was to remember that distant afternoon when his father took him to discover ice.' Márquez starts telling his story by making his reader aware of the direction the narrative will take. The first sentence anticipates the future. In the first sentence of the novel Márquez tells the reader what will happen in the story. Therefore, we know how events will unfold and Márquez is able to control how we read to these events; we are left wondering what will happen and how Colonel Buendia will be led to his inevitable meeting with a firing squad. Another tremendous opening is Ford Madox Ford's *The Good Soldier*: 'This is the saddest story I have ever heard.'

Some writers take this idea of playing with narrative even further. You will now read the famous opening of Italo Calvino's novel *If on a Winter's Night a Traveller*.

Text 3.7 *If on a Winter's Night a Traveller*, Italo Calvino, 1979

You are about to begin reading Italo Calvino's new novel, *If on a winter's night a traveller*. Relax. Concentrate. Dispel every other thought. Let the world around you fade. Best to close the door; the TV is always on in the next room. Tell the others right away, 'No, I don't want to watch TV!' Raise your voice – they won't hear you otherwise – 'I'm reading! I don't want to be disturbed!' Maybe they haven't heard you, with all that racket; speak louder, yell: 'I'm beginning to read Italo Calvino's new novel!' Or if you prefer, don't say anything; just hope they'll leave you alone.

Find the most comfortable position: seated, stretched out, curled up, or lying flat. Flat on your back, on your side, on your stomach. In an easy chair, on the sofa, in the rocker, the deck chair, on the hassock. In the hammock, if you have a hammock. On top of your bed, of course, or in the bed. You can even stand on your hands, head down, in the yoga position. With the book upside down, naturally.

As you will immediately have noticed, Calvino is using a very unusual narrative technique. His narrator is directly addressing the reader. In fact, his narrator is telling the reader how to read. Writers have done this in various ways in the past but almost never with the directness or wit of Calvino. By making a joke out of his instructions to the reader – by telling him how to sit, for example – the narrator sends out a powerful message that he expects his reader to respond to his many narrative clues and be guided on how to read the story he is telling.

How do writers end their narratives?

You've looked at the openings of various stories; now you should think about how writers end narratives. Charles Dickens famously wrote three different endings to *Great Expectations*. He would not have been surprised by the Hollywood practice of filming different endings for films and showing each of them to a target audience before deciding which one is likely to be commercially most successful. Some writers appease their readers – they give them the happy ending they secretly desire – others deliberately disappoint. The classic conclusion – the marriage at the end of a Jane Austen novel, the death of Fagin at the end of *Oliver Twist* – is often subverted as writers play around with readers' expectations. The final sentence of the novel is the trump card in the writer's narrative hand.

The Remains of the Day, a 1989 novel by Kazuo Ishiguro, is narrated (it's a first person narrative) by a butler called Stevens. As the novel ends, Stevens is desperately trying to 'keep up appearances'. His aim is to continue to present a resolutely correct facade. The novel ends with his resolve: 'I should hope, then, that by the time of my employer's return, I shall be in a position to pleasantly surprise him.' And yet, even at this moment of optimism, Ishiguro has provided us with the clue that things are not as resolved as they might seem. Stevens is a snob and a pedant and the final line includes a solecism (a grammatical 'mistake') which would upset just such a pedantic snob: he splits an infinitive when he says 'to pleasantly surprise'. This is a good example of how the ostensible narrative direction can be offset by the language writers use. Ishiguro has crafted the end of his narrative with extreme care and you should take equal care in your reading and writing to respond fully to the language choices all writers make.

You will now look at another strategy writers use to end their narratives. Isabel Allende's novel *The House of the Spirits* is rightly praised as a ground-breaking magic realist novel. Now read the final paragraph of this novel.

> ### Key term
>
> **Magic realism** A style of writing where writers include elements of magic or the supernatural in otherwise realistic situations.

Text 3.8 *The House of the Spirits*, Isabel Allende, 1985

My grandmother wrote in her notebooks that bore witness to life for fifty years. Smuggled out by certain friendly spirits, they miraculously escaped the miraculous pyre in which so many other family papers perished. I have them here at my feet, bound with coloured ribbons, divided according to events and not in chronological order, just as she arranged them before she left. Clara wrote them so they would help me now to reclaim the past and overcome terrors of my own. The first is an ordinary school copybook with twenty pages, written in a child's delicate calligraphy. It begins like this: *Barrabas came to us by sea …*

As the novel ends, it comes back to its starting point. There is a pleasing circularity, a sense of returning to the beginning which gives the narrative closure and completeness. The novel started with the lines: '*Barrabas came to us by sea*, the child Clara wrote in her delicate calligraphy.' Almost 500 pages later, we have joined the narrator and have shared a moment of omniscience – of understanding what happened, when, how and, possibly, why. Other novelists leave their endings open: inviting the reader to speculate about what will happen when the story comes to an end. Zadie Smith ends her 2005 novel *On Beauty* with an 'intimation of what is to come'. This closing phrase looks outwards rather than backwards and acknowledges the inevitability of more stories, that narrative can only ever be temporarily postponed. In the same way that Jean Rhys took up the story of *Jane Eyre* in *Wide Sargasso Sea*, other writers might return to a narrative, perhaps to tell it from another perspective, or in another order, or for another time.

Activity 3.4

Having looked at the different narrative decisions writers make, you should now review your notes. They should serve as a quick reminder of what you've learned so that you can ask the right questions of the Part 3 texts you will be studying.

How do writers of prose use settings?

Writers often use places and settings with particular care in their stories. Sometimes a place is described in such a way as to evoke a particular mood. Dickens was a master at this: the marshes at the start of *Great Expectations* suggest Pip's desolation, and the foggy London air at the opening to *Bleak House* suggests confusion, uncertainty and a lack of clarity. Gabriel García Márquez's novel *One Hundred Years of Solitude* is set in a fictional small town in South America called Macondo. Márquez uses a third person narrator to tell this story. Read Text 3.9 and think about how the writer creates a sense of the place Macondo as a setting for the novel.

Figure 3.1 Gabriel García Márquez at Santa Marta, Columbia, travelling to Aracataca, 2007.

Text 3.9 *One Hundred Years of Solitude*, Gabriel García Márquez, 1967

Born in Colombia, Márquez is famous for the style of writing that has come to be known as magic realism and this passage has some very realistic features: the newly arrived railway station and the record players (phonographs) that the townspeople are suspicious of. However, the presence of a ghost suggests that there will also be an important magical element in the novel. In some ways this surreal town is hardened against change; the wider world, as you will see from this passage, is constantly asserting itself.

Something similar happened with the cylinder phonographs that the merry matrons from France brought with them as a substitute for the antiquated hand organs and that for a time had serious effects on the livelihood of the band of musicians. At first curiosity increased the clientele on the forbidden street and there was even word of respectable ladies who disguised themselves as workers in order to observe the novelty of the phonograph from first hand, but from so much and such close observation they soon reached the conclusion that it was not an enchanted mill as everyone had thought and as the matrons had said, but a mechanical trick that could not be compared with something so moving, so human, and so full of everyday truth as a band of musicians. It was a serious disappointment that when phonographs became so popular that there was one in every house they were not considered objects for amusement for adults but as something good for children to take apart. On the other hand,

Extended essay

EE

Gabriel García Márquez, known colloquially as Gabo, won the Nobel Prize in Literature in 1982. He is the author of many novels and short stories, including *Love in the Time of Cholera*, *The General in his Labyrinth* and *Chronicle of a Death Foretold*. As one of the leading proponents of the style that has come to be known as magic realism, his work could form the basis of a very interesting extended essay. If you want more information, this website would be a good starting point: http://www.themodernword.com/gabo/.

when someone from the town had the opportunity to test the crude reality of the telephone installed in the railway station, which was thought to be a rudimentary version of the phonograph because of its crank, even the most incredulous were upset. It was as if God had decided to put to test every capacity for surprise and was keeping the inhabitants of Macondo in a permanent alternation between excitement and disappointment, doubt and revelation, to such an extreme that no one knew for certain where the limits of reality lay. It was an intricate stew of truths and mirages that convulsed the ghost of Jose Arcadio Buendia under the chestnut tree with impatience and made him wander through the house even in broad daylight.

Márquez does not sentimentalise his setting of Macondo in this extract. He presents it as different but certainly not ideal. On the ominous-sounding 'forbidden street' everything is not as it would seem to an outsider. We find that there are 'respectable' ladies (the description is surely ironic) who are 'disguised' in order to observe the record player. They are imitating reality in the same way that the phonograph is imitating it. But the people of Macondo do not respond well to this imitation and it lacks the 'everyday truth' of live musicians. The people of Macondo don't trust the music because it is recorded and they can't see it being performed in front of their own eyes. They have to take it on trust that it was really produced by live musicians. Their suspicion is that it is an 'imitation' and, therefore, not real.

The population of this town is challenged to find the 'limits of reality'. The telephone is seen not as a technological advance but rather as a test set by God. A strange overlapping of time-frames is going on when 20th century realities are being interpreted as Old Testament trials and punishments. The ultimate effect of this 'permanent alternation between excitement and disappointment' is to disturb one of the town's ghosts. If the future is invading the town in the form of innovations brought in on the train, then it is also a community haunted by the past. The ghost is 'convulsed' and this very physical image gives the reader a tangible sense of Macondo being wrenched into a different age. It is as if the town of Macondo becomes a character in the story.

The next extract we'll examine is from Bharati Mukherjee's 1989 novel *Jasmine*. The passage forms a bridge between this section and the next, on character: the settings the writer uses are critically important in this extract because they are formative in the development of the central character. We'll look at how Mukherjee uses settings in this extract, before moving on to look at how she and other writers construct characters in novels and short stories.

Text 3.10 *Jasmine*, Bharati Mukherjee, 1989

Lifetimes ago, under a banyan tree in the village of Hasnapur, an astrologer cupped his ears – his satellite dish to the stars – and foretold my widowhood and exile. I was only seven then, fast and venturesome, scabrous-armed from leaves and thorns.

'No!' I shouted. 'You're a crazy old man. You don't know what my future holds!'

'Suit yourself,' the astrologer cackled. 'What is to happen will happen.' Then he chucked me hard on the head.

I fell. My teeth cut into my tongue. A twig sticking out of the bundle of firewood I'd scavenged punched a star-shaped wound into my forehead. I lay still. The astrologer re-entered his trance. I was nothing, a speck in the solar system. Bad times were on their way. I was helpless, doomed. The star bled.

'I don't believe you,' I whispered.

[...]

I dragged my bundle to the river bend. I hated that river bend. The water pooled there, sludgy brown, and was choked with hyacinths and faeces from the buffaloes that village boys washed upstream. Women were scouring brass pots with ashes. Dhobis were whomping clothes clean on stone slabs. Housewives squabbled whilst lowering their pails into a drying well. My older sisters, slow, happy girls with butter-smooth arms, were bathing on the steps that led down to the river.

'What happened?' my sisters shrieked as they sponged the bleeding star on my forehead with the wetted ends of their veils. 'Now your face is scarred for life! How will the family ever find you a husband?'

I broke away from their solicitous grip. 'It's not a scar,' I shouted, 'it's my third eye.' In the stories that my mother recited, the holiest sages developed an extra eye right in the middle of their foreheads. Through that eye they peered out into invisible worlds. 'Now I'm a sage.'

My sisters scampered up the slippery steps, grabbed their pitchers and my bundle of firewood, and ran to get help from the women at the well.

I swam to where the river was a sun-gold haze. I kicked and paddled in a rage. Suddenly my fingers scraped the soft waterlogged carcass of a small dog. The body was rotten, the eyes had been eaten. The moment I touched it, the body broke in two, as though the water had been its glue. A stench leaked out of the broken body, and then both pieces quickly sank.

That stench stays with me. I'm twenty-four now, I live in Baden, Elsa County, Iowa, but every time I lift a glass of water to my lips, fleetingly I smell it. I know what I don't want to become.

Activity 3.5

Read the response on *Jasmine* that follows. In groups, discuss the following questions and consider how you might make these techniques a feature of your own writing:

- How are quotations used in this commentary?
- How long are the quotations that are used?
- What tense is used in this commentary?
- What do you notice about the first sentence of each paragraph?

(Note: the extract this student is writing about is not identical to the one above.)

The passage features two discrete settings. The first is an Indian village and at a seminal moment in a young girl's early life. It begins under the banyan tree, a traditional place of meeting. The second is the United States several years on and in the 'now' of the novel. As this girl looks back to an event that happened 'lifetimes ago', she realises the extent to which she is haunted by her past and how this informs her present. Despite her uncertainties, she is at least definite that she knows 'what I don't want to become'.

In the first sentence of the extract Mukerjee makes us aware of the contrast between the modern world of the United States and the world of her childhood. The metaphor she uses to describe the astrologer's ears – 'his satellite dish to the stars' – highlights the very different practices of reading the world she has experienced in her life. They are also hugely divergent experiences; indeed, they are not even considered to have happened within the history of one individual: this narrative started 'lifetimes ago'. We might then read the central character as a representative figure or a hybrid shaped by one culture and living in another. She is also pushed forward as a rebel. The passage starts with the rejection of one tradition, when the girl shouts: 'You're a crazy old man. You don't know what my future holds!'

At this moment in her childhood the girl experiences a strange mingling of past and future. The wound – which is 'punched' into her forehead – is a violent reminder of the predictions that have been made for her. On the other hand she is haunted by the past. As we begin reading this novel we do so in the knowledge that history is written indelibly into this girl's life. The 'she-ghosts' will always be with her as a haunting presence and she never will be able entirely to escape the past.

This extract also creates a vivid sense of a journey being started. And it is a journey that leads away from home. This girl is 'wandering' and she is given direction by the astrologer when he points her to a trail that leads out of the woods. The woods might easily represent her state of confusion and anxiety and the flowing river is certainly a symbol of the onward-moving passage of life. She passes the traditional activities, perhaps ready to leave them behind, and the narrator foregrounds her differences from her sisters. She is 'fast and venturesome'; her sisters are 'slow, happy girls'. They are content with their lives; she needs to move on.

Those differences are reinforced by her sisters' reaction to the wound. They respond within conventional parameters. They worry only that the family may not now find her a husband. They cannot envisage a different narrative for their lives from the one they have grown up with. Their 'solicitous' reaction refuses to allow the possibility of rebellion. The narrator, however, is embarking on a re-write or re-imagination of the story of her life. It will still be informed by her background – she delves into Hindu mythology – but the interpretation is all hers: 'it's my third eye ... Now I'm a sage.' Whilst the sisters revert to a traditional source of advice – 'the women at the well' – the narrator is already moving off down the river, angrily breaking loose from the past: 'I kicked and paddled in a rage.'

Perhaps the narrator sees the country in which she has grown up as diseased and rotten. Like the carcass of the dog it is broken and has lost sight of where it is going: 'the eyes had been eaten'. When she touches this state, 'the body broke in two' and it is almost as if she reads this as a warning that she does not fit in. However, there is no escaping the influence of the country of her birth. Her cultural make-up is always there, and she is reminded by the stench of the dog's rotting body: 'That stench stays with me.'

As this extract begins we meet a young girl: 'I'm twenty-four now, I live in Baden, Elsa County, Iowa.' However, the bare bones of identity are informed by a complex history we have been allowed to peep at. This girl is 'scarred for life' but she is also a 'sage'. A hybrid identity is run through with haunting images from a very different past. Here is a young immigrant motivated by a passionate desire not to conform: 'I know what I don't want to become.' At the heart of this novel we expect to find the complications we face when we try to construct our identities and the difficulties we encounter when we address the question 'Who am I?'

This question is, of course, fundamental to the construction of character, which leads us into the next section of this unit.

How do writers of prose construct characters?

It is always worth remembering that there is no such thing as a real person in a novel. What we refer to as a character is merely a collection of words arranged in a particular order. If you are aware of the strangeness of this artifice then you will be better equipped to write about the ways in which writers construct characters. They narrate an often very narrow series of events and let the reader overhear particular snippets of dialogue in order for them to form a powerful impression of 'character'. When the artifice works we are caught up in it and believe the character to be a real person.

One way of making characters convincing is to give the reader a privileged glimpse into their history. In Text 3.11, from *The God of Small Things* by Arundhati Roy, we find out about Rahel's schooldays.

Text 3.11 *The God of Small Things*, Arundhati Roy, 1997

In this extract from *The God of Small Things*, Arundhati Roy is telling part of the 'back story' of a character called Rahel. Like her twin brother, Estha, she does not conform easily to society's expectations. She is unconventional, just like Roy's narrative which helps to delineate her central characters: Rahel, Estha and their mother, Ammu.

Six months later she was expelled after repeated complaints from senior girls. She was accused (quite rightly) of hiding behind doors and deliberately colliding with her seniors. When she was questioned by the Principal about her behaviour (cajoled, caned, starved), she eventually admitted she had done it ...

In each of the schools she went to, the teachers noted that she:

a   Was an extremely polite child.

b   Had no friends.

It appeared to be a civil, solitary form of corruption. And for this very reason, they all agreed (savouring their teacherly disapproval, touching it with their tongues, sucking it like a sweet) – all the more serious.

You will already have noticed that Arundhati Roy is using a third person narrator; however, from time to time that narrative slips into telling the story from one of the character's perspectives, sometimes only for a few words. This is a very interesting technique which is usually referred to as **free indirect style** or **free indirect narrative**. You can spot when this technique is being used by asking yourself: 'Who is thinking this?' If you look at the sections in parenthesis (in brackets) in Text 3.11, you'll notice that the tone is slightly different from the rest of the passage. These are someone else's

Key term

Free indirect style/narrative A technique where a third person narrative temporarily assumes the voice of one of the characters so that the reader sees the world through their eyes.

Figure 3.5 Archie Jones, played by Phil Davis in the Channel 4 adaptation of *White Teeth* by Zadie Smith. He is a troubled, multi-layered character.

thoughts; it's almost as if they are providing a commentary on the narrative. In fact, it is probably reasonable to assume that these are the thoughts of the adult Rahel seeping into the narrative, but Roy doesn't tell us this directly (although the brackets are a clue) – the reader has to work it out by asking the right questions.

Zadie Smith is another modern writer adept at crafting multi-faceted and hugely believable characters. Her comic novel *White Teeth* starts with the tellingly named chapter 'The Peculiar Second Marriage of Archie Jones'. From the verb-less first sentence (suggesting this character is going nowhere fast) onwards, the reader is assaulted by impressions of Archie. We are left asking all sorts of questions but, even by the end of this one paragraph, we have a sense in our heads of who Archie Jones is. You should now read Text 3.12 and attempt the activity that follows it.

Text 3.12 *White Teeth*, Zadie Smith, 2000

Early in the morning, late in the century, Cricklewood Broadway. At 06.27 hours on 1 January 1975, Alfred Archibald Jones was dressed in corduroy and sat in a fume-filled Cavalier Musketeer Estate face down on the steering wheel, hoping the judgement would not be too heavy upon him. He lay forward in a prostrate cross, jaw slack, arms splayed either side like some fallen angel; scrunched up in each fist he held his army service medals (left) and his marriage licence (right), for he had decided to take his mistakes with him. A little green light flashed in his eye, signalling a right turn he had resolved never to make. He was resigned to it. He was prepared for it. He had flipped a coin and stood staunchly by its conclusions. This was a decided-upon suicide. In fact it was a New Year's resolution.

Activity 3.6

Read the extract from *White Teeth* carefully. Make a list of all of the things the reader discovers about Archie in this paragraph. In groups discuss why you think Zadie Smith has included this information (as opposed to other things she could have told us) and how this contributes to the reader's sense of Archie's character.

What are the key features of prose texts other than novels and short stories?

Writers of novels and short stories write fiction: their stories are made up. However, much prose is non-fiction. For Part 3 you might be studying non-fiction texts such as travel writing, memoirs or essays. You will have noticed, however, that writers of such texts use many of the same features as writers of novels and short stories. Writers of non-fiction also construct narratives and are similarly concerned with the presentation of setting and character. Read the two extracts which follow (Texts 3.13 and 3.14). They are both from non-fiction texts: one is from a memoir, the other from a piece of travel writing. As you read, look carefully for the many literary features the writers employ.

Text 3.13 *Out of Place: a Memoir*, Edward W. Said, 1999

Edward W. Said was a Palestinian writer and critic. *Out of Place* is his memoir, published not long before he died in 2003. In this extract he recalls his childhood memories of his father.

My father's strength, moral and physical, dominated the early part of my life. He had a massive back and a barrel chest, and although he was quite short he communicated indomitability and, at least to me, a sense of overpowering confidence. His most striking physical feature was his ramrod-stiff, nearly caricature like upright carriage. And with that, in contrast to my shrinking, nervous timidity and shyness, went a kind of swagger that furnished another browbeating contrast with me: he never seemed to be afraid to go anywhere or do anything. I was, always.

Figure 3.6 Edward W. Said, 1935–2003.

Text 3.14 *The Great Railway Bazaar*, Paul Theroux, 1975

Paul Theroux is a prolific travel writer. He chronicles his solo journeys, often by train, memorably re creating the people and places he visits. In this extract he is travelling through Turkey during a train journey across Asia which started in London.

Large grey dogs, a pack of seven, presumably wild, were chasing across the harsh steppes of northwestern Turkey, barking at the train. They woke me in Thrace, which Hagel calls 'rather unattractive', and when the wild dogs slackened their pace and fell behind the fleeing train there was little else to see but a dreary monotony of unambitious hills. The occasional army posts, the men shovelling sugar beets caked with dirt into steel hoppers, and the absence of trees made the dreariness emphatic. And I couldn't bear those hairless hills.

Figure 3.7 The steppes of Thrace, Northern Turkey, as described in *The Great Railway Bazaar*.

Activity 3.7

Read Texts 3.13 and 3.14 very carefully. Choose one to write about. You should write two or three paragraphs of analysis, looking carefully at how the writer constructs either character or setting. You should aim to write about the writer's use of literary features and to look closely at his language. Pick out the words and phrases that you think are most interesting, most surprising or most unusual. What can you say about each? You should ask yourself how and why the writer uses the words you have selected.

tip

If your Part 3 genre is prose then this section will have suggested a range of questions to ask about the various texts you are studying. Don't worry about there being right answers – there are usually no such things. If you ask thoughtful questions about your texts then you will be on track for successful study.

What are the key features of drama texts?

There are many advantages of studying drama as your chosen genre for Part 3:

- You will be able to read the plays together in class.
- You will be able to watch performed versions of the play on film or, if you are lucky, live in the theatre.
- You may find it easier to learn quotations from plays than from novels.
- There is a wealth of critical material to support your study.

   Although you will be studying drama texts in printed form you should always remember that drama is written to be performed. You should write about drama as if you were watching it on stage in performance. Rather than talking about the 'reader' you should imagine yourself as the 'audience' and write about the way in which the unfolding action of the play would affect the audience watching it.

Figure 3.8 Drama is written to be performed. A scene from a production of *Macbeth*, Globe Theatre, London, 2001.

Figure 3.9 The tension mounts between Blanche and Stella in this production of *A Streetcar Named Desire*, Donmar Warehouse Theatre, London, 2009.

The interaction between the audience and the actors performing the various roles on stage is key to the success of a play. When analysing drama texts you should describe how the writer's choices of language and structure help the actors to establish this relationship with the audience. In looking at drama, you should also consider the various key features which are common to this genre. In this section you will look at how playwrights create character, how they use setting; we will offer you advice on writing about **dramatic irony** and subtext. You should also consider stagecraft: stage directions, movement, dramatic tension, costume, voice and pauses.

How do playwrights create character?

You should remember that all art is crafted; it is not real, but the creation of a writer. Your job as a student of literature is to write about the ways in which the playwright's choices have created an impression of a believable human being. Ask yourself: 'What is it about these lines that give this character the illusion of reality?'

In Tennessee Williams's play *A Streetcar Named Desire,* two sisters, Blanche and Stella, are reunited at Stella's house in New Orleans. They grew up on a wealthy plantation so Blanche is shocked to find Stella living in what she considers to be relative poverty, although we later find out that Blanche is in pretty straightened circumstances herself. Read the dialogue in Text 3.15, in which Blanche challenges her sister about the conditions she is living in.

Text 3.15 *A Streetcar Named Desire*, Tennessee Williams, 1947

Blanche	Oh, I'm not going to be hypocritical, I'm going to be honestly critical about it! Never, never, never in my worst dreams could I picture – Only Poe! Only Mr Edgar Allan Poe! – could do it justice! Out there I suppose is the ghoul-haunted woodland of Weir! (*She laughs.*)
Stella	No, honey, those are the L&N tracks.
Blanche	No, now seriously, putting joking aside. Why didn't you tell me, why didn't you write me, honey, why didn't you let me know?
Stella	(*carefully, pouring herself a drink*) Tell you what, Blanche?
Blanche	Why, that you had to live in these conditions!

Activity 3.8

Some critics think that when playwrights include stage directions they are interfering in what should be the job of the director and the actors. Others argue that these directions give crucial advice to the actors. The extract above contains two stage directions. Discuss what you think their effect is.

- Why does Williams include these directions?
- What, if anything, do they tell us about the characters that we don't find out from the language they use?
- How might the scene be played differently if they hadn't been included?

Blanche (who has been an English teacher) initially uses metaphor to describe the surroundings of New Orleans, representing it as a 'ghoul-haunted woodland'. Stella contradicts this very literally: 'those are the L&N [the railway company] tracks'. Blanche thinks she's joking – 'now seriously' – but the audience is left unsure. Their language is one very clear clue as to what sort of characters the writer is presenting. Blanche's reliance on metaphor suggests that she is unworldly and wary of confronting the truth. Stella, on the other hand, is represented as grounded and straightforward.

Another tool that writers can use when creating characters and which can help to let the audience know what a character is thinking is the soliloquy. Shakespeare famously used soliloquies as a way of letting us know what that character is actually thinking in comparison with what they might be saying to other characters. You may well know several of Shakespeare's famous soliloquies, such as Hamlet's meditation on life and death which starts: 'To be, or not to be: that is the question'.

A close relation of the soliloquy is the aside, which is when a character steps out of the action momentarily and shares his or her thoughts with the audience. Shakespeare's characters Hamlet and Cordelia (in *King Lear*) both have first lines which are asides, as if to suggest that they are, or will be, somehow closer to the audience than the other characters; we are encouraged to sympathise with them through this theatrical device.

Figure 3.10 Soliloquies and asides are key tools for a playwright. Here Shakespeare's character Malvolio in *Twelfth Night* believes he is not overheard which adds to the comedy. (Royal Shakespeare Company, Stratford-Upon-Avon, UK, 1997)

Most characters in a play are active participants in it. Sometimes, however, writers use characters who stand outside the drama, perhaps in the role of a narrator, in order to guide the audience and to give us a different perspective on the action that is unfolding onstage. Classical Greek theatre used a chorus to help tell the story and to give the audience clues and hints about what was happening in a play. When the American playwright Arthur Miller sat down to write *A View from the Bridge* he set out to write a modern-day tragedy. In imitation of Greek tragedy he used a chorus-style figure – a lawyer, Alfieri – who is both a character in the play and a narrator who steps out of the action from time to time to talk directly to the audience.

Key term

Tragedy A literary genre which ends unhappily and often ends with a death usually because of the central character's flaws.

Figure 3.11 A scene from *A View from the Bridge*, University of South Carolina Theatre, USA, 2005.

Text 3.16 *A View from the Bridge*, Arthur Miller, 1955

A View from the Bridge starts with a speech by Alfieri – as the narrator – which sets the tone and introduces the context for the action of the play. This is his opening speech. The play is set in Brooklyn, New York City, in the 1950s. Alfieri speaks directly to the audience.

You wouldn't have known it, but something amusing has just happened. You see how uneasily they nod to me? That's because I am a lawyer. In this neighbourhood to meet a lawyer or a priest on the street is unlucky. We're only thought of in connexon with disasters, and they'd rather not get too close.

I often think that behind that suspicious little nod of theirs lie three thousand years of distrust. A lawyer means the law, and in Sicily, from where their fathers came, the law has not been a friendly idea since the Greeks were beaten.

I am inclined to notice the ruins in things, perhaps because I was born in Italy ... I only came here when I was twenty-five. In those days, Al Capone, the greatest Carthaginian of all, was learning his trade on these pavements, and Frankie Yale himself was cut precisely in half by a machine-gun on the corner of Union Street, two blocks away. Oh, there were many here who were justly shot by unjust men. Justice is very important here.

But this is Red Hook, not Sicily. This is the slum that faces the bay on the seaward side of Brooklyn Bridge. This is the gullet of New York swallowing the tonnage of the world. And now we are quite civilized, quite American. Now we settle for half, and I like it better. I no longer keep a pistol in my filing cabinet.

And my practice is entirely unromantic.

My wife has warned me, so have my friends; they tell me the people in this neighbourhood lack elegance, glamour. After all, who have I dealt with in my life? Longshoremen and their wives, and fathers, and grandfathers, compensation cases, evictions, family squabbles – the petty troubles of the poor – and yet ... every few years there is still a case, and as the parties tell me what the trouble is, the flat air in my office suddenly washes in with the green scent of the sea, the dust in this air is blown away and the thought comes that in some Caesar's year, in Calabria perhaps or on the cliff at Syracuse, another lawyer, quite differently dressed, heard the same complaint and sat there as powerless as I, and watched it run its bloody course.

It is dramatically important that Alfieri is a lawyer. His tells us that 'In this neighbourhood to meet a lawyer or a priest on the street is unlucky'. The familiarity that is suggested by the colloquial 'In this neighbourhood' is immediately contrasted with the sense of Alfieri as an outsider: one whose role, like that of a priest, is to hear confessions – to be in the know but on the outside. This is a play that also announces that – like its Greek tragedy precursor – it will concern itself with fate: meeting with Alfieri will prove 'unlucky'.

The 'machinery' behind the play can be found in the stage directions. Miller's detailed instructions paint the picture of both an apartment and a law office. It is also 'skeletal entirely' suggesting that the location for the action (the 'Bridge' of the title) is merely the bare bones of a story that is re-enacted with different inflections throughout history. In Alfieri's terms, this is a case that could have been heard 'in Calabria perhaps' but one that – for all its historical differences – would have been heard by a lawyer 'as powerless as I'. Alfieri establishes himself as a teller of stories (like a Greek chorus, the intermediary between the audience and the action) but one who can no more change the course of the tragedy than those who came before him. He ends with the image of the play running its 'bloody course.' It is inevitable that this drama, being a tragedy, will end in bloodshed. This is, in part, because Miller wrote it in the tradition of tragedy, from the Greeks, through Shakespeare, to this tragedy of the modern man. In this tradition, tragedy ends in suffering and often death whereas comedy ends in resolution and often marriage.

How do playwrights use setting?

Both Miller and Williams carefully construct their settings: the contexts the plays are set in have a direct impact on characterisation and plot. Both *Death of a Salesman* by Miller and *A Streetcar Named Desire* by Williams begin with a description of the setting, and both writers try to create an atmosphere of claustrophobia. They want the audience to realise that their characters are trapped, and the settings play an important role in conveying this.

Text 3.17 *A Streetcar Named Desire*, Tennessee Williams, 1947

The exterior of a two-storey corner building on a street in New Orleans which is named Elysian Fields and runs between the L&N tracks and the river. The section is poor but, unlike corresponding sections in other American cities, it has a raffish charm. The houses are mostly white frame, weathered grey, with rickety outside stairs and galleries and quaintly ornamented gables to the entrances of both. It is first dark of an evening early in May. The sky that shows around the dim white building is a peculiarly tender blue, almost turquoise, which invests the scene with a kind of lyricism and gracefully attenuates the atmosphere of decay. You can almost feel the warm breath of the brown river beyond the river warehouses with their faint redolences of bananas and coffee. A corresponding air is evoked by the music of Negro entertainers at a bar-room around the corner. In this part of New Orleans you are practically always just around the corner, or a few doors down the street, from a tinny piano being played with the infatuated fluency of brown fingers. This 'Blue Piano' expresses the spirit of the life which goes on here.

Text 3.18 *Death of a Salesman*, Arthur Miller, 1949

A melody is heard, played upon a flute. It is small and fine, telling of grass and trees and the horizon. The curtain rises.

Before us is the salesman's house. We are aware of towering, angular shapes behind it, surrounding it on all sides. Only the blue light of the sky falls upon the house and forestage; the surrounding area shows an angry glow of orange. As more light appears, we see a solid vault of apartment houses around the small, fragile-seeming home. An air of the dream clings to the place, a dream rising out of reality. The kitchen at centre seems actual enough, for there is a kitchen table with three chairs, and a refrigerator. But no other fixtures are seen. At the back of the kitchen there is a draped entrance, which leads to the living-room. To the right of the kitchen, on a level raised two feet, is a bedroom furnished only with a brass bedstead and a straight chair. On a shelf over the bed a silver athletic trophy stands. A window opens on to the apartment house at the side.

Figure 3.12a A set from a production of *A Streetcar Named Desire*, Lyttelton Theatre/National Theatre, UK, 2002.

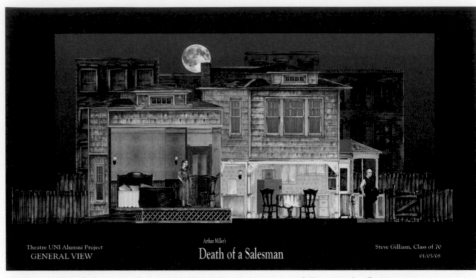

Figure 3.12b Stage set design for the opening scene of *Death of a Salesman*.

Activity 3.9

In groups, compare the pictures of the stage sets in Figures 3.12a and b with the playwrights' instructions, and discuss the following questions:

- In what ways have the set directors followed the playwright's instructions?
- What have they done that is different from the instructions?
- What do you think is most effective and why?

Both writers include detailed stage directions and instructions for the set at the beginning of their plays. Other playwrights do not include this sort of detailed instruction, believing that these are decisions for the set designer and the director rather than the writer. Williams and Miller, however, are exacting in their demands. They want to make sure that any performance of their plays creates a setting that is in line with their intentions.

These two examples are interesting because the writers have similar concerns in creating these settings, although the plays are, ostensibly, very different. Both playwrights want the set to suggest that the characters are trapped in their environments; to do this they create a sense of claustrophobia: Miller describes the 'towering, angular shapes behind [Willy's house], surrounding it on all sides'; it is a 'small, fragile-seeming home'. Williams uses the ubiquitous jazz music as a tool to suggest an atmosphere of claustrophobia, of there being very little room for private space. In this play the sounds of other people are always imposing themselves as a constant reminder of the outside world. The instructions both writers include for the lighting effects to suggest the sky are uncannily similar. Williams tells us that: 'The sky that shows around the dim white building is a particularly tender blue, almost turquoise'. Miller describes how 'Only the blue light of the sky falls upon the house and forestage'.

How do playwrights use dramatic irony?

Irony is when the intended meaning is the opposite of what is actually said. In other words, it requires the audience to interpret the words spoken on stage and not to accept them at face value. The audience might reinterpret a character's words if, for example, they are at odds with his body language or facial expression, or if the context or what is already known about a character makes it unlikely or surprising that he really means what he says. Dramatic irony is when the audience knows more than one or more of the characters on stage.

In *A Streetcar Named Desire*, Blanche du Bois' lines are often ironic, sometimes consciously, sometimes not. The audience knows that she drinks, for instance, so when she says to Mitch 'I – rarely touch it', the line is ironic because the audience is privileged to know something that one of the characters on stage doesn't. The audience knows that Blanche often thinks and talks in metaphor; she also speaks French. Mitch is both literal and ignorant of French. Therefore, when Blanche is talking to Mitch late at night on the way back from a date, you might be able to spot the dramatic irony in the lines: 'Is that streetcar named Desire still grinding along the tracks at this hour?' and 'Voulez-vous coucher avec moi ce soir? Vous ne comprenez pas? Ah, quel dommage!'

How do playwrights use stagecraft?

If you are studying the genre of drama you should consider the full range of theatrical techniques that are available to dramatists. In this section you will look at a number of features; the list of approaches suggested here is not exhaustive, but aims to encourage you to start asking the right questions.

Activity 3.10

Try to find out as much as possible about elements of stagecraft, such as stage directions, movement, dramatic tension, costume, voice and pauses, and many other features. Do some research in the library or on the Internet and you will find lots of helpful information.

In Samuel Beckett's play *Waiting for Godot*, two characters, Estragon and Vladimir, are waiting on stage for another character called Godot, whom, it transpires, they don't actually know. The Irish critic Vivian Mercier famously quipped that this is a play 'in which nothing happens ... twice' because Godot doesn't arrive in either the first or second Act. In Act 1 two other characters, Pozzo (and Lucky who rarely speaks on stage), do arrive on stage. After a sequence of exchanges and disagreements it is soon time for them to move on, but nothing is as easy as it seems, as you will see when you read this extract.

Further resources

A good place to start your research on stagecraft techniques might be the websites of the Royal Shakespeare Company and London's National Theatre, and others:

- http://www.rsc.org.uk/
- http://www.nationaltheatre.org.uk/
- http://www.sydneytheatre.com.au/
- http://www.roundabouttheatre.org/index.html

Text 3.19 *Waiting for Godot*, Samuel Beckett, 1956

Estragon	I hear something.
Pozzo	Where?
Vladimir	It's the heart.
Pozzo	(*Disappointed.*) Damnation!
Vladimir	Silence!
Estragon	Perhaps it has stopped.
	(*They straighten up.*)
Pozzo	Which of you smells so bad?
Estragon	He has stinking breath and I have stinking feet.
Pozzo	I must go.

Figure 3.13 A scene from *Waiting for Godot* featuring Pozzo, Vladimir and Estragon (Theatre Royal Haymarket, UK, 2009).

Estragon	And your half-hunter?
Pozzo	I must have left it at the manor.
	(*Silence.*)
Estragon	Then adieu.
Pozzo	Adieu.
Vladimir	Adieu.
Pozzo	Adieu.
	(*Silence. No one moves.*)
Vladimir	Adieu.
Pozzo	Adieu.
Estragon	Adieu.
	(*Silence.*)
Pozzo	And thank you.
Vladimir	Thank *you.*
Pozzo	Not at all.
Estragon	Yes yes.
Pozzo	No no.
Vladimir	Yes yes.
Estragon	No no.
	(*Silence.*)
Pozzo	I don't seem to be able ... (*Long hesitation*) ... to depart.
Estragon	Such is life.

Key term

Stichomythia The exchange of alternating single lines between characters in dramatic dialogue.

One of the dramatic techniques being used here is stichomythia, which is the rapid exchange of single lines, often featuring repetition and contradiction; when using this term you should be aware that stichomythia is a word from Greek tragedy. There is no obvious reason for the characters to be conversing in this way: perhaps it is a parody of conventional manners of saying goodbye. The pauses are clearly important as well.

Activity 3.11

Working in a group, one of you takes on the role of directing the scene in Text 3.19. The director should tell the actors what to do for each line:

- where they should stand
- where they should be looking
- how long they should wait before saying the line
- what tone they should use to say it
- how fast they should say it.

The director then explains to the actors why they have asked them to do these things for each line. You should all find that in making these decisions, you are starting to analyse the scene. By asking the right questions you will begin to find meaning.

What makes plays powerful and dramatic?

Drama is most powerful when it captures and holds an audience's attention and makes them believe absolutely in the characters on stage and in their concerns and problems. Two key moments for establishing this dramatic suspension of disbelief are the opening and concluding scenes of a play. When we looked at settings, we considered first impressions. You will now read part of the final scene of *Death of a Salesman* by Arthur Miller (Text 3.20).

Activity 3.12

Read and make notes on Text 3.20 before reading the analysis of the text that follows. Use the following guiding questions to help structure your notes:

- Why do you think Miller chooses to end the play with a twilight funeral?
- How does Miller present the characters' different response to the funeral?
- Which character do you think is presented most sympathetically?
- Do the stage directions add to our understanding of the characters?

Text 3.20 *Death of a Salesman*, Arthur Miller, 1949

The salesman, Willy Loman, has committed suicide by crashing his car and at his funeral he is mourned by his wife, Linda, his friend, Charley, and his two sons, Biff and Happy. Miller calls this final scene a 'requiem' which is traditionally a mass offering prayers for someone who has died. The title 'Requiem' sends a very clear message that Miller expects his audience to mourn and to feel sorry for Willy. The last lines of the play sound a note of darkly ironic closure when Linda repeats 'We're free' four times. She is free of debt but that freedom is worthless as Willy is not alive to share it.

Charley	It's getting dark, Linda.
	(LINDA *doesn't react. She stares at the grave.*)
Biff	How about it, Mom? Better get some rest, heh? They'll be closing the gate soon.
	(LINDA *makes no move. Pause.*)
Happy	(*deeply angered*) He had no right to do that. There was no necessity for it. We would've helped him.
Charley	(*grunting*) Hmmm.
Biff	Come along, Mom.
Linda	Why didn't anybody come?
Charley	It was a very nice funeral.
Linda	But where are all the people he knew? Maybe they blame him.
Charley	Naa. It's a rough world, Linda. They wouldn't blame him.
Linda	I can't understand it. At this time especially. First time in thirty-five years we were just about free and clear. He only needed a little salary. He was even finished with the dentist.
Charley	No man only needs a little salary.
Linda	I can't understand it.

Figure 3.14 The final scene of *Death of a Salesman* from the 1985 Castle Hill Productions film version.

Biff	There were a lot of nice days. When he'd come home from a trip; or on Sundays, making the stoop; finishing the cellar; putting on the new porch; when he built the extra bathroom; and put up the garage. You know something, Charley, there's more of him in that front stoop than in all the sales he ever made.
Charley	Yeah. He was a happy man with a batch of cement.
Linda	He was so wonderful with his hands.
Biff	He had the wrong dreams. All, all, wrong.
Happy	*(almost ready to fight* Biff) Don't say that!
Biff	He never knew who he was.
Charley	*(stopping* Happy's *movement and reply. To* Biff) Nobody dast blame this man. You don't understand; Willy was a salesman. And for a salesman, there is no rock bottom to the life. He don't put a bolt to a nut, he don't tell you the law or give you medicine. He's a man way out there in the blue, riding on a smile and a shoeshine. And when they start not smiling back – that's an earthquake. And then you get yourself a couple of spots on your hat, and you're finished. Nobody dast blame this man. A salesman is got to dream, boy. It comes with the territory.
Biff	Charley, the man didn't know who he was.

Death of a Salesman is a play that moves inevitably towards darkness. Charley opens with the line: 'It's getting dark', and we know that there is no new light for the Loman family. The dominant mood of the Requiem is unsatisfactory closure. Biff tells us: 'They'll be closing the gate soon'. The line captures both a tone of helplessness ('they' is indefinite, ambiguous) and a sense of inevitable failure: the metaphorical gate will close on their 'massive dreams'.

However, Happy (and his name never seems more ironic than now) is still angry and this works in counterpoint to the dominant mood. His hopeless: 'He had no right … We would've helped him' captures both a futile sense of moral 'right' and a failure to acknowledge the truth, which is underlined in his use of the past conditional: he claims he 'would've helped', when the audience knows that he didn't. Biff is nostalgic in this scene. He remembers that 'There were a lot of nice days' but he is also ready to admit to some truths when he says of his dead father: 'He had the wrong dreams. All, all, wrong'. There is also an air of wistful acceptance ('All, all' is a sigh of despondency) which Happy swiftly resists when he counters with: 'Don't say that!' Happy's vehemence amplifies Miller's stage direction which picks up on the simmering undercurrent of violence: Happy is *'almost ready to fight'*.

It is left to Charley to adopt the tone of a eulogy, to compose his words of respect for Willy: 'Nobody dast blame this man. A salesman is got to dream, boy. It comes with the territory.' The colloquial tone ('dast'; 'is got') combined with the weighted, elegiac sentences suggest finality and that maybe some sort of closure is possible. But the Lomans will not let this stand. Biff rudely interjects with: 'the man [Willy] didn't know who he was' as if now is somehow the moment for unwanted and unnecessary truth.

tip

If your Part 3 genre is drama then this section will have suggested a range of questions to ask about the various texts you are studying. Don't worry about there being right answers – there are usually no such things. If you ask thoughtful questions about your texts then you will be on track for successful study.

What are the key features of poetry texts?

There are many advantages to studying poetry as your chosen genre for Part 3:

- You will be able to study all of the poems in class with your teacher and you will get to know them all extremely well.
- You will be able to study the language and form of the poems in detail and compare a range of different interpretations.
- Many students find it easier to memorise lines of poetry than quotations from prose texts.
- There is a wealth of critical material to support your study.

The possibilities for poetry as a genre are limitless. It is a good idea to remember Coleridge's phrase that 'Poetry is the best words in the best order' (see page 113). There are no rules about which words or which order, although many poets choose to write in traditional forms such as the sonnet or to use conventional line structures, such as iambic pentameters, which you will look at in Unit 3.3; others write in 'free' verse which can differ wildly in style.

There are many valid approaches to writing about poetry in Part 3 which have been successful for students in the past and there is no one preferred route to the study of this genre. Nevertheless, these general strategies are recommended:

- Pay particular attention to the form and structure of the poems you are studying.
- Consider whether a poem is expressing a particular idea or experience.
- Consider the ways in which writers use literary features in order to produce the 'heightened' language of poetry.
- Consider whether the poem is, in some way, about the process of creating or about the process of writing itself.

In this section you will be given lots of advice about studying poetry. There is a lot more material to support your study of poetry elsewhere in this coursebook and if this is your chosen genre you are strongly advised to use this section in conjunction with other chapters. If you are thinking about how poets use literary features in their work, for instance, you should refer to Unit 5.2 in Chapter 5 on preparing poetry for Paper 1: Commentary. The key skills tested throughout this literature course are transferable and you should use this coursebook in its entirety to help support your study.

It is likely, although not a condition of Part 3, that you will be studying collections of relatively short poems, sometimes referred to as **lyric poems**. If you are studying longer, narrative poetry, you might want to turn back to Chapter 2 to have a look again at the advice on tackling longer poems and the examples from *Paradise Lost*.

In the sense that poems are more concerned with ideas than stories, the genre of poetry is very different from drama and prose because it is often not a narrative, although it will often use narrators in noteworthy ways. One important feature of this genre is the way in which poems often look afresh at the world around us, as you will see in the example by Louis MacNeice in the next section.

Key term

Lyric poem A poem less concerned with telling a story than with capturing a mood or an idea.

How do poets use structure and form in their writing?

Poetry – which is sometimes referred to as 'verse' – is always carefully structured. Prose (which is the form of language used in most novels, short stories, essays and drama) is continuous and organised into sentences and paragraphs. Poetry is organised into lines and stanzas. The term *stanza* is often used interchangeably with *verse*; you should use *stanza* to refer to groups of lines of poetry. Don't forget though that poetry is usually also written in sentences, which often don't stop at the end of lines! Sometimes writers use particular forms; in Unit 3.3, for example, you will look at two examples of sonnets: a 14-line poem of iambic pentameters with a particular rhyme scheme. Sometimes poets use their own, unique form. Whenever you come across a new poem try to work out what its structure is. You should ask the following questions:

- Is the poem written in a recognisable form such as a sonnet?
- How long are the lines? Do they have a particular rhythm? Are the lines different lengths?
- Are the lines organised into stanzas? If so, are these all the same length?
- Is there a rhyme scheme?

You should then ask yourself:
- Why do you think the poet has made these decisions?
- How do they affect your experience of reading the poem?
- What does the form tell us about the meaning of the poem?

Even when poets write in 'free verse' (which means they don't follow a particular form and don't use rhyme) they still make important decisions about when to start new lines and how to organise and structure their poems.

One of the most impressive elements of effective student responses to poetry is a discussion of the relationship between the content of a poem and its form and structure. With every poem you study you should aim to think about the writer's decisions about form and structure – the order of words and lines and other technical aspects of the poem – and how these decisions work with the content (what the poem is about). Now read the short but richly suggestive poem 'Snow' by Louis MacNeice (Text 3.21).

You should always analyse poets' language choices in your writing. However, remember that whilst good students talk about language, outstanding students also go on to talk about structure and form and their relationship with the content of the poem.

Text 3.21 *Snow*, Louis MacNeice

The room was suddenly rich and the great bay-window was
Spawning snow and pink roses against it
Soundlessly collateral and incompatible:
World is suddener than we fancy it.

World is crazier and more of it than we think,
Incorrigibly plural. I peel and portion
A tangerine and spit the pips and feel
The drunkenness of things being various.

And the fire flames with a bubbling sound for world
Is more spiteful and gay than one supposes –
On the tongue on the eyes on the ears in the palms of one's hands –
There is more than glass between the snow and the huge roses.

The poem is about an epiphany (a sudden realisation about the world around us); MacNeice describes how we experience the 'incorrigibly plural' world through each of our five senses, a sensation he refers to as the 'drunkenness of things being various'. In the final stanza he describes a fire burning in a nearby fireplace. However, because the narrator is not looking directly at the fire, he describes the sound it makes. He tells us that the 'fire flames with a bubbling sound'.

Poets have a number of different techniques at their disposal to draw attention to particular sounds. Two of these are alliteration and onomatopoeia; these literary techniques are explained in Chapter 5 in Unit 5.2, about preparing poetry for Paper 1: Commentary. You will remember that alliteration is the repetition of letters at the beginning or two or more words in a line; onomatopoeia is when the sound you make when saying the word is the same sound that is being described. What these techniques do is to draw attention to the sounds; when you read the line you are forced to make the sounds being described. What better techniques to use if you are a poet interested in highlighting particular sounds! MacNeice does exactly this in 'Snow'. He focuses on the sound of the fire so he employs alliteration – 'fire flames' – and onomatopoeia – 'bubbling' – in order to draw attention to the sounds that are being made. This is a good example of structure and content interacting to reinforce meaning.

Key term

Onomatopoeia Using a word that sounds like the thing it describes (for example 'bang', 'crash' etc.).

Activity 3.13

Think about the way in which the poem 'Snow' is organised into three stanzas. Can you detect three distinct stages to the poet's thinking in this short poem? In your notes write down three sentences which describe the narrator's state of mind in each of the stanzas. Discuss in groups how these thought processes develop throughout the poem.

The next poem (Text 3.22) has 30 words in total and is by the Australian poet Clive James. We have included it to show you how responding successfully to poetry is less about finding the 'right answer' than about asking the most interesting questions.

Text 3.22 *As I see you*, Clive James

As I see you
Crystals grow
Leaves chime
Roses flow

As I touch you
Tables turn
Towers lean
Witches burn

As I leave you
Lenses shiver
Flags fall
Show's over

tip

Ask the right questions about poetry. Poems rarely offer up easy answers; if they do then they're probably not very good. You shouldn't expect to 'get' a poem on first reading; perhaps you will never fully understand its complexities: this is one of the joys of returning to a poem and seeing new things in it with every reading. Rather than look for an answer you should aim to ask the right questions. Those suggested in this chapter are a very good starting point.

Activity 3.14

Read *As I see you* by Clive James then think about and discuss the following questions:

- Why do you think this poem has no punctuation?
- There is only one line with a linking verb and an adverb; all the other lines have a main verb. Why do you think this is? Is it significant that this line comes when it does?
- The stanzas are structured with an opening line followed by three two-word responses: what do you think each of these two-word lines suggests?
- If you had to come up with a two-word phrase to capture what you think the theme of the poem is, what would it be?

If you can answer some of these questions then you already have many of the analytical skills you need to approach the study of poetry.

Do poems express a single idea or experience?

Emily Dickinson lived a reclusive life in 19th century Amherst, Massachusetts, USA. She wrote many poems, very few of which were published during her lifetime. Her poems are often very short and are characterised by a proliferation of dashes, which was often the only punctuation Dickinson used. The poem you will read next (Text 3.23) starts with an image of 'a certain Slant of light' on a winter's afternoon which triggers a particular experience or emotion. When you read the poem – and you'll probably need to read it several times – try to imagine what the poet is feeling in response to that thought of the light.

Text 3.23 *There's a certain Slant of light*, Emily Dickinson, c. 1861

There's a certain Slant of light,
Winter Afternoons –
That oppresses, like the Heft
Of Cathedral Tunes –

Heavenly Hurt, it gives us –
We can find no scar,
But internal difference,
Where the Meanings, are –

None may teach it – Any –
'Tis the Seal Despair –
An imperial affliction
Sent us of the Air –

When it comes, the Landscape listens –
Shadows – hold their breath –
When it goes, 'tis like the Distance
On the look of Death –

Activity 3.15

You should often trust your initial judgements about poetry. Does Emily Dickinson's poem make you feel happy or sad? Before you continue reading, write down as quickly as possible all the words that come into your head when you read this poem.

Don't worry if you don't find this poem easy: it is complex and the examiner won't expect you to 'get' everything that's happening in the poem immediately. Many critics disagree about what it might mean. Many of the best responses about poetry are formed by students asking interesting questions about the poems. If you thought that this poem was sad, was it because you picked up on the vocabulary: 'despair', 'affliction', shadow', 'death'? Emily Dickinson is certainly talking about suffering. However, she makes it clear that this is not physical, in the lines: 'Heavenly Hurt, it gives us –/ We can find no scar'. There is no outward sign or 'scar' as a mark of her 'hurt'. It is also strange that she feels oppressed by the thoughts associated with the light 'like the Heft/ Of Cathedral Tunes'. This odd simile might suggest that the despair is moral or spiritual. Perhaps the central idea of the poem is to be found at its physical centre: 'Where the Meanings, are –/ None may teach it'. Dickinson despairs that nothing and no one is able to give her a sense of what her life might mean; and perhaps this is why the poem ends with an image of death and why its final word is 'death'.

The poem springs from a single idea, the 'Slant of light', and it goes on to explore the narrator's emotional response to this idea. This is true of so many poems; it is true of 'Snow' and, as you will find out in Unit 3.3, it is true of the two sonnets you will examine there.

How do poets use literary features in their poems?

One key element you should analyse in your writing about poetry is the writer's use of literary features. Writing about these will be important whatever genre you are preparing for Part 3; however, poetry tends to be relatively dense with such features because the language of poetry is generally more stylised and more 'heightened'. For this reason you might consider such devices to be one of the conventions of poetry as a genre; you will certainly want to write about such features in the exam. You should use the Glossary to remind yourself of the literary terms and features referred to throughout this coursebook.

Is poetry about the craft of writing poetry?

Poetry often celebrates the craft of writing itself and in Unit 3.3 you will look at two sonnets which esteem the power of poetry and celebrate the skill of the poet and the potential for the written word to last for all time (Percy Bysshe Shelley said that 'Poets are the unacknowledged legislators of the world'). One of the features of many poems is the writing about writing itself. Ted Hughes's *The Thought-Fox*, for instance, is a famous celebration of the power of poetry.

Text 3.24 *The Thought-Fox*, Ted Hughes

I imagine this midnight moment's forest:
Something else is alive
Beside the clock's loneliness
And this blank page where my fingers move.

Through the window I see no star:
Something more near
Though deeper within darkness
Is entering the loneliness:

Cold, delicately as the dark snow
A fox's nose touches twig, leaf;
Two eyes serve a movement, that now
And again now, and now, and now

Sets neat prints into the snow
Between trees, and warily a lame
Shadow lags by stump and in hollow
Of a body that is bold to come

Across clearings, an eye,
A widening deepening greenness,
Brilliantly, concentratedly,
Coming about its own business

Till, with a sudden sharp hot stink of fox
It enters the dark hole of the head.
The window is starless still; the clock ticks,
The page is printed.

TOK

Edward Bulwer-Lytton wrote in 1839 'The pen is mightier than the sword.' To what extent do you think that the written word has the power to effect social and political change? Does history show us that the written word is more powerful than violence?

The poem charts two simultaneous events: a fox crossing some country side and the writing of a poem. It is about the movement from 'this blank page' to 'The page is printed'. Although this poem is obviously about a fox it is perhaps even more powerfully about the 'thought' of the fox: about the process of poetic creation. When you re-read it you notice more and more clues. The 'Something more near' that is 'entering the loneliness' is the poem on the page. The act of writing, of putting down words 'now/ And again now, and now, and now', is responsible for setting 'neat prints' on the paper. It is the writer who works 'concentratedly' and it is the poem that 'enters the dark hole of the head'. Crafting a poem is an incredibly self-conscious process. Writers spend hours choosing the right words and revising what they have written. Sometimes the act of writing becomes as much a part of the theme of the poem as the thing being described.

Activity 3.16

Have a go at writing a poem yourself. You should write about a recent experience or emotion but make sure that you think and write about the process of writing. Think carefully about the structure of each line and how you organise your ideas. In writing your own poem you will realise just how careful poets are with their choices of language, structure and form.

tip

If your Part 3 genre is poetry then this section will have suggested a range of questions to ask about the various texts you are studying. Don't worry about there being right answers – there are usually no such things. If you ask thoughtful questions about your texts then you will be on track for successful study.

Unit 3.3 What does an effective comparative literary essay look like?

In studying Part 3 of the course and in preparing for Paper 2 you should make sure that you are very confident about the form your exam answer will take. The expectation is that you will write a formal comparative literary essay, and the better you understand this form and the more you practise it, the better prepared you will be. There is one piece of advice which you should remember before all others: *answer the question!* The questions should guide you to write about the conventions and features of the genre you have been studying; however, you should remember at all times that the best responses always answer the question with clarity and focus.

This unit suggests a structure for writing essays which will enable you to answer the question as directly and as effectively as possible. You'll be guided through how to write a really clear introduction which sets out a thesis for the essay. The main body of your essay will be composed of analytical paragraphs, all with a very similar structure, always focusing on the conventions and features of the genre you are studying. You'll be given a model for writing a good analytical paragraph which you can then use in your own writing. At the end of the unit you'll be given some advice on how to conclude your essay and some ideas of what you might write in a final paragraph.

What should you include in the Introduction?

The introduction is the first thing an examiner reads, so it's your first opportunity to impress. You may have been advised that introductions are unnecessary; however, the advice given here is that the very best essays have a focus and directness which needs to be established from the very first paragraph and you should, therefore, include an introduction.

You should keep introductions as short as possible, and aim to write about three sentences. However, you should make sure that you do the following:
• Mention the texts and the writers you will be talking about in your essay.
• Show that you understand the question and include a thesis or argument in response to that question.

Let's look at these points one by one:

1   You need to tell the examiner as soon as possible which texts you will be writing about. Remember that the examiner won't necessarily know which texts you've been studying. Therefore, in the introduction you need to include the writer's name (just their surname will do) and the title of each text. Remember that when you are handwriting, the convention for indicating

tip

Answer the question! This is the simplest and best advice you will get for this exam. One of the chief qualities of any successful essay is that it answers the question. You should avoid the temptation to tell the examiner everything you know about a text: always stay focused on the question.

that something is a title is to place it in inverted commas. (When typing, it's italics for novels and plays and inverted commas for poems.) Imagine your genre is drama; your introduction might start: 'In Beckett's *Waiting for Godot*, Albee's *Who's Afraid of Virginia Woolf?* and Williams's *A Streetcar Named Desire* …' you've immediately let the examiner know which texts you will be writing about.

2   All effective essays answer the question. If you show from your very first paragraph that you understand the terms of the question and that you are going to answer it in a focused and tightly argued way then you have taken the first important steps to ensuring that your essay is effectively structured. You should aim to set out a thesis, or argument; this will set out as clearly and in as few words as possible the focus of your essay. It will tell the examiner how you intend to answer the question. You should avoid anything vague; everything you write should be text or question specific. We would particularly advise against 'clearing your throat' type statements. Imagine you are writing an essay on the opening scenes of three plays you have studied. You should avoid writing things like: 'In the essay I will examine the opening scenes of three different plays and look at the various techniques the different playwrights use to make their openings as effective as possible.' This is vague and unnecessary. Don't tell the examiner what you're going to say. Just say it; and say it as directly and specifically as possible. Using the same drama examples as above, you might write something like: 'We are immediately aware of the claustrophobic neighbour in *A Streetcar Named Desire* and Albee's opening dialogue presents a relationship under strain. From the opening moments of each drama both playwrights make it obvious to their audiences that their plays will be dramatically tense.'

An introduction does not need to include analysis of the language of the texts. However, this doesn't necessarily mean that it should never include a quotation. There are times when a very short (two- or three-word) quotation dropped into the introduction can send out the message that you know the texts you are writing about intimately and that your essay will be constantly referencing the primary texts.

How should you structure an analytical and comparative paragraph?

With the exception of the introduction and the conclusion, most of the paragraphs in your essays will be structured in a similar way. Here, we suggest a structure for paragraphs which aim to be both analytical and comparative. Analytical, when we are talking about literary essays, means writing about the writers' decisions and showing how and why they make specific choices about language and structure. Comparative, in this sense, means writing about the similarities and differences between the various texts. Most of the paragraphs you write in your Paper 2 essay should aim to be both of these things.

Read through the guide to structuring a paragraph that is both analytical and comparative below. You will then have a chance to look at a worked example and, in Unit 3.4, some sample student responses to show you how you might adapt this structure to your chosen genre.

We suggest that you break down each paragraph into six or seven parts, as follows:

1 **The first sentence needs to tell the reader what the focus of the paragraph is going to be as clearly and in as few words as possible.** Make sure that it directly addresses the question. If your essay is very well structured then you should be able to summarise it by reading the first sentence of each paragraph. The first sentence is vital in signposting what the paragraph is going to be about. Some teachers call this the *topic sentence*; others refer to it as the *point*.

2 **The second sentence should include your first piece of evidence.** This will usually be a quotation from one of the texts. The rule of thumb for quotations is that they should be as short as possible: you should quote only the sections that you intend to discuss and, in an essay like this, they should never be longer than a couple of lines of poetry or a prose sentence. They should also be *embedded* – the sentence should read naturally and flow continuously if you were to take the quotation marks away.

3 **The next part of the paragraph will usually be two or three sentences of analysis of the first quotation.** In these sentences you should write about the writer's choices of language, structure and form. You will need to quote certain individual words again in order to focus on them and to show how and why the writer has used them. You should use technical language in your analysis to show that you understand how and why the writer uses various literary devices.

4 **You will then need to link into the next section of the paragraph** which will often be a comparison with another text. This will usually be one sentence and will often use a linking word or phrase. The tip box at the bottom of page 112 gives some examples of the sorts of words and phrases you might use to link to the next part of the paragraph.

5 **You now need to provide some evidence from the text you are comparing,** so you will normally include another quotation here. You should follow the advice given in point 2 above.

6 **Once again you will analyse the quotation**, following the advice in point 3 above. In this section of the paragraph you may draw the two texts together and write about the similarities and differences between the two pieces of evidence you have selected.

7 **It may be appropriate to end the paragraph with a sentence which brings the reader back to the point of focus set out in the first sentence.** However, if you have stuck to the point of the paragraph and focused on answering the question throughout, this may not be necessary.

tip

You should always aim to embed quotations in your writing. The quotation should be part of the sentence; in order to help you to achieve this it is usually a good idea to avoid starting a sentence with a quotation. Instead, you could say something as simple as: 'We can see this when the writer says: "…".' Remember that everything that you put inside quotation marks should be exactly what appears in the text. You can't add extra words or punctuation of your own unless you put these in square brackets [like this] but you should avoid doing this if possible. If you want to leave out a few words you can replace them with an ellipsis: this means just putting three dots [...] where the words you've left out would have been.

Key term

Volte face An about-turn where at the end of a poem the argument is challenged or turned on its head.

tip

Link words or phrases are a very powerful tool, especially when you are writing comparative essays. Make sure you have a few at your disposal. You could use: *however*, *on the other hand*, *in contrast*, *alternatively*, *in a similar vein*. If used at the start of a sentence, linking words or phrases are usually followed by a comma.

Having looked at a suggested structure for this type of paragraph, let's look at how you might tackle this in practice. As an example, we'll work through a comparative paragraph about two sonnets by Shakespeare. In Unit 3.4, we'll look at some student sample material that compares drama, poetry and prose texts. First, read the following two sonnets by Shakespeare (Text 3.25), which are both about time and the effects of the passing of time.

Text 3.25 *Sonnets 15* and *19*, William Shakespeare

Sonnet 15

When I consider every thing that grows
Holds in perfection but a little moment,
That this huge stage presenteth nought but shows
Whereon the stars in secret influence comment;
When I perceive that men as plants increase, 5
Cheered and check even by the self-same sky,
Vaunt in their youthful sap, at height decrease,
And wear their brave state out of memory;
Then the conceit of this inconstant stay
Sets you most rich in youth before my sight, 10
Where wasteful Time debateth with Decay,
To change your day of youth to sullied night;
And all in war with Time for love of you,
As he takes from you, I engraft you new.

Sonnet 19

Devouring Time, blunt thou the lion's paws,
And make the earth devour her own sweet brood;
Pluck the keen teeth from the fierce tiger's jaws,
And burn the long-liv'd phoenix in her blood;
Make glad and sorry seasons as thou fleet'st, 5
And do whate'er thou wilt, swift-footed Time,
To the wide world and all her fading sweets;
But I forbid thee one most heinous crime:
O, carve not with thy hours my love's fair brow,
Nor draw no lines there with thine antique pen; 10
Him in thy course untainted do allow
For beauty's pattern to succeeding men.
Yet, do thy worst, old Time. Despite thy wrong,
My love shall in my verse ever live young.

Paragraph structure: a worked example

These two poems are both sonnets. That is, they have 14 lines, each line has 10 syllables (each is an iambic pentameter) and they follow a specific rhyme scheme. One of the interesting features of that rhyme scheme is that the final two lines rhyme, which has the effect of making that final rhyming couplet stand out. Indeed, in Shakespeare's sonnets, the final rhyming couplet often has the effect of a conclusion or, to use the technical term, a *volte face*: the argument turns around and the poet shows us a new way of looking at the 'problem' of the poem.

The problem in both of these sonnets is the onset of time. Both poems are addressed to a young man whom the poet realises will soon become old and lose his beauty. As the poems unfold, Shakespeare bemoans the way that time always catches up with us and makes us old and destroys what was previously beautiful. However, both sonnets finish with a very similar argument: that although the passage of time is inevitable, there is one way of winning the war against time. In those final couplets, Shakespeare argues that by writing about beauty we manage to make it immortal and protect it from the passage of time. In many ways he's correct: we're still reading the poems now, over 400 years after they were written, so he has managed a degree of immortality at least.

So far, you have looked at *what* Shakespeare is doing; however, the examiner wants to see evidence that you can write about *how* and *why* Shakespeare makes the decisions he does. Let's think about how you would go about writing this comparative paragraph. You've already made one important decision; you know what evidence you're going to be using: the final two lines from each poem (although you won't necessarily have to quote every word). Your next important task is to write the opening sentence of the paragraph, remembering that this should tell the reader what the paragraph is going to be about in as clear a way as possible. You should also aim to do this in as few words as possible. So you might write something like:

In the final rhyming couplets Shakespeare turns the argument of each sonnet on its head and argues that, by writing about the young man's beauty, he has conferred on him a type of immortality.

After that first sentence you need to find evidence from the text to show that you are grounding your points in the language and structure choices the writer makes. You're going to need to embed the quotations you use very carefully to make sure that the sentences still read clearly. In this way, you might write something like this:

Although the sonnet has been about a 'war with Time for love of' the young man, the last line is a direct challenge to time: 'As he takes from you, I engraft you new.'

Remembering that your writing should aim to show how and why the writer makes the choices he does, you now need to write some analytical sentences. In this part of the paragraph you should be aiming to use technical vocabulary (where appropriate) and to look at individual words and phrase choices (and re-quote these where necessary) in order to unravel how and why Shakespeare makes the choices he does. You might write something like this:

We are told that the poet is at 'war' with time and the force of this metaphor is underlined by the ongoing personification of 'Time', which has a capital letter. This has the effect of making the contest personal which is reinforced in the repeated pronouns of the final line: 'he ... you ... I ... you'. This struggle swings one way and then the other. However, the *volte face* is achieved in the final idea where Shakespeare argues that the poem itself can 'engraft you new'. The verb 'engraft' suggests the physical act of writing but also a force which implies that the poem will be a permanent reminder of the young man's beauty and, therefore, will be able easily to defeat 'wasteful Time' and 'Decay'.

So far you have written a section of a paragraph that successfully analyses the idea in one poem. You'll remember, however, that this exam requires you to compare. The next

> **tip**
>
> Samuel Taylor Coleridge said that poetry is the 'best words in the best order'. If you are ever stuck on how to analyse language and structure you can always write about why you think a particular word is the best choice and why you think the writer has chosen the best order for the words he or she has used.

thing you need, therefore, is a link to the next piece of evidence. Often this will be simply a linking word or phrase. If you can pick up on something specific then your link will be more effective. Here the link might be the act of writing, so you might continue in this way:

In Sonnet 19, on the other hand, time's 'antique pen' is mocked in the final couplet: 'Yet, do thy worst, old Time: despite thy wrong,/ My love shall in my verse ever live young.'

All you need to do now is to write several sentences about how and why Shakespeare makes the choices he does in this couplet and then bring the paragraph to a conclusion. What you should end up with is an effective paragraph which is both analytical and comparative. Let's put it all together and see what it looks like:

In the final rhyming couplets Shakespeare turns the argument of each sonnet on its head and argues that, by writing about the young man's beauty, he has conferred on him a type of immortality. Although the poem has been about a 'war with Time for love of' the young man, the last line is a direct challenge to time: 'As he takes from you, I engraft you new.' We are told that the poet is at 'war' with time and the force of this metaphor is underlined by the ongoing personification of 'Time', which has a capital letter. This has the effect of making the contest personal which is reinforced in the repeated pronouns of the final line: 'he ... you ... I ... you'. This struggle swings one way and then the other. However, the volte face is achieved in the final idea where Shakespeare argues that the poem itself can 'engraft you new'. The verb 'engraft' suggests the physical act of writing but also a force which implies that the poem will be a permanent reminder of the young man's beauty and, therefore, will be able easily to defeat 'wasteful Time' and 'Decay'. In Sonnet 19, on the other hand, time's 'antique pen' is mocked in the final couplet: 'Yet, do thy worst, old Time. Despite thy wrong,/ My love shall in my verse ever live young.' Shakespeare mocks Time with the dismissive phrase 'do thy worst' and by using the adjective 'old' to describe him. The final rhyme is also important as it underlines the way in which the poem defeats 'devouring time'. Time is 'wrong', but in direct contrast to this the poem keeps the subject 'young'. The immortality Shakespeare is claiming for his verse is powerfully underlined by the word 'ever' as the final couple turns the argument on its head and challenges the power of time.

After having worked through this example, you should have a clearer idea of how to structure an effective paragraph that is both analytical and comparative. Now you will need to think about how this might work for the particular genre you are studying; you will also need to start practising writing paragraphs of your own.

tip

Practise writing individual paragraphs in preparation for the exam. Although you will need to write full essays in order to get used to writing for 1½ or 2 hours in exam conditions, sometimes it will be a good idea to write just one paragraph. By focusing on detail in this way you will be able to improve the structure of your writing and your analytical technique.

Activity 3.17

Have a go at writing a paragraph of your own based on Shakespeare's *Sonnets 15* and *19*. You should choose an idea from each which lends itself to comparison and then follow the structure for writing an effective paragraph which is both analytical and comparative. To help you, we have included one further example which has been marked up to make its structure as clear as possible.

Shakespeare presents time as a destroyer of beauty by metaphorically representing him as a cruel writer and a negligent timewaster.[1] In *Sonnet 19*, Time is, metaphorically, a draughtsman whom Shakespeare challenges to: 'draw no lines … with thine antique pen'.[2] The 'lines' are literally the marks of ageing that Time leaves on the man's 'brow'; that Time writes them there suggests his active enjoyment in the destruction of beauty. Time's pen is 'antique' – it is literally ageing – but we might also hear the word 'antic' when we read the poem aloud, which would suggest the callousness of the ageing process. There is a clever irony in presenting Time as a writer because, as we know, he will be defeated by Shakespeare's own writing, his 'verse'.[3] In *Sonnet 15*, on the other hand,[4] Time is painted as being neglectful. We see this when Shakespeare describes how: 'wasteful Time debateth with Decay,/To change your day of youth to sullied night'.[5] Both 'Time' and 'Decay' are personified here to give the sense of two human figures chatting away, neglectful and unaware of the passing time; this is underlined by the use of the adjective 'wasteful' to describe Time. Their negligence turns the day of beauty to the metaphorical night of ageing and decay. Shakespeare uses the powerful adjective 'sullied' to describe this night to convey the absence of former glory and beauty.[6] Both sonnets use metaphors to demonstrate the inevitable power of time which makes its defeat in the final couplet even more impressive.[7]

What should you include in a conclusion?

A conclusion should be one short paragraph which aims to tie up any threads of your argument that are still unresolved. Although most effective essays will include a conclusion, it is important to avoid it becoming simply a short summary of the essay. In your conclusion you should aim to return to the thesis you set out in the introduction to convince the examiner that you really have answered the question in the way you said you would. Although you shouldn't be introducing anything entirely new, it may be appropriate to use a specific textual example or a short quotation from one of the texts you have been writing about in order to keep your argument focused and directed.

Unit 3.4 **Assessment: Sample student responses**

In this unit you will read some sample student essays. The commentaries on the responses are designed to help you to see how these essays address the various assessment criteria. You will read two Paper 2 essays here: one is on the genre of drama and the other is on the genre of prose (the novel and the short story). The first essay is written by an SL student; the second by an HL student. Both essays were awarded good marks and have been marked up to show how they addressed the various assessment criteria. Your teacher will be able to provide you with sample essays and examiner's commentaries for other genres that are not included in this coursebook.

Drama: SL sample student response

'Drama is full of interesting characters who barely know themselves.' To what extent do you find this statement applicable in **at least two plays** you have studied?

1. This first sentence attempts to point out as clearly and in as few words as possible what the paragraph is going to focus on.

2. The first piece of evidence is embedded into this sentence.

3. The paragraph then offers some analysis of the quotation. It aims to use technical language wherever possible and to focus on Shakespeare's word choices, sometimes quoting individual words again to draw attention to them.

4. The paragraph then uses a linking phrase to take the reader into an analysis of the comparative example.

5. The second piece of evidence is embedded into this sentence.

6. The paragraph here analyses the second example.

7. The paragraph draws to a conclusion, returning to its central theme. It won't always be necessary to add a final sentence like this but it can sometimes give even more focus and clarity to your writing.

Chapter 3 – Literary genres

1. The student immediately signals an intention to answer the question (Criterion B).
2. A clear, focused introduction helps to ensure that the essay will be organised and developed (Criterion D).
3. This paragraph uses language very effectively (Criterion E). It is also analytical and demonstrates good understanding (Criterion A); however, it is not always clear from this paragraph that the techniques and conventions being discussed are specifically those associated with the genre of drama. For this reason, Criterion C is not addressed as effectively as it might be in this paragraph.
4. By referring to a convention that is specifically dramatic, this paragraph is immediately more successful in terms of addressing Criterion C.
5. The student continues to focus effectively on responding to the question (Criterion B).
6. In talking about the playwright's construction of the scene, the student addresses Criterion C although there may be more room to explore how this might be performed and how a director might approach it in order to focus even more specifically on the conventions of drama.

Eddie Carbone and Blanche DuBois barely know themselves. The central characters of *A View from the Bridge* and *A Streetcar Named Desire* live in a world of self-deception which ultimately leads to their tragic downfalls.[1] The audience is engaged by Eddie and Blanche – both playwrights present them as basically good characters who are nevertheless flawed – but the dramatic power of the plays is established because the audience experiences the catharsis of watching their downfalls. Like Alfieri we are 'powerless to stop' even as we see events on stage spiralling out of control because of the central characters' lack of self-knowledge.[2]

Blanche and Eddie's language is shrouded in ambiguity. Eddie's feelings for Catherine are deeply problematic and his language reflects this. At the start of the play he says to his niece: 'Listen, you been givin' me the willies the way you walk down the street, I mean it.' The phrase 'the willies' is strangely inappropriate. It is as if Eddie is incapable of articulating how he actually feels and is reverting to the language of childhood. His lack of self-knowledge is reinforced in the final phrase: 'I mean it'. It is almost as if he is trying to convince himself. Miller also shows us how Eddie is challenged by Rodolpho but is unable to acknowledge how; Eddie says: 'He give me the heeby-jeebies the first minute I saw him'. 'Heeby-jeebies' is also ambiguous. In the same way, Blanche hides from reality through her language. She talks and thinks in metaphor – always one stage removed from the truth – and describes how, 'The soft people have got to – shimmer and glow – put a – paper lantern over the light … And I – I'm fading now!' The irony here is that at the same time that she is trying to tell the truth (she is 'soft' – she's a victim; the lights are beginning to go out), in the ambiguity of her language she is also trying to protect herself from the harsh glare of reality.[3]

Williams and Miller both use dramatic irony: as the action progresses the audience gains greater knowledge than some of the characters on the stage.[4] Blanche's irony stems from her brutal self-realisation: 'I tell what ought to be the truth' combined with her lack of desire to deal with the truth of her situation: 'I don't want realism'.[5] The audience sees her suffering and her self-deception as one and the same. Blanche can be vehement and forceful. She warns Stella, '*Don't – don't hang back with the brutes*', desperately trying to convince her to leave Stanley. However, Williams constructs this scene so that Stanley is positioned so that he overhears her tirade against him and, ironically, the audience is more aware than Blanche of the effects of her behaviour.[6] The critic James Wood has argued that one definition of dramatic irony is 'to see through a character's eyes while being encouraged to see more than the character can see'. This is certainly true in *A View from the Bridge* when Eddie tells Alfieri about Rodolpho, saying: 'The guy ain't right, Mr Alfieri.' The audience hears Eddie's pain in the haunting phrase 'ain't right' but we recognise that, ironically, these words apply more to Eddie who demonstrates yet again that he barely knows himself. A further irony is that his lack of self-knowledge ultimately means that, as Alfieri puts it: 'He allowed himself to be wholly known'. 'Wholly known' by the audience but barely known by himself.

Both playwrights use setting and stage directions in order to underline the extent to which their characters barely know themselves. At the start of *A Streetcar Named Desire* the stage directions and the setting suggest the incompatibility of Blanche and her surroundings. She is the '*Tender blue*' light Williams describes that '*invests the scene with a kind of lyricism*'. The clear suggestion that this 'lyricism' doesn't fit in with the noisy realities of New Orleans underlines the sense that Blanche is out of place. Her actions also demonstrate her lack of self-knowledge. Williams's stage directions for Blanche on arrival in Stella and Stanley's flat are interesting. Firstly, he describes how '*Blanche sits in a chair very stiffly with her shoulders slightly hunched and her legs pressed close together*'. She is playing a role, trying to be proper in a way that refutes the truth of the situation – although the 'slightly hunched' shoulders belie this. It is not until she '*pours half a tumbler of whisky and tosses it down*' that she is able to be truer to herself. In the same way, Miller's stage directions demonstrate Eddie's lack of self-awareness. At the end of Act 1 he describes how Eddie '*has been unconsciously twisting the newspaper in a tight roll*.' The word 'unconsciously' shows his lack of perception of the reality of the situation just as the adverb 'weirdly' does in the stage direction: '*He is weirdly elated*.' It is weird because even Eddie doesn't know why he feels the way he does.[7]

The supporting cast play a critical role in showing the audience Eddie's and Blanche's lack of self-knowledge and self-awareness. In *A View from the Bridge* the narrator, Alfieri, guides the audience, in much the same way as a Greek chorus, and suggests that the audience might be 'as powerless as I' as we watch the tragedy 'run its bloody course'. We are unable to affect the characters' self-awareness. Perhaps only Beatrice understands the truth. She is forced to remind Catherine: 'I told you fifty times already, you can't act the way you act. You still walk around in front of him in your slip'. There is desperation in the 'fifty times already'. And, of course, it is Beatrice who utters the devastating line: 'You want somethin' else Eddie, and you can never have her!' The powerful dramatic effect of this line is that the audience is unsure what she is actually going to say until the very last word. In *Streetcar*, on the other hand, the supporting cast underline Blanche's lack of awareness. She chooses Mitch to confide in, knowing that he won't understand her – just as he doesn't understand when she speaks French to him. He responds to the tale of Allan's death with the line: 'You need somebody. And I need somebody, too. Could it be – you and me, Blanche?' Blanche can only stare 'vacantly' at his lack of self-awareness. She may want to 'speak – plainly' but she never really manages to confront the truth consistently.[8]

Alfieri tells the audience that 'Eddie Carbone had never expected to have a destiny'; he is a common man but he is trapped in a modern tragedy because of a single tragic flaw ('too much love for the niece'). His lack of self-knowledge is mirrored by his incompatible presence in this tragic drama. Blanche remains ironically blind even at the last, telling the doctor: 'I have always depended on the kindness of strangers.' The audience suffers with these two tragic characters, whose lack of self-knowledge and refusal to change lead inexorably to their downfalls.[9]

7 This paragraph is more effective in addressing Criterion C (stage directions particularly are conventions specific to drama). However, the student could place more emphasis on the theatricality of the scene and how it might play out in performance.

8 This paragraph demonstrates excellent knowledge and understanding (Criterion A) and effective and precise use of language (Criterion D). Perhaps it could do more to address the specific conventions of drama (Criterion C).

9 The conclusion draws the argument together. The essay has responded to the question (Criterion B) throughout and its organisation and development (Criterion D) have been very effective: each of the paragraphs has been coherently structured. Reference to the audience shows an awareness of the need to address Criterion C although this criterion is tackled less successfully than the others in this essay.

Prose (the novel and the short story): HL sample student response

> Discuss the ways in which **at least two** novels or short stories you have studied demonstrate that the search for identity can be a complex and difficult process.

1. The essay starts with a clear focus on the question (Criterion B), and in specifically referencing some of the key characters from the novels it will focus on it demonstrates good knowledge and understanding (Criterion A).

2. References to genre-specific conventions (such as narrative, in this case) help to address Criterion C; however, the reference could, perhaps, be more persuasively developed.

3. The comparative structure of the paragraph works very well (Criterion D) and the essay continues to be well focused on responding to the question (Criterion B).

4. In writing about the construction of narrative, the student is more successful here at addressing Criterion C (Appreciation of the literary conventions of the genre).

Arundhati Roy's *The God of Small Things* is a novel where characters are forced to conform against their will. When they refuse because their individual sense of identity clashes with society's expectations, they suffer. Estha, Rahel, Ammu and Velutha are torn and struggle to construct a coherent sense of their own identities in the context of the worlds they find themselves in. Bharati Mukherjee's *Jasmine*, on the other hand, consciously shifts context throughout her novel: the novel's heroine, Jasmine, moves from India to the US; however, her shifting identity remains confused: each new sense of self simply adds a layer of complexity.[1]

Roy and Mukherjee's central characters don't fit in to the models of identity expected by the societies they live in. Roy's central protagonists are Estha and Rahel, a 'two-egg ... rare breed of Siamese twins'. They think of themselves, as we are told in the opening chapter by the third person narrator, 'individually as We or Us'. Roy opens her narrative[2] with a pair of characters who are both genetically and temperamentally ill-suited to the community in which they grow up. She alludes to the simple binary divisions of Noah's Ark to describe the twins: 'And nearby in the jungle, in the eerie, storm-coming light, animals queued up in pairs:/ Girlboy./Girlboy./Girlboy./Girlboy./ Twins were not allowed.' They are incompatible and alienated.[3] In a similar vein, Jasmine is defined in contrast to her 'older sisters' whom she characterises as 'slow, happy girls'. The juxtaposition of 'slow' and 'happy' – one a negative quality, the other positive – is a powerful representation of Jasmine's sense of not fitting in. She tells the reader that, 'My body was merely the shell': she is not prepared to accept an identity which is imposed upon her by society, but will go out and forge her own. This sense of empowerment makes her feel 'potent, a goddess'. She is narrating her own story but also taking charge of her life's narrative.

The narrative movement of *Jasmine* is forward whereas Roy's narrative moves back into the past. *Jasmine* follows a traditionally chronological narrative: it starts with a seminal moment in the narrator's childhood and ends in the present.[4] But this forward-moving narrative is in tension with the 'she-ghosts' we meet in the opening section of the novel and which continue to haunt the narrator throughout. In the novel mother and mother-country are one and the same, and Jasmine recognises the unbreakable bond between her past and present when she tells us to: 'Blame the mother. Insanity has to come from somewhere. It's the mother who is mad ... The girl is mad. Her mother is mad. The whole country is mad.' The manic repetition of 'mad' demonstrates the difficulties she encounters in cohering her various different experiences. The narrative is also circular: the astrologer of the first episode 'floats cross-legged above my kitchen stove' on the last page of the book. The opening chapter of *The God of Small Things*, on the other hand, relates the events on the eve of the last day described by the narrative. The novel is mostly retrospective: the twins' lives – in Chapter One – have a 'size and shape now' (albeit tragic) and the story reaches back into the past to unearth the 'bleached bones' and to unpick a narrative which 'really began in the days when the Love Laws were made'. Roy uses the phrase 'Love Laws' to stand for the unwritten social conventions which bind characters into certain patterns of behaviour and deny Estha and Rahel the identities they feel are their birthrights.[5]

The strengths of various characters' identities are bound up in the manner in which their stories are told. *Jasmine* is narrated by the eponymous heroine. It is a first person narrative and very much Jasmine's story.[6] As the narrator moves through diverse communities and environments the 'I' changes and adapts, and Jasmine makes the reader aware of this: 'ghosts float toward me. Jane, Jasmine, Jyoti.' Mukherjee even has her change her name as an obvious symbol of the ways in which her identity is shifting. Jasmine is a survivor. Her assertive narrative voice tells the reader that, 'in surviving I was already Jane, a fighter and adaptor'. In contrast, Roy employs a third person omniscient narrator to tell her story. The narrative is knowing and ironic. At times it slips into the heads of various characters, using the technique of free indirect style[7] to allow us to view the events from a number of different perspectives. Rahel – as a schoolgirl – is described by the narrator as an 'extremely polite child' (this is society's judgement) but the narrative moves on to say of her behaviour: 'It was, they whispered to each other, *as though she didn't know how to be a girl.*' In this instance the reader is in the minds of disapproving gossips, teachers and traditionalists. That voice is countered (in parenthesis) by a narrative interjection which sounds like the child Rahel knowingly commenting on her critics, as they are seen '(savouring their teacherly disapproval, touching it with their tongues, sucking it like a sweet)'. Estha's uncertain identity is revealed through his handwriting. He scrawls 'Un-known' on his school exercise book, 'His surname postponed for the Time Being'.

Both writers use setting to underline the difficulties their characters face in their search for identity.[8] *Jasmine* starts in India ('Lifetimes ago, under a Banyam tree' – the traditional centre of a community) and moves to the US; the narrator tells us that, in the present, 'I live in Baden … Iowa'. These two settings are described in contrasting and antithetical ways, but both inform each other. At the start of the novel – in India – Jasmine is swimming in a river when she sees a dead dog. The memory haunts her; India – the first setting for the novel – is present 'every time I lift a glass of water to my lips' because, as Jasmine tells us, 'fleetingly I smell it'. She is represented as being 'On the edge of the world', a product of a number of different settings and environments. In *The God of Small Things* the settings add to the sense that there are no clear boundaries. 'Boundaries blur as tapioca fences take root and bloom' and the walls of an old house, personified in the opening section of the novel, 'bulged a little with dampness'.[9] Roy uses settings

---

5	This paragraph uses language clearly and precisely (Criterion E) and is persuasively organised and developed (Criteria D). This student does a very good job of addressing Criteria D and E throughout the essay.
6	The analysis of how the writer has constructed narrative helps to address Criterion C.
7	This is another example of a perceptive identification of a literary convention used by novelists and so can be effectively rewarded for Criterion C.
8	Each paragraph starts with a clear, focused sentence which not only responds to the question (Criterion B) but also signals that the paragraph will be persuasively structured (Criterion D).
9	The skilful embedding of quotations into the argument of the essay demonstrates a high degree of accuracy in sentence construction (Criterion E: Language).

10 Perceptive knowledge and understanding of these texts are very clearly in evidence in this paragraph (Criterion A).

11 Perhaps there is a little more room to explore how novelists create character in order to be even more specific about the literary conventions novelists adhere to (Criterion C). Nevertheless, the excellent knowledge and understanding (Criterion A) and the very effective use of language (Criterion E) in this paragraph are highly rewarded.

12 The student concludes the essay effectively, drawing the focus back to the question (Criterion B) and reminding the reader of the high degree of organisation which has been in evidence throughout (Criterion D).

to foreground the blurring of boundaries which the twins feel as an assault on their sense of identity. Similarly, she represents them, using a powerful metaphor, as 'A pair of actors trapped in a recondite play with no hint of plot or narrative'. Rahel can walk back into the 'play' but even then she is only a small part: 'A flower perhaps. Or a tree ... A townspeople.' The narrative that society wants to impose on the twins' lives does not cohere with the story inside their heads.[10]

The identities of many characters in both novels are presented as confused and complex.[11] The problems with authority in *The God of Small Things* are represented by the ironic references to the police. When the twins' mother, Ammu, is forced to go to a police station, the officer 'tapped her breasts with his baton' in a symbolically charged 'attempt to instill order into a world gone wrong.' Similarly, the section with the Kathakali dancer (a traditional South Indian art form) introduces us to Kunti: 'She too was a man ... a man with breasts, from doing female parts for years.' He might appear to have a confused identity, but even he subscribes to certain of society's patriarchal norms: 'The Kathakali men took off their make up and went home to beat their wives. Even Kunti, the soft one with breasts.' In *Jasmine*, on the other hand, the narrator sees her own crises of identity reflected in her husband's: 'My transformation has been genetic; Du's was hyphenated.' She picks up on how the language we use to describe our identity helps shape our realities, just as she is constructing a narrative to forge a new reality. Her husband is 'a hybrid, like the fantasy appliances he wants to build.' And perhaps in this line we have a metaphor for the narrative itself: a 'fantasy' that the narrator 'wants to build'.

At the beginning of *Jasmine*, the eponymous heroine tells the reader: 'I know what I don't want to become.' She sets about constructing a hybrid sense of identity to shape up to the modern world. It is difficult and complex, but she is – to some degree – in control. Arundhati Roy's characters, on the other hand, are moulded by the cruel status quo of the 'Love Laws'. Hers is a narrative of suffering and despair: a tragic exploration of the difficulties of asserting a sense of identity which is unconventional and problematic.[12]

Chapter 3 summary

In the course of this chapter, we hope that you have:
- understood what you will study in Part 3 and how it is assessed
- become confident in working within the particular genre that you are studying for Part 3
- looked at a number of extracts from a variety of different literary genres and responded to them analytically
- found out about Paper 2 and what you will be asked to do in the exam.

By now you should feel confident about this part of the course. As you study the texts from your chosen genre you should refer back to this chapter in order to ensure that you are asking the right questions about the books you are reading.

4 Options

Objectives

In this chapter you will:

- learn what studying Part 4 involves and how it is assessed through presentations to class
- explore strategies for preparing, planning and practising this exciting and varied part of your course
- consider new possibilities for your presentation
- engage with a number of genres from a variety of different perspectives and practise analysing how particular effects are achieved through artists' choices of language, structure and form
- consider how different factors affect our analysis of a written, drawn, performed or filmed 'text'
- consider how the subject of your presentation may develop as its aspect becomes more focused
- develop a closer understanding of the critical vocabulary required in areas of study such as the graphic novel, film, and new forms of expression such as hypertext narratives.

How is this chapter structured?

This chapter follows the shape of Part 4: Options. There are four quite distinct options in this part of the course, and the breadth of choice available is almost unlimited. We will focus on each of these four options in turn in Units 4.2 to 4.5 of this chapter, providing ideas, and asking you to develop skills that will result in your presentation being as well prepared and coherent as possible.

1   Unit 4.1 gives a general outline of what is expected of students in Part 4 of the course.

2   In Unit 4.2 we look at the **school's free choice** option and possible texts which your teacher may consider appropriate to widen your understanding of different writers and literary traditions. This part of the course is a free choice, and allows a school to balance its choices from elsewhere.

3   In Unit 4.3 we look at **Option 1: The study of prose other than fiction leading to various forms of student writing**. For this part of the course you will be provided with suggestions of texts by writers whom you may not otherwise have encountered, and this will deepen and enrich your understanding of the course and the conventions of the genre you are studying. This part of the course will enable you to explore these different forms through your own personal writing.

4   In Unit 4.4 we look at **Option 2: New textualities**. In this part of the course the IB syllabus allows students to explore 'rapidly evolving text forms', which includes genres as varied as graphic novels, hypertext narratives and fan fiction. Again, the choice is almost limitless and you will focus on skills and ideas rather than set texts.

5 **Option 3: Literature and film**, which we look at in Unit 4.5, allows you to study how a literary work is adapted for the screen. The choices made by the writer and the film maker are very different, but developing a critical vocabulary which allows you to objectively evaluate the effectiveness of both methods of expression is central to this unit.

For this part of the course you will be required to make a presentation to the class. Remember that this part of the course is assessed internally and has no written component. But it is also important to remember that assessment criteria will be applied, and throughout the chapter we will be helping you to understand how and when this is done. Like every part of this course the focus is on the text's *literary* qualities, even if the genre itself (such as film) does not immediately appear 'literary'. As in other chapters we provide you with a range of study tips, as well as Theory of Knowledge and extended essay suggestions, which will give you ideas not only for Part 4: Options, but for the rest of the English Literature course, and for the Core too.

Unit 4.1 **What is Part 4: Options?**

Part 4 of the English Literature course is called Options. The IB Diploma has depth *and* breadth, not just in your studying of six subjects (plus the Core) but also, within those six subjects, it provides you with the opportunity to research a writer in real depth (in Part 1) and also to study a vast range of different authors and genres. Part 4: Options is the part of the course that allows schools an almost entirely free choice in what they study. However, there are some limitations, and you need to be aware of these before you begin to prepare for your presentation, but the parameters are wide, and you should really enjoy exploring genuinely different texts from very different perspectives.

The texts you will present on must be taught. Your teacher may discuss the various options with you before this part of the course is studied, so there may be the possibility of exploring an enthusiasm with the rest of the class. If you have an enthusiasm for films then now is your chance to develop it here; if you enjoy reading graphic novels then this part of the course allows you to share that interest with your classmates; or if you have already developed a blog, or have a growing interest in social networking websites, then – provided there is a literary aspect to your presentation – you will be able to present on these areas and be formally assessed.

The IB learner profile states that students should strive to be, among other things, inquirers, thinkers, communicators, knowledgeable and risk-takers. You should of course aspire to each of these qualities not just in English, but in every part of your studies, as well as beyond; but it is certainly the case that in Part 4 these qualities are especially important. Take those risks, but prepare for them in advance by thinking, by becoming increasingly knowledgeable in your area, and by inquiring … if you do this then in your presentation you will communicate your understanding as effectively as you possibly can.

What is literature?

In his important book *Literary Theory: An Introduction* (published 1983) the critic Terry Eagleton proposed the idea that we all recognise the difference between the literary and the non-literary. The example he suggested was the person who, standing at a bus stop, whispers to a stranger the famous line from a John Keats poem: 'Thou still unravished bride of quietness'. Although if someone were to confront you with this line you'd probably think they were weird, you'd also probably acknowledge that, at some level, these words are 'literary'. Asking: 'When does the next bus arrive?' is not literary. But does this help us to say what literature is? It's certainly helpful. Eagleton's introduction 'What is literature?' is as good an essay on the subject as any, and we would highly recommend it.

Many modern 'literary' plays, poems and novels have been written in very un-'literary' language. Does this stop them from being literature? Much of Shakespeare is actually very rude. Does this affect the way we read or watch the plays? For many students, literature is whatever their teachers tell them is literature. The problem with this is that often they then distinguish between the literary texts they study in class and the non-literary texts they read for pleasure. Millions of people have read the Harry Potter stories in many different languages. But are these books literary? Possibly.

The IB course you are following encourages you to study distinctly literary texts. But what does this mean? Many well-qualified academics have spent much time trying to explain this distinction. And perhaps it is impossible, ultimately, to distinguish between literary and non-literary writing.

However, in this coursebook we hope that the passages that we've selected and the texts that we're encouraging you to read are literary in the sense that they make you think differently about the world.

We would argue that something is literary because it is crafted.

One of the most frequent complaints with which students confront their English teachers is: 'The writer can't possibly have thought about that; she can't possibly have meant that when she was writing.' We would argue differently. Perhaps the most important defining characteristic of 'literary' texts is that – yes – most words really have been decided upon, thought about and judiciously included. Is this what makes a text literary?

A note on 'literary' texts

The course you are studying is essentially *literary*. This means that the majority of texts you are studying have to be literary. The IB syllabus includes the prescribed literature in translation list and prescribed list of authors in order to guide students and teachers in their choices; in this respect a canon has been defined by the IB organisation and has to be adhered to: in other words the texts on these lists are defined as literary enough for study. Anything which is described as 'literature' has qualitative connotations: we assume that the work in question has integral worth, and that it is somehow 'better' than other texts. Such judgements are fraught with difficulties: one person's idea of what constitutes 'literature' may not agree with anyone else's: you may like a particular poem but a classmate might think it is a simple piece of doggerel. You can see how easy it is to get drawn into a relativistic argument which can lead nowhere: if Shakespeare is great literature what about Dan Brown? Are the lyrics of Michael Jackson as 'literary' as Goethe's verse? If not, why not? We can agree, though, that literature is made up of major genres: the novel, poetry, drama, short stories, and within these broad genres are other classifications (there are epic poems, and odes, haiku, and so on).

Key terms

Doggerel Badly written verse, or verse expressed in a clumsy, plodding metre; often done for effect

Epic poem A long poem, traditionally one that narrates the adventures of legendary figures from the ancient myths.

Ode From the Greek word for 'song'; usually regularly and formally structured, expressing sentiments of profound importance.

Haiku A Japanese form of poetry which consists of 17 syllables. Traditionally line 1 has five syllables, line 2 has seven syllables, and the 3rd and final line has five syllables.

TOK

To what extent is a picture a 'language'? Does a film or a graphic novel communicate to us in the same way as a novel or poem? How do we interpret language differently if it is conveyed visually and aurally?`

Extended essay

EE

Film is now a Group 6 subject and so you can write an extended essay on this subject, even if you are not studying it as a part of your Diploma. If you are interested in doing this, be sure to read the course guidelines, published by the IB organisation, so that you know the requirements.

Key term

Hypertext narrative A new genre which exists in different media (CD, Internet), which has no fixed narrative centre, and can be collaborative in composition.

It is important to remember that any other media you analyse must be approached from a literary perspective. For example, if you are going to do your presentation on 'Literature and film', the starting point for your research should be a literary text. You could look at how a particular novel or play has been adapted for the screen, but what you couldn't do is to do an entire presentation on a particular film: your focus should be on the process of adaptation, so that you deepen your understanding of both the text and the film. If you decide to do a presentation on a graphic novel you have to do one which is an original text so that you focus on its *literary* strengths (the author's use of language, plot development, characterisation and so on) *as well as* its visual structure and impact.

Activity 4.1

Look at the following openings of four different texts and answer the following questions:

- Which would you consider the most 'literary' and why?
- Can you rank them in order of quality? What guides you in this process?
- If you were to rank them by preference, would this list be any different from the list you compiled on their quality? If so, why might this be?

1 **A quest is not to be undertaken lightly – or at all! – pondered Hlothgar, Thrag of the Western Boglands, son of Glothar, nephew of Garthol, known far and wide as Skull Dunker, as he wielded his chesty stallion Hralgoth through the ever-darkening Thlargwood, beyond which, if he survived its horrors and if Hroglath the royal spittle reader spoke true, his destiny awaited – all this though his years numbered but fourteen.** (Stuart Greenman)

2 **She walked into my office on legs as long as one of those long-legged birds that you see in Florida – the pink ones, not the white ones – except that she was standing on both of them, not just one of them, like those birds, the pink ones, and she wasn't wearing pink, but I knew right away that she was trouble, which those birds usually aren't.** (Eric Rice)

3 **I am an invisible man. No, I am not a spook like those who haunted Edgar Allan Poe; nor am I one of your Hollywood-movie ectoplasms. I am a man of substance, of flesh and bone, fibre and liquids – and I might even be said to possess a mind. I am invisible, understand, simply because people refuse to see me.** (Ralph Ellison)

4 **1801. – I have just returned from a visit to my landlord – the solitary neighbour that I shall be troubled with. This is certainly a beautiful country! In all England, I do not believe that I could have fixed on a situation so completely removed from the stir of society.** (Emily Brontë)

By being able to read a text closely so that you can interpret and draw out different shades of meaning is a skill which can be transferred to other media. Film, television, graphic texts and **hypertext narratives** will all be easier to deconstruct because you will have developed a critical approach, a language and a method of constructing a coherent analysis, and each are appropriate to making meaning of often very diverse genres. In doing so you will be able to assess – and evaluate – the quality of what you are studying and, perhaps as importantly, be able to explain your judgements. In other words, approaching widely different media from a literary perspective should not be viewed as limiting; instead, it should be seen as ideal preparation for a range of different approaches.

How should you prepare for Part 4

To get the most out of Part 4 you will have to seek advice from your teacher, talk to your classmates, and trust your own judgement. Some of the best presentations are those in which the student has followed his or her own enthusiasms: a love of the subject can make a critical difference, not only in the delivery of the presentation itself, but also in the preparation time given over to it. However, enthusiasm alone can only take you so far: you have to make sure the presentation conforms to the IB's requirements, and you also have to do enough research to merit a good mark in this part of the course. It is expected that much of the preparation time for your presentation will be completed outside class.

It is also important to remember that:

• although Part 4 is assessed by your teacher and in class, it should be approached with the rigour you would bring to any other part of the course
• it is your responsibility to select appropriate material for the presentation
• you should organise the material into a coherent structure
• you should choose and rehearse your presentation so that the linguistic register is appropriate for the presentation.

How will you be assessed on Part 4?

This part of the course is the only one in which SL and HL students study the same number of texts. In addition to the four different options available, you are also allowed to choose texts in translation.

SL and HL students	**Individual oral presentation** lasting between 10 and 15 minutes. It is assessed by your teacher. All texts must be taught in lessons.	Worth 15% of your final mark in English Literature.

There are no limitations placed on the format you are allowed to use, but remember this is a presentation to your classmates and your teacher and so you should avoid overusing PowerPoint, Keynote or equivalent programs. Remember, too, that you should not read your presentation from a pre-prepared script: notes or prompts are fine, but a teacher will be unable to assess an essay that is spoken aloud.

SL and HL students' presentations will be assessed using three criteria. Here they are again, but with some explanation about what they might mean to you:

Criterion A	*Knowledge and understanding of the work(s)* Although you have to study all three texts you can do your presentation on an aspect of one. You should show your teacher that you not only know the text very well, but can also *interpret* its meaning and construct a convincing analysis.	10 marks

Figure 4.1 A confident and thorough presentation will help you merit a good mark.

Discussion

How can you use your experiences and interests outside your studies to help you in your presentation? What do you spend most of your time doing outside class? Can this be turned into a presentation within the available options? For instance: what sort of films do you like watching? What is your favourite sort of book? Travel? Biography? Do you read blogs? Talk to members of your family, to friends and classmates about their interests: in doing so you will begin to reflect on areas which might be of interest, or may connect with something you are already thinking about. Now think about how you might present on these – from a literary perspective – to your class: why would others find your subject area interesting?

Key term

Nomenclature A system of names or terms, often in technical vocabulary.

tip

When you are selecting a work (or works) to do your presentation on, choose something that allows for many different interpretations. That 'hard' or 'difficult' text you have studied might be the one which has the richness of themes and language which will stand up to real scrutiny.

Criterion B	*Presentation* Your presentation should be well structured: you only have 10–15 minutes so ensure that you do not waste time on a lengthy introduction, and that your main points are clear and linked. Engage your audience: convince them that the subject you are talking about is a valid area for exploration and discussion.	10 marks
Criterion C	*Language* Your language – like each part of the course – has to be appropriate to the task. Remember that the focus is literary, so include in your analysis appropriate literary terms; if your presentation is on a genre – such as film – which has its own quite distinctive nomenclature then use this when appropriate too.	10 marks
Total		30 marks

Although the descriptors are the same for SL and HL students they differ by degree in Criteria A and B: the same skills are assessed but HL students will have to show more depth and understanding of how their topic will match their style of presentation.

You also need to keep in mind that all four options share the same learning and teaching aims. This means that all students should:
- develop a *knowledge* and *understanding* of the works studied
- present an *individual*, independent response to the works studied
- develop *powers of expression* through oral presentation
- learn how to *interest* and hold the attention of the audience.

There is a clear emphasis here not only on what you know but on *how* you present it to others; not only that, but your presentation has to be individual and distinctive. Bear this in mind as you research your work and keep your teacher – who will have an overview of your class's work – informed throughout the process.

The choice available for this part of the course is extremely wide. Getting the tone and approach right is essential for a good presentation.

What areas could you explore in your presentation?
Ideally, you should choose a topic that reflects your own personal interest. You could choose to present on any aspect of a work, or works, including the following:
- The cultural setting of the work: this would include its historical, biographical, cultural, literary and sociological background, its origins and development as a work of literature.
- A thematic focus: for example, you may want to look at the representation of journeying in two of the texts you have studied, or how two writers have explored faith or class. There as many possibilities here as themes in the texts themselves.
- Characterisation: comparing and contrasting character development can be a very rewarding area for exploration (the representation of children in two texts, or father figures, and so on).
- Techniques and style: what stands out as being most interesting, or characteristic, about the writing style of the authors you are studying? Can you compare them? Do they share similarities? If you're studying works from the same genre then this might be particularly appropriate.

- Setting: compare and contrast the setting of the texts you are studying. How have the writers differed in their use of setting? Does the setting affect the plot? Does it shape the main themes? To what extent does it influence our reading of these texts?

What could you do for your presentation?

The following lists give examples of the wide range of activities which are acceptable for the presentation. Please do bear in mind that these lists are neither exhaustive nor prescriptive: they are only suggestions and may be added to by your teacher, or by students with the approval of their teachers. You should select the activity most appropriate to the topic you have chosen to work on.

Structured discussions

The class discussion

You could host a class discussion, but remember that this should be distinct from the interactive oral you have to do in Part 1 of the course. To be properly assessed in Part 4 you should have special responsibilities: advance preparation will be needed and key subject areas researched. The whole class may participate but only you – the chairperson or host – will be assessed. Within this structure you could present two opposing interpretations and take questions from the class, or you could advocate a position that has not been considered by the class before.

Individual discussions

If you would prefer a more individually focused presentation then you could do one of the following activities.

- Be interviewed by your teacher on an agreed topic or work(s).
- Provide an introduction to a writer or work(s).
- Give an analysis of a particular aspect of an author's work.
- Scrutinise a particular interpretation of a work. This doesn't have to be a straightforward depiction; instead it could be something much more rigorous. For example, many people have interpreted Mary Shelley's *Frankenstein* as an early feminist text: you could give a presentation in which you reject this position whilst offering an alternative – and more valid – analysis.
- Explore the setting of a particular writer's work against another body of material, such as details on social background or political views, and argue that one area is more important to that writer's development than the others.
- Provide a commentary on the use of a particular image, idea or symbol, or motif in one text or in a writer's work.
- Compare and contrast two key passages from either one work, or two (or three): what are their relative strengths and weaknesses? Are they principally concerned with the same themes?
- Present on how your understanding and appreciation has developed over the course of reading a text. If you decide that this might appeal to you then start taking reflective notes from the very beginning of your studies.

Role play

Some students relish the opportunity to be more creative in their study of a particular text and their presentations to the class can be very illuminating. Part 4 allows you to respond to a text by using, amongst other approaches, role play. Remember, though, that simply acting a passage from a play you are studying is not enough to satisfy the assessment criteria (and indeed you should always keep in

Monologue A speech in which a character speaks at length alone.

mind how you are being assessed in this unit). Some approaches which you could find interesting are:

- a monologue by a character given at an important point in the work
- reminiscences by a character from a point in later life, perhaps reflecting on the action in the text
- an author's reaction to a particular interpretation of elements of his or her work in a given context; for example, a critical defence of the work against a charge of subversion, or immorality, before a censorship board.

If you do choose to do role play you should write a rationale of what you have done, and why you approached it in this way. This rationale should form a part of your presentation: in this way the teacher can assess the choices made by you before you performed your role play.

Unit 4.2 The 'school's free choice' option

If your school has opted to supplement your course with texts from other regions or periods it will have done so to widen your understanding of text choices in other parts of the course. Remember to approach each text with an open mind, to take notes from the beginning of your studies, and to be prepared to work independently on your presentation topic. Your teacher could provide you with the titles of the texts you will be studying at the beginning of term. Read them carefully and begin to think about how you might approach them.

Here are some consideration points for this option:

- If there are 'classic' texts in this part of your course (for example *Pride and Prejudice, Great Expectations, The Scarlet Letter*) you will find that there is a wealth of secondary material published on them, and this could help you in your preparation. These texts have retained their durability for many reasons, but one of them is that they are rich in possibilities for analysis and comment.
- If there are texts that relate specifically to your background or the region that the school is in you will find good supportive material which would allow for a contextual reading and presentation. Your teacher will have done this deliberately of course, but you will already be at an advantage because of your innate understanding of the setting, as well as other factors. Don't overlook your inherited expertise.
- If there are texts which are very much outside your area of understanding and experience you could make this marked difference a starting point for your presentation rather than a possible obstacle: how is it (or they) different from your own experience of life ? What particular aspect of the text challenged you the most? What similarities in experience did you encounter as you read? Did your response develop over time? If so, how? Are there any universal truths – which transcend cultural, social, historical and political boundaries – that you have enjoyed exploring?
- Do the texts you are studying have links with other parts of your Diploma? For example, a study of *Wild Swans* by Jung Chang will be enriched if you are also studying Mao for your History course. Subjects in Groups 2, 3 and 6 are other areas where connections could be made. Make the most of such possibilities: the IB Diploma actively encourages this holistic approach to learning.

If you have decided to do a creative presentation you may wish to consider:

- a dramatic performance of a scene of a play with a particular focus or interpretation in mind, perhaps performing a scene in more than one way to show different possible interpretations

- a dialogue in the style of a particular writer (an extra scene from a novel or play)
- a performance of a scene from a pre-20th century play in modern language and setting
- a performed piece of dialogue or monologue, or an interview between a character and journalist, or between the character and the writer, or between you and the writer
- a character's thoughts or feelings expressed in poetic form
- art work, a poem, song, short story, musical composition linked to/inspired by a text which has been studied
- a visual explanation or accompaniment to some aspect of a text
- a visual linking of the texts studied by theme, style, etc.

Remember: it is essential that you are constantly aware that you are being assessed on the texts you have studied, so any creative piece must allow for the assessment criteria to be fully applied. Look carefully at the time allocated, and talk to your teacher throughout the planning process.

Here are ten examples of memorable student presentations:
- A student compared Ted Hughes's *Wuthering Heights* with Sylvia Plath's poem of the same name.
- A student wrote a monologue based on Kafka's *The Trial*. He then answered questions about his character and actions.
- A student discussed Mary Shelley's *Frankenstein* from different critical positions.
- A student compared the significance of everyday objects in Raymond Carver's short stories.
- A student compared the changing role of women in Sebastian Faulks's *Birdsong*, arguing that both central female characters are equally oppressed.
- A student compared dictatorships in Ken Kesey's *One Flew Over the Cuckoo's Nest* and George Orwell's *Nineteen Eighty-Four*.
- A student compared Cormac McCarthy's representation of travelling in *The Road* with Jack Kerouac's description in *On the Road*.
- A student gave a presentation on whether Bruce Chatwin was guilty of exploiting Aboriginal culture in *The Songlines*.
- A student discussed William Blake's view of love in *The Songs of Innocence and Experience*.
- A student gave a talk on the representation of racism in J.M. Coetzee's *Disgrace*.

The range of texts you could study in this option is almost limitless. However, here are some very common text choices made by teachers and students with some guiding themes added; taken together they may further clarify your thoughts should you choose to present on them. They are frequently chosen by schools because they work so well in this part of the course. Those that have been grouped together work, we think, especially well as they are connected, very often, not just by theme, but by other techniques as well (for instance, *Mister Pip* by Lloyd Jones, although set on a tiny island in the Pacific, is heavily influenced by Charles Dickens's *Great Expectations*). This is only a suggested list, and we are sure that you and your teacher will be able to compile alternatives; indeed your list may more effectively balance the rest of your course. Poetry has been omitted because the number of different themes in a collection of verse can be too many to reduce to a manageable few.

Main themes	Genre	Title	Author	Country/region of origin
Alienation, identity, justice	Novel	*Heart of Darkness*	Joseph Conrad	England
		The Outsider	Albert Camus	France
		Perfume	Patrick Suskind	Germany
Dystopia	Novel	*The Handmaid's Tale*	Margaret Atwood	Canada
		Nineteen Eighty-Four	George Orwell	England
Education	Novel	*Mister Pip*	Lloyd Jones	Pacific
		Great Expectations	Charles Dickens	England
Fate, love	Novel	*Ethan Frome*	Edith Wharton	USA
	Drama	*Oedipus Rex*	Sophocles	Greece
Faith, betrayal	Novel	*Silence*	Shusaku Endo	Japan
Heroism	Novel	*The Guide*	R.K. Narayan	India
Identity, love, madness	Novel	*Wide Sargasso Sea*	Jean Rhys	Caribbean
		Jane Eyre	Charlotte Brontë	England
Identity, imperialism	Drama	*Translations*	Brian Friel	Ireland
Imperialism	Non-fiction	*The Songlines*	Bruce Chatwin	Australia
Social responsibility	Novel	*Chronicle of a Death Foretold*	Gabriel García Márquez	Colombia

Unit 4.3 The 'prose other than fiction' option

In this unit you will look at prose other than fiction. Among other sub-genres, you will study speeches, autobiographical writing, creative non-fiction, and travel writing. We will suggest different ways of approaching genres which you may not have studied previously and we hope this will provide you with some new ideas for your own presentations. As its title makes clear, there is a very strong written element to this option, and this unit will ask you to write in a number of different styles: in addition to writing analytically we will ask you to **pastiche** the genres you are studying so that you are fully aware not just of the language appropriate to that genre, but also of the conventions that shape it. As children we learn by imitating, and many students learn a great deal about the writers they are studying by imitating their technique.

Speeches

Every great speech is initially set within a clearly defined historical context; the best **oratory** plays within a great arena and resonates not only with its immediate audience, but with countless generations that follow. In other words, they exist beyond that initial context. The journalist Gary Younge has written of Martin Luther King's 'I have a dream' speech:

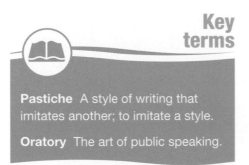

Key terms

Pastiche A style of writing that imitates another; to imitate a style.

Oratory The art of public speaking.

'Like all great oratory its brilliance was in its simplicity. Like all great speeches it understood its audience. And like all great performances it owed as much to delivery as content. But it stands out because it was both timely in its message and timeless in its appeal.'

Activity 4.2
Preliminary preparation
How many great speeches do you know? Make a list. What characterises them as 'great'? Do they share the qualities Gary Younge singles out as typical of great pieces of oratory? You may find this website a useful resource for accessing other famous speeches of the 20th century: http://www.guardian.co.uk/theguardian/series/greatspeeches

We are lucky to be able to watch and listen to many of the most important speeches made; and although many only exist on paper we can still evaluate not just their importance, but also their linguistic power: we can analyse the rhythms of the speech, their use of imagery, as well as other rhetorical devices used to achieve their objectives.

For this unit we have chosen two very different speeches made by two highly influential Americans: the first is John F. Kennedy's inauguration speech; the second is William Faulkner's acceptance speech for the Nobel Prize in Literature. Both speeches reach beyond their immediate arena – or contexts – and both articulate something more important than even the historic events they are marking.

Text 4.1 'Ask not what your country can do for you', President John F. Kennedy, 20 January 1961

It was a bitterly cold day in January when the young, charismatic John F. Kennedy was sworn in as President of the United States of America. At 43 he was the youngest President ever elected. As a speech it has been described as 'world changing' because it changed the West's foreign policy with its Cold War enemy, the Communist Soviet Union. It was a speech of great hope, heralding a new era of openness, and, tragically, 1000 days later, his personal vision ended when the President was assassinated in Texas. Ted Sorensen, who advised Kennedy, and was his primary speechwriter (the speech was a joint effort) has written that 'it was a statement of core values'.

Figure 4.2 John F. Kennedy speaking at his inauguration as President of the United States of America.

Vice-president Johnson, Mr Speaker, Mr Chief Justice, President Eisenhower, Vice-president Nixon, President Truman, reverend clergy, fellow citizens.
We observe today not a victory of party, but a celebration of freedom – symbolising an end, as well as a beginning – signifying renewal, as well as

change. For I have sworn before you and almighty God the same solemn oath our forebears prescribed nearly a century and three-quarters ago.

The world is very different now. For man holds in his mortal hands the power to abolish all forms of human poverty and all forms of human life. And yet the same revolutionary beliefs for which our forebears fought are still at issue around the globe – the belief that the rights of man come not from the generosity of the state, but from the hand of God.

We dare not forget today that we are the heirs of that first revolution. Let the word go forth from this time and place, to friend and foe alike, that the torch has been passed to a new generation of Americans – born in this century, tempered by war, disciplined by a hard and bitter peace, proud of our ancient heritage and unwilling to witness or permit the slow undoing of those human rights to which this nation has always been committed, and to which we are committed today at home and around the world. Let every nation know, whether it wishes us well or ill, that we shall pay any price, bear any burden, meet any hardship, support any friend, oppose any foe, to assure the survival and the success of liberty.

This much we pledge – and more.

To those old allies whose cultural and spiritual origins we share, we pledge the loyalty of faithful friends. United, there is little we cannot do in a host of cooperative ventures. Divided, there is little we can do – for we dare not meet a powerful challenge at odds and split asunder.

To those new states whom we welcome to the ranks of the free, we pledge our word that one form of colonial control shall not have passed away merely to be replaced by a far more iron tyranny. We shall not always expect to find them supporting our view. But we shall always hope to find them strongly supporting their own freedom – and to remember that, in the past, those who foolishly sought power by riding the back of the tiger ended up inside.

To those people in the huts and villages of half the globe struggling to break the bonds of mass misery, we pledge our best efforts to help them help themselves, for whatever period is required – not because the communists may be doing it, not because we seek their votes, but because it is right. If a free society cannot help the many who are poor, it cannot save the few who are rich.

To our sister republics south of our border, we offer a special pledge: to convert our good words into good deeds, in a new alliance for progress, to assist free men and free governments in casting off the chains of poverty. But this peaceful revolution of hope cannot become the prey of hostile powers. Let all our neighbours know that we shall join with them to oppose aggression or subversion anywhere in the Americas. And let every other power know that this hemisphere intends to remain the master of its own house.

To that world assembly of sovereign states, the United Nations, our last best hope in an age where the instruments of war have far outpaced the instruments of peace, we renew our pledge of support – to prevent it from becoming merely a forum for invective, to strengthen its shield of the new and the weak, and to enlarge the area in which its writ may run.

Finally, to those nations who would make themselves our adversary, we offer not a pledge but a request: that both sides begin anew the quest for peace, before the dark powers of destruction unleashed by science engulf all humanity in planned or accidental self-destruction. We dare not tempt them with weakness. For only when our arms are sufficient beyond doubt can we be certain beyond doubt that they will never be employed.

But neither can two great and powerful groups of nations take comfort from our present course – both sides overburdened by the cost of modern weapons, both rightly alarmed by the steady spread of the deadly atom, yet both racing to alter that uncertain balance of terror that stays the hand of mankind's final war.

So let us begin anew – remembering on both sides that civility is not a sign of weakness, and sincerity is always subject to proof. Let us never negotiate out of fear, but let us never fear to negotiate.

Let both sides explore what problems unite us instead of belabouring those problems which divide us. Let both sides, for the first time, formulate serious and precise proposals for the inspection and control of arms, and bring the absolute power to destroy other nations under the absolute control of all nations. Let both sides seek to invoke the wonders of science instead of its terrors.

Together let us explore the stars, conquer the deserts, eradicate disease, tap the ocean depths, and encourage the arts and commerce. Let both sides unite to heed, in all corners of the earth, the command of Isaiah – to 'undo the heavy burdens, and to let the oppressed go free'. And, if a beachhead of cooperation may push back the jungle of suspicion, let both sides join in creating a new endeavour – not a new balance of power, but a new world of law – where the strong are just, and the weak secure, and the peace preserved.

All this will not be finished in the first 100 days. Nor will it be finished in the first 1000 days, nor in the life of this administration, nor even perhaps in our lifetime on this planet. But let us begin.

In your hands, my fellow citizens, more than in mine, will rest the final success or failure of our course. Since this country was founded, each generation of Americans has been summoned to give testimony to its national loyalty. The graves of young Americans who answered the call to service surround the globe. Now the trumpet summons us again – not as a call to bear arms, though arms we need; not as a call to battle, though embattled we are, but a call to bear the burden of a long twilight struggle, year in and year out, 'rejoicing in hope, patient in tribulation', a struggle against the common enemies of man: tyranny, poverty, disease, and war itself.

Can we forge against these enemies a grand and global alliance, north and south, east and west, that can assure a more fruitful life for all mankind? Will you join in that historic effort?

In the long history of the world, only a few generations have been granted the role of defending freedom in its hour of maximum danger. I do not shrink from this responsibility – I welcome it.

I do not believe that any of us would exchange places with any other people or any other generation. The energy, the faith, the devotion which we bring to this endeavour will light our country and all who serve it. And the glow from that fire can truly light the world.

And so, my fellow Americans, ask not what your country can do for you; ask what you can do for your country. My fellow citizens of the world, ask not what America will do for you, but what, together, we can do for the freedom of man.

Finally, whether you are citizens of America or citizens of the world, ask of us here the same high standards of strength and sacrifice which we ask of you. With a good conscience our only sure reward, with history the final judge of our deeds, let us go forth to lead the land we love, asking His blessing and His help, but knowing that here on earth, God's work must truly be our own.

Activity 4.3

Preliminary research

Your teacher will be able to provide you with a copy of President John F. Kennedy's speech to mark up.

Read this speech, commonly referred to as 'Ask not what your country can do for you'.

1 Would you describe Kennedy's speech as:

persuasive	emotive	pessimistic
divisive	dignified	pragmatic
unifying	complicated	idealistic
visionary	straightforward	moral?
inward-looking	optimistic	

   What other adjectives could you apply? Now be specific: mark up your copy of the speech so that you begin to link the qualities you feel the speech has with Kennedy's words. For example, if you think it is visionary, find the words and phrases that support your point.

2 Now look at the speech as a *literary* text: does he use any figurative language (metaphors, similes, imagery)? If so, what are their effects? Does he use any other literary techniques to make his speech vivid and memorable?

3 Continue to mark up this speech using the skills you have developed with exercises in other chapters. Think about how you might be able to draw out different meanings from this speech; could its meaning be interpreted in different ways? Is there any deliberate ambiguity here?

4 What is the speech's purpose? Is it purely constitutional: to inaugurate the new President? Is it to introduce the President's policies to the American people? Or is it wider than that?

5 Who is Kennedy's audience? The crowd? The American people? People in other countries?

6 Now read the following notes on Kennedy's speech made by a teacher for his class. After reading it, write a 10-minute presentation on the speech in which you bring in the initial research you did on it with your response to these notes. You could take any position you want. For example:

   - You could argue that this speech's lasting power relies as much on its style as on its content.
   - You could argue that Kennedy's speech, although a powerful piece of rhetoric, has very little content.

Notes

- Rhetorical devices – lists of three, use of metaphors, imperative verbs and parenthesis: what is the effect of these?
- Speech begins with a direct address, showing respect, singling people out, but he ends with 'my fellow Americans': what is the effect of making everyone end up sounding equal?
- Note use of antithetical parallelism: not … but …: 'we observe today not a victory of party, but a celebration of freedom – symbolising an end, as well as a beginning – signifying renewal, as well as change'. Can you find any more?
- What is the effect of using inclusive 'we' so often? 'We dare not forget today', 'We dare not tempt them with weakness'. Who is the 'we' – the

Key term

Antithetical parallelism Images and ideas used in opposition to display respective differences.

American people? Those living in the 'free world'? Can you find any more examples?

- Think of JFK echoing the Bible's language, e.g. 'let there be light', 'let every nation know', 'let the word go forth' (what does the 'word' mean in this context – allusion to the book of Genesis?).
- The 'rights of man' is a reference to the Declaration of Independence.
- Allusion to Jean-Jacques Rousseau ('Man is born free but everywhere he is in chains')? But changes it so that he promises to 'assist free men and free governments in casting off the chains of poverty'. What is the point of this reference and what is the effect of this statement?
- Alliteration: 'dark powers of destruction' – effect?
- Poetic rhythm of some his statements: 'For man holds in his mortal hands the power' and 'have far outpaced the instruments of peace'. Both are iambic pentameter. Effect?
- Most of the words are simple (count how many are more than three syllables).

William Faulkner (1897–1962) was born in New Albany, Mississippi. When he was a child he moved with his family to a small town in Mississippi; it was here that he found the inspiration for many of his greatest works, including *As I Lay Dying*, *Sanctuary* and *Light in August*.

Now read Faulkner's speech. Your teacher may be able to give you a clean copy for you to mark up as you read.

Key term

Allusion A reference to another work of art.

Extended essay

EE

You can find out more about the Nobel Prize at http://nobelprize.org/ It's an excellent resource bank in itself, and could be the starting point for your research into some of the most influential individuals of our (and previous) times.

Text 4.2 Nobel Prize in Literature acceptance speech, William Faulkner, 10 December 1950

Figure 4.3 William Faulkner was awarded the 1949 Nobel Prize in Literature.

1 Antithetical parallelism: use of 'but' here in opposition to the 'I' at the beginning of the sentence: moving from the personal to the universal in one sentence.
2 Again, moving from his work to 'life's work', as if his work has a greater importance beyond the individual author. Theme developing here: the universal importance of literature.
3 Long, complex opening sentence: distilled to 'art creates something finer than that which is created out of mere sweat and profit'.

<table>
<tr><td valign="top">4</td><td>Altruistic: Faulkner is not the winner, he is the guardian for the prize. Again, developing theme of the universality of human experience over the personal and individual.</td></tr>
<tr><td valign="top">5</td><td>We have the universal and the individual as a theme; now we have the old and the young in this sentence.</td></tr>
<tr><td valign="top">6</td><td>Language seems old-fashioned: 'anguish and travail' is biblical in its imagery, evoking scenes of great suffering, but Faulkner here describes it as voluntary, chosen by the individual for the common good. Again, the main theme of the universality of experience is explored here.</td></tr>
<tr><td valign="top">7</td><td>Faulkner cleverly bridges any perceived divide between young and old by making them the equal of him (and his generation): somebody (young) listening to him will one day be as great as him, and receive an equal reward.</td></tr>
<tr><td valign="top">8</td><td>Tragedy has many connotations: it is Shakespearean in its scope (man is master of his own fate).</td></tr>
<tr><td valign="top">9</td><td>Key theme: making the individual experience universal.</td></tr>
<tr><td valign="top">10</td><td>A strange statement: it is as if Faulkner is dismissing all spiritual concerns of man and focusing purely on the physical fear of nuclear war. Is this a simplification of the situation?</td></tr>
<tr><td valign="top">11</td><td>His argument becomes clearer: as a result of fearing nuclear war we neglect the other great questions which continue to face us all.</td></tr>
</table>

In recognition of 'his powerful and artistically unique contribution to the modern American novel', Faulkner was awarded the 1949 Nobel Prize in Literature. His acceptance speech (below), given at the Nobel Banquet at the City Hall in Stockholm on 10 December 1950, gave voice to the growing fear of a nuclear war between the West and the Soviet Union. These fears would reach their peak in October 1962 when President John F. Kennedy challenged the Soviet leader, Nikita Khrushchev, to withdraw his country's missiles from Cuba.

Ladies and gentleman, I feel that this award was not made to me as a man, but[1] to my work – a life's work[2] in the agony and sweat of the human spirit, not for glory and least of all for profit, but to create out of the materials of the human spirit something which did not exist before.[3] So this award is only mine in trust.[4] It will not be difficult to find a dedication for the money part of it commensurate with the purpose and significance of its origin. But I would like to do the same with the acclaim too, by using this moment as a pinnacle from which I might be listened to by the young men and women[5] already dedicated to the same anguish and travail,[6] among whom is already that one who will some day stand here where I am standing.[7]

Our tragedy[8] today is a general and universal[9] physical fear so long sustained by now that we can even bear it. There are no longer problems of the spirit.[10] There is only the question: When will I be blown up? Because of this, the young man or woman writing today has forgotten the problems of the human heart in conflict with itself which alone can make good writing because only that is worth writing about, worth the agony and the sweat.[11]

He must learn them again. He must teach himself that the basest of all things is to be afraid; and, teaching himself that, forget it forever, leaving no room in his workshop for anything but the old verities and truths of the heart, the old universal truths lacking which any story is ephemeral and doomed – love and honor and pity and pride and compassion and sacrifice. Until he does so, he labors under a curse. He writes not of love but of lust, of defeats in which nobody loses anything of value, of victories without hope and, worst of all, without pity or compassion. His griefs grieve on no universal bones, leaving no scars. He writes not of the heart but of the glands.

Until he relearns these things, he will write as though he stood among and watched the end of man. I decline to accept the end of man. It is easy enough to say that man is immortal simply because he will endure: that when the last dingdong of doom has clanged and faded from the last worthless rock hanging tideless in the last red and dying evening, that even then there will still be one more sound: that of his puny inexhaustible voice, still talking.

I refuse to accept this. I believe that man will not merely endure: he will prevail. He is immortal, not because he alone among creatures has an inexhaustible voice, but because he has a soul, a spirit capable of compassion and sacrifice and endurance. The poet's, the writer's, duty is to write about these things. It is his privilege to help man endure by lifting his heart, by reminding him of the courage and honor and hope and pride and compassion and pity and sacrifice which have been the glory of his past. The poet's voice need not merely be the record of man, it can be one of the props, the pillars to help him endure and prevail.

Activity 4.4

Preliminary research

Read the speech by William Faulkner. Analyse this speech as a *literary* text.

1 Look at the mark-ups already provided here and, on your clean copy, begin to add to them as you analyse Faulkner's final third paragraph.

2 How are the themes that have already been explored through the initial mark-up points developed by Faulkner? Does he add to them?

3 What imagery does he use to convey his points?

4 Analyse the language: how would you describe the mood? Reflective? Emotive?

5 Start to link your ideas from these mark-ups so that you begin to construct a clear analysis of the author's aims: you may find it useful to apply the simple mnemonic you learned in Chapter 1, TECT:

- Time & place: how does context affect our understanding of the speech?
- Easy & difficult: what is easy to understand and what is difficult? Why?
- Connections: what links are there between your views and the author's?
- Technique: what is interesting about the author's technique?

Preparing for a mini-presentation

Write a short presentation on this speech. Remember that in the real presentation you will be focusing on a key text (or texts). This short presentation is simply an exercise in getting you to analyse a non-fiction text, and to construct a meaningful presentation from it. Your topic could be specifically on Faulkner's message, or it could be on something more general:

- Writers are fundamental to humankind's self-preservation.
- The Nobel Prize has always been completely irrelevant to human progress.
- Writers are vain self-promoters who can say nothing to society.
- Without writers our society would slowly become increasingly stupid and we would end up not knowing what was important.

Creative non-fiction

Creative non-fiction sounds like an oxymoron: surely non-fiction is concerned with reporting facts, or giving personal opinions? As soon as it becomes 'creative' it must inevitably become fictional. Creative non-fiction is a sub-genre of both fiction and non-fiction, melding qualities of both. One creative non-fiction writer, Brian Doyle, defines it as 'true stories about people and the world … small true odd interesting unusual voice-laden funny poignant detailed musical sweet sad stories'. Lee Gutkind, in his introduction to *Keep it Real: Everything You Need to Know About Researching and Writing Creative Nonfiction* (2008), has written that the term creative non-fiction:

> …precisely describes what the form is all about. The word 'creative' refers simply to the use of literary craft in presenting nonfiction – that is, factually accurate prose about real people and events – in a compelling, vivid manner. To put it another way, creative nonfiction writers do not make things up; they make ideas and information that already exist more interesting and, often, more accessible. It is important to remember that there are lines – real demarcation

Key terms

By using the Glossary at the back of the coursebook you will be able to pin down your meaning by applying key literary terms.

Creative non-fiction A genre of writing which fictionalises aspects of real events.

Oxymoron A short phrase which appears to be contradictory but makes sense in context (such as 'bittersweet').

tip

Record and time your presentation and mark it according to the criteria provided at the beginning of this chapter. What mark would you give yourself? Where did you gain marks and where did you lose them? Now try doing it again and focus on the areas where you felt you lost most marks.

Discussion

Imagine that you had Faulkner's speech for your Paper 1: Commentary examination: SL and HL students might find it useful to discuss the sorts of guiding questions that might follow this speech.

points between fiction, which is or can be mostly imagination; traditional nonfiction (journalism and scholarship), which is mostly information; and creative nonfiction, which presents or treats information using the tools of the fiction writer while maintaining allegiance to fact. Creative nonfiction offers flexibility and freedom while adhering to the basic tenets of reportage. It is a genre in which writers can be poetic and journalistic simultaneously.

This mixture of journalism and fiction allows for great freedom, flexibility, insight and narrative development. For this section we are going to look at three very different examples by two quite different writers: Truman Capote and Maya Angelou.

Read the following extract from Capote's novel *In Cold Blood*.

Text 4.3 *In Cold Blood*, Truman Capote, 1966

One of the first – and still most famous – examples of creative non-fiction is Truman Capote's *In Cold Blood*. This 'non-fiction novel' tells the story of the 1959 murder of four members of the same family by Dick Hickock and Perry Smith. Instead of writing the story with journalistic objectivity, Capote went to the town where the crime was committed and interviewed as many people as he could who had an opinion on the incident. Capote spent six years writing the book, and in that time he got to know the murderers, and wrote at great length about their backgrounds and motives. The book received a lot of criticism when it was published because many felt that it was too sympathetic towards Hickock and Smith. It is now regarded as a pioneering work of this new genre, and has been adapted into several film versions.

Figure 4.4 Still from the film version of *In Cold Blood*, 1967.

The distance between Olathe, a suburb of Kansas City, and Holcomb, which might be called a suburb of Garden City, is approximately four hundred miles.

A town of eleven thousand, Garden City began assembling its founders soon after the Civil War. An itinerant buffalo hunter, Mr C.J. (Buffalo) Jones, had much to do with its subsequent expansion from a collection of huts and hitching posts into an opulent ranching centre with razzle-dazzle saloons, an opera house, and the plushiest hotel anywhere between Kansas City and Denver – in brief, a specimen of frontier fanciness that rivalled a more famous settlement fifty miles east of it, Dodge City. Along with Buffalo Jones, who lost his money and then his mind (the last years of his life were spent haranguing street groups against the wanton extermination of the beasts he himself had so profitably slaughtered), the glamours of the past are today entombed. Some souvenirs exist; a moderately colourful row of commercial buildings is known as the Buffalo Block, and the once splendid

Windsor Hotel, with its still splendid high-ceilinged saloon and its atmosphere of spittoons and potted palms, endures amid the variety stores and supermarkets as a Main Street landmark – one comparatively unpatronised, for the Windsor's dark, huge chambers and echoing hallways, evocative as they are, cannot compete with the air-conditioned amenities offered at the trim little Hotel Warren, or with the Wheat Lands Motel's individual television sets and 'Heated Swimming Pool'.

Anyone who has made the coast-to-coast journey across America, whether by train or by car, has probably passed through Garden City, but it is reasonable to assume that few travellers remember the event. It seems just another fair-sized town in the middle – almost the exact middle – of the continental United States. Not that the inhabitants would tolerate such an opinion – perhaps rightly. Though they may overstate the case ('Look all over the world, and you won't find friendlier people or fresher air or sweeter drinking water,' and 'I could go to Denver at triple the salary, but I've got five kids, and I figure there's no better place to raise kids than right here. Swell schools with every kind of sport. We even have a junior college,' and 'I came out here to practise law. A temporary thing, I never planned to stay. But when the chance came to move, I thought, Why go? What the hell for? Maybe it's not New York – but who wants New York? Good neighbours, people who care about each other, that's what counts. And everything else a decent man needs – we've got that, too. Beautiful churches. A golf course'), the newcomer to Garden City, once he has adjusted to the nightly after-eight silence of Main Street, discovers much to support the defensive boastings of the citizenry: a well-run public library, a competent daily newspaper, green-lawned and shady squares here and there, placid residential streets where animals and children are safe to run free, a big, rambling park complete with a small menagerie ("See the Polar Bears!" "See Penny the Elephant!"), and a swimming pool that consumes several acres ("World's Largest FREE Swim-pool!"). Such accessories, and the dust and the winds and the ever-calling train whistles, add up to a "home town" that is probably remembered with nostalgia by those who have left it, and that, for those who have remained, provides a sense of roots and contentment.

Activity 4.5

Preliminary research

Answer the following questions on the extract from Capote's novel.

1 What is Capote's purpose in describing the town and its inhabitants in this way? Is it to convey purely factual details or to give greater depth?

2 To what extent has Capote's writing style compromised the truth of the story he is telling?

Now look more closely at the techniques Capote uses and comment on:
- the sentence lengths (ranging from long, complex sentences to two-word sentences) and their effect
- the use of parenthesis
- the use of direct speech (what does it add to the narrative?)
- the use of colloquial language
- the use of imagery.

Capote's tone: is it respectful, or patronising?

Preparing for a presentation
Read Capote's description again.
3   Try to condense it from 561 words to 250: in doing so simply stick to the facts and cut out everything that you think is personal, fictional, exaggerated or not important to understanding the town being described.
4   What has been lost in doing this? Would you say that Capote's description reveals a greater – or deeper – truth than your draft?
5   What has been gained in your draft? Is it always better to remain purely factual? Is succinctness a good thing which all writers should aspire to?

Now write two pages bringing together your notes from the first three activities. Your presentation title is:

'Truman Capote's *In Cold Blood* shows us that creative non-fiction gets us closer to reality than pure, factual journalism.'

Maya Angelou's *I Know Why the Caged Bird Sings* is difficult to define. Although it has enjoyed lasting popularity, in its depiction of racism and exploitation it is not a book which flinches from difficult subjects.

Figure 4.5 Maya Angelou, 2002.

Text 4.4 *I Know Why the Caged Bird Sings*, Maya Angelou, 1969

I Know Why the Caged Bird Sings is another book that mixes reality and fiction. Published in 1969, some critics view it as autobiographical fiction, others as creative non-fiction.

The mourners on the front benches sat in a blue-serge, black-crepe-dress gloom. A funeral hymn made its way around the church tediously but successfully. It eased into the heart of every gay thought, into the care of each happy memory. Shattering the light and hopeful: "On the other side of Jordan, there is a peace for the weary, there is a peace for me." The inevitable destination of all living things seemed but a short step away. I had never considered before that dying, death, dead, passed away, were words and phrases that might be even faintly connected with me.

But on that onerous day, oppressed beyond relief, my own mortality was borne in upon me on sluggish tides of doom.

No sooner had the mournful song run its course than the minister took to the altar and delivered a sermon that in my state gave little comfort. Its subject was, "Thou art my good and faithful servant with whom I am well pleased." His voice enweaved itself through the somber vapors left by the dirge. In a monotonous tone he warned the listeners that "this day might be your last," and the best insurance against dying a sinner was to "make yourself right with God" so that on the fateful day He would say, "Thou art my good and faithful servant with whom I am well pleased." ...

Mr. Taylor and the high church officials were the first to file around the bier to wave farewell to the departed and get a glimpse of what lay in store for all men. Then on heavy feet, made more ponderous by the guilt of the living viewing the dead, the adult church marched up to the coffin and back to their seats. Their faces, which showed apprehension before reaching the coffin, revealed, on the way down the opposite aisle, a final confrontation of their fears. Watching them was a little like peeping through a window when the shade is not drawn flush. Although I didn't try, it was impossible not to record their roles in the drama.

And then a black-dressed usher stuck her hand out woodenly toward the children's rows. There was the shifty rustling of unreadiness but finally a boy of fourteen led us off and I dared not hang back, as much as I hated the idea of seeing Mrs. Taylor. Up the aisle, the moans and screams merged with the sickening smell of woolen black clothes worn in summer weather and green leaves wilting over yellow flowers. I couldn't distinguish whether I was smelling the clutching sound of misery or hearing the cloying odor of death.

It would have been easier to see her through the gauze, but instead I looked down on the stark face that seemed suddenly so empty and evil. It knew secrets that I never wanted to share.

Activity 4.6
Preliminary research
Read the extract from *I Know Why the Caged Bird Sings*.

1   Adverbs such as 'tediously', 'successfully'; verbs such as 'shattering', 'enweaved'; and adjectives such as 'black-crepe dress', 'onerous', 'sluggish' are emotive words. How would you describe the atmosphere they help create?

2   Re-read this sentence: 'I couldn't distinguish whether I was smelling the clutching sound of misery or hearing the cloying odor of death.' Some critics have argued that such vivid recollections are fictional, and that this is an adult projecting her views onto those of a child for the benefit of a compelling narrative. In this sense, such sentiments are imaginary and even deceptive. To what extent would you agree with such a view? Is the writer deceiving her audience? Or is she allowing us to more fully understand the scene's importance?

3   Analyse the last two sentences. There is an intentional ambiguity here which is difficult to interpret. Answer the following questions:
   *   How can something be both empty and evil?
   *   What secrets do you think the child sees?
   *   Why would a writer not wish to share such insights with her audience?

Preparing for a presentation
Spend 1 hour preparing for a 10–15 minute presentation:

'Memory is at the heart of imagination: an analysis of creative non-fiction responses to the past.'

You should use the notes you have written on the passage above to guide you in your preparation, but in order to make this presentation comparative you should also refer to any other creative non-fiction text that you have studied, either for your Diploma or at another stage in your education (if you find this difficult to do then you could use the extracts used in this chapter).

> **tip**
>
> You could do this with a friend: simply record your presentations and exchange them when you have finished. Mark each other's and then compare and contrast the marks you awarded each other: if they differ a great deal then discuss why this might be so. You could then ask your teacher to 'moderate' the marks: in other words he or she will listen to both and award a mark felt appropriate to the level you are studying for.

Remember to record your presentation and to mark it according to the criteria:

Criterion A	Knowledge and understanding of the work(s)	10 marks
Criterion B	Presentation	10 marks
Criterion C	Language	10 marks
Total		30 marks

How many marks did you give yourself out of 30? Again, where did you lose most marks and where did you gain most?

Autobiography

Autobiographies often become best-sellers. We like to read about other people's lives, and in particular we like to learn about those who have overcome sometimes difficult personal circumstances to become successful in their chosen fields. These autobiographies are enjoyable to read, but you have to be very clear about what you are being asked to present on in this part of the course. If you are studying autobiographies then they have to be of a suitably high literary standard to merit serious analysis: your teacher will have selected a number of appropriate texts to study.

But what makes an autobiography successful? A fascinating human story is central to this: we would not read somebody's life story if we were not interested in that person or, at the very least, the field he or she is successful in. But, perhaps more importantly, they have to be written well enough to keep us reading beyond our initial interest: how many of us have started reading the autobiography of a favourite sportsperson, singer or actor only to find that it does not engage us? This is the fault of the writing, rather than the story.

Activity 4.7
Preliminary research

Read the following opening sentences of an autobiography written by an IB student:

I was born in 1992 in Hong Kong. My father works in an office, and my mother does some part-time work in the local school. I have two brothers, a sister, and a dog called Zak. I go to school and study the IB Diploma, which is fun, but sometimes a lot of work.

There is nothing in this opening which really grabs our attention: it could be anybody. Now compare it with this opening:

The day I was born I nearly died. I arrived into this world two thousand miles from home, in a city called Hong Kong. My father was absent, and my mother, who was visiting a friend, went into labor six weeks early. She was rushed through a tropical storm to an anonymous, grey building which she had never seen before, to be met by endless, strange faces speaking a language she did not understand. All the time, she told me later, she prayed that I would live, and that the rest of the family – my two brothers, my sister, and my ancient dog – would be able to welcome me home.

Both are by the same student, but the second is far more memorable than the first: he has had to think about what is distinctive about his story and it has become not only more personal, but also more vivid in its depiction of the event (the strangeness of the place is very well described). Analysing autobiographical writing can be a lot easier once you have gone through the process yourself: writing about yourself in an original and engaging way is not as easy as it might appear, and many of us can be reticent about our own successes (and failures).

Can you make your own life story interesting to others? With your teacher's agreement try the following as a class activity:

Write, in 250 words, your own potted autobiography, without mentioning your name. You should write about:
- your family
- your character strengths
- you character weaknesses
- your likes
- your dislikes
- your hopes
- your fears.

Now exchange your autobiography with another member of the class. Make sure they are anonymous. Either your classmates or your teacher should then read out the autobiographies and the class has to guess who has written each one.

Further research
Read the following extracts from five well-known autobiographies. You are not given any information about them so that you can assess them on their own terms rather than judge them by their reputations.
1   Talk with your classmates about these openings: Can you tell which writers are male and female? Can you tell their ethnicity? What can you say about their cultural identities, or their personalities? Can you tell when they were written? Explain your answers with references to the texts.
2   Which of the openings interest you the most? Why?
3   Which of the openings do not interest you enough to read on? Why?

(For the last two questions, do your answers depend more on the subject matter than the style? If you don't like the style of writing, think about why you have not engaged with it: when did you lose interest?)

Extract 1
The very first thing I remember in my early childhood is a flame, a blue flame jumping off a gas stove somebody lit. It might have been me playing around with the stove. I don't remember who it was. Anyway, I remember being shocked by the whoosh of the blue flame jumping off the burner, the suddenness of it. That's as far back as I can remember; any further back than

this is just fog, you know, just mystery. But that stove flame is as clear as music is in my mind. I was three years old.

Extract 2

Childhood is looked upon as the happiest time of life. Is that always true? No, only a few have a happy childhood. The idealization of childhood originated in the old literature of the privileged. A secure, affluent, and unclouded childhood, spent in a home of inherited wealth and culture, a childhood of affection and play, brings back to one memories of a sunny meadow at the beginning of the road of life. The grandees of literature, or the plebions who glorify the grandees, have canonized this purely aristocratic view of childhood. But the majority of the people, if it looks back at all, sees, on the contrary, a childhood of darkness, hunger and dependence. Life strikes the weak – and who is weaker than a child?

Extract 3

Lou Levey, top man of Leeds Music Publishing company, took me up in a taxi to the Pythian Temple on West 70th Street to show me the pocket sized recording studio where Bill Haley and His Comets had recorded 'Rock Around the Clock' – then down to Jack Dempsey's restaurant on 58th and Broadway, where we sat down in a red leather upholstered booth facing the front window.

Lou introduced me to Jack Dempsey, the great boxer. Jack shook his fist at me.

'You look too light for a heavyweight kid, you'll have to put on a few pounds. You're gonna have to dress a little finer, look a little sharper – not that you'll need much in the way of clothes when you're in the ring – don't be afraid of hitting somebody too hard.'

"He's not a boxer, Jack, he's a songwriter and we'll be publishing his songs."

"Oh, yeah, well I hope to hear 'em some of these days. Good luck to you kid."

Extract 4

It was my good fortune to be deported to Auschwitz only in 1944, that is, after the German Government had decided, owing to the growing scarcity of labour, to lengthen the average lifespan of the prisoners destined for elimination; it conceded noticeable improvements in the camp routine and temporarily suspended killings at the whim of individuals.

Extract 5

Apart from life, a strong constitution and an abiding connection to the Thembu royal house, the only thing my father bestowed upon me at birth was a name, Rolihlahla. In Xhosa, Rolihlahla literally means 'pulling the branch of a tree', but its colloquial meaning more accurately would be 'troublemaker'. I do not believe that names are destiny or that my father somehow divined my future, but in later years, friends and relatives would ascribe to my birth name the many storms I have both caused and weathered. My more familiar English or Christian name was not given to me until my first day of school. But I am getting ahead of myself.

Literary autobiography

The literary autobiography is seen by many as a sub-genre in its own right. Literature is, like much art, autobiographical in flavour, and for many writers an autobiography allows them the opportunity to further explore – in a much more explicit way – episodes and themes which shape their writings. They can be hugely rewarding to read because they allow the reader to make connections with the writer and his or her art, and, because they are written by professional writers, their language is often richer and more sophisticated than the language in autobiographies written by people from other professions.

The following extract is by one of the greatest playwrights of the 20th century. Arthur Miller's autobiography *Timebends* is a valuable insight into the author of seminal works such as *The Crucible, A View from the Bridge* and *Death of a Salesman*. Miller not only became a highly influential figure on the American liberal left, but he also lived a life that could be viewed by many as the encapsulation of the American Dream: coming from a relatively poor immigrant background he reached the peak of his fame by marrying perhaps the most famous and glamorous woman in the world at that time, Marilyn Monroe.

Text 4.5 *Timebends*, Arthur Miller, 1987

Glamour is a youth's form of blindness that lets in light, incoherent color, but nothing defined. Like the rainbow, it is a once uplifting vision that moves away the closer you come to it.

My father, on the other hand, got more glamour-struck the older he became. He loved to stand in front of a theatre where a play of mine was on and every once in a while stroll in to chat with the box office men about business. 'How do you know they're giving you the right count?' he would ask me. Indeed, how did I?

In 1962, after our divorce, Marilyn took him as her escort to John Kennedy's birthday party in Madison Square Garden and introduced him to the president. My father would treasure a news photographer's picture of the occasion: Marilyn stands laughing with her head thrown back while Kennedy shakes hands with him, laughing with spontaneous, innocent enjoyment at what I am sure must have been one of my father's surprising remarks. I was not aware that for the rest of his life, which lasted some four more years, he spent considerable time on the lookout for his name in the gossip columns and entertainment news, until one day he gravely asked me – he was about eighty then – 'Do you look like me or do I look like you?'

This was serious. 'I guess I look like you,' I said. He seemed to like that answer.

How strange it was – not only had I competed with him but he with me. And the fact that this vaguely disappointed me signaled that even now I saw him partly shrouded in his myth.

He was an American and saw all things competitively. Once our old basset, Hugo, an immense dog whose incontinence was matched only by his lassitude, rose like a senator from one of his naps and unaccountably attacked a rag doll, throwing it up in the air and growling menacingly at it and charging at it again and again until he settled down once more into his habitual torpor with one ear covering his eyes. My father had watched in surprise all this uncustomary activity and then said, 'Well…everybody has to be better than somebody.'

Figure 4.6 Marilyn Monroe and Arthur Miller.

Activity 4.8

Read the extract from *Timebends* and answer the following questions.

1   The first two sentences are clearly figurative in their use of language, but what do they mean?

2   How would you describe Miller's relationship with his father? Tense? Respectful? Competitive? Is this an affectionate portrayal of the older man, or is there an underlying darkness to the relationship depicted here?

3   Why was Miller disappointed in his father's attitude towards him?

4   The description of Hugo, the basset hound, attacking the doll is clearly meant to be humorous, but there is seriousness to the anecdote as well: what is it?

5   There are many themes explored here:
   • the struggle for supremacy between father and son
   • the nature of the American Dream
   • ageing
   • status.

   Look closely at the extract to see if you can find where Miller introduces these themes, and see if you can find any more.

It's clear from approaching this text as a piece of literature that we can get more from it: themes, characterisation, figurative language … such qualities are shared with fictional prose, poetry and drama, but they are not out of place here either.

Now write a short essay of 400 words on: 'Why is the extract from Miller's autobiography literary in its style?' You should refer to the answers you have given to the previous questions.

Preparing for a presentation

Write a presentation on one of the following topics. You can use Miller's extract above as part of your presentation, or any of the texts given in this chapter, or you can use texts that you are studying in class:
   • 'The autobiographical impulse in literature: a desire to explain the self'
   • 'The fictionalisation of the self: truth and lies in two autobiographical texts'
   • 'The poetry of identity: literary techniques in two autobiographical texts'
   • 'Selective representation: how the writer re-writes himself in two literary texts'
   • 'At war with ourselves: generational conflict in two autobiographical texts'
   • 'Literary autobiography explains but does not excuse the actions of the authors': an analysis of motive in two literary autobiographies

Further research

Now try to write about one incident from your childhood as vividly as you can. Think about the literary devices you could use: you could use metaphor and simile; you could bring people to life with evocative physical descriptions and the use of direct speech; you could adopt a quiet, reflective tone, or a more upbeat, optimistic voice which might better reflect your character. You could experiment with your style, choosing between using suspense, humour, surrealism, third person, or the more traditional first person … the list goes on. Don't be limited in your choices: be a risk-taker in your writing.

Essays and travel writing

As a student of English Literature you will be used to writing essays. But this option allows you to study formal essays written by other writers, something which you may not do otherwise (the critical essay which focuses on a particular work or writer is rather different). It is not much of an exaggeration to say that the most significant writers of English – novelists, poets or playwrights – have written essays. The form itself probably dates back to a French philosopher, Michel de Montaigne who published his *Essais* in 1580. In this collection of 'essais' – or trials – Montaigne reflected on his own thoughts and tested them against his own counter-arguments. It was a process of self-inquiry. But it was an Englishman, the philosopher and politician Francis Bacon, who it could be argued made the form his own. His *Essayes: Religious Meditations. Places of Perswasion and Disswasion. Seene and Allowed,* published in 1597, is a masterpiece of the craft: it is polemical and personal, wide-ranging and clearly focused on apparently incidental observations, and covers subjects as varied as gardens, love, death, lying and disability.

With the growth in the West of newspapers and magazines throughout the 18th and 19th centuries, essays grew in popularity: they were ideally fitted to the format, and, in their apparent immediacy, also suited the more transient nature of the medium (as opposed to the novel). Indeed, in the 18th century in Great Britain magazines such as *The Reader, The Weekly Gazette* and *The Rambler* were created specifically for the essay.

In English literature the highpoint of the essay came in the 19th century when writers as celebrated and influential as William Hazlitt, Matthew Arnold, Walter Pater, Oscar Wilde and John Ruskin not only articulated an astonishing range of ideas and personal thoughts, but in turn shaped how their societies saw themselves (they influenced architecture, political theory, economics, art, amongst many other things). Indeed, so powerful and all-pervasive did the essay form become that some writers took against it: for some, even those who reverted to it to express a clear opinion, it lacked the richness and openness of creative literature. Charles Dickens, in *Our Mutual Friend,* attacks the art form, characterising it through a depiction of Miss Peecher as 'small, shining, neat, methodical ... a little pincushion, a little workbox, a little set of tables and weights and measures'. This 'littleness', this precision and insularity, was, perhaps for a writer with the scope of Dickens, something to be suspicious of.

Many believed that the essay – along with other literary forms – would be threatened by the growing ubiquity of the Internet, but the opposite appears to be true. Magazines and newspapers have moved a lot of their content online (including archived material), and new websites dedicated to polemical writing have become very popular. Blogs – perhaps the latest manifestation of the essay – continue to grow rapidly as growing numbers of people find they have an appetite not just for strongly-worded, direct arguments, but also for writing them as well. With mobile technology providing a growing number of ways in which we can access the Internet, it is safe to say that the essay has an assured future.

Essays can contain many different elements – in combination with each other or in splendid isolation – and these could include review, interpretation, and argument. The essay does not always have to be balanced: indeed, some of the best essays written have been biased responses to issues of great seriousness. They should, first and foremost, as the novelist and essayist Virginia Woolf wrote, 'give pleasure' but they should also, according to Woolf, be 'pure like water or pure like wine, but pure from dullness, deadness and deposits of extraneous matter'. In other words a good essay has to be unambiguous and succinct, direct and engaging.

We have included travel writing and the essay in the same section because they can so often be inseparable: writers often use the essay not only to describe a new place

Further resources

There are many websites which have essays published on them. Some are classics of the genre, others personal blogs which may be of interest to a much smaller audience. You may find the following websites interesting:

http://www.aldaily.com/#classics

http://www.theawl.com/

http://longform.org/

they have visited, but also to express ideas and opinions about the culture they see. Travel writing has always been popular: in the days before travelling vast distances was nothing more than a dream for the majority of people, the early explorers who recounted their experiences met a need that could not have otherwise have been filled. When the camera – first still and then moving – was able to relay pictures of distant lands to those fortunate enough to be able to visit a cinema, then some feared that the travel writer might become as endangered as the cultures he (and it was more often than not a male writer) was describing. This has not happened, and even with cheaper flights, and better roads and rail links, not to mention webcams set up in public squares and private roads, we still have a desire to read about other cultures and traditions through the eyes of an expert guide, or at least a guide we have some sympathy for. We have chosen several extracts from famous essays, and we have included essays written by writers as they try to come to terms with new contexts.

The essay can be highly opinionated, but it should always entertain and be clearly written. The essays that you will study will have to be analysed as literary texts, which means that they must have a level of sophistication which can withstand analysis.

Read the following openings of two famous essays on the English language.

Text 4.6 *On Getting Respected in Inns and Hotels*, Hilaire Belloc, 1908

Hilaire Belloc (1870–1953) was an English essayist and politician. He wrote on a number of subjects, including poetry, history and religion.

To begin at the beginning is, next to ending at the end, the whole art of writing; as for the middle you may fill it in with any rubble that you choose. But the beginning and the end, like the strong stone outer walls of medieval buildings, contain and define the whole.

And there is more than this: since writing is a human and a living art, the beginning being the motive and the end the object of the work, each inspires it; each runs through organically, and the two between them give life to what you do.

So I will begin at the beginning and I will lay down this first principle: that religion and the full meaning of things has nowhere more disappeared from the modern world than in the department of Guide Books.

Text 4.7 *Politics and the English Language*, George Orwell, 1946

George Orwell (1903–50) is perhaps best known for two novels: *Animal Farm* (1945) and *Nineteen Eighty-Four* (1950). He is also one of the most celebrated and influential essayists in the language.

Most people who bother with the matter at all would admit that the English language is in a bad way, but it is generally assumed that we cannot by conscious action do anything about it. Our civilization is decadent, and our language – so the argument runs – must inevitably share in the general collapse. It follows that any struggle against the abuse of language is a sentimental archaism, like preferring candles to electric light or hansom cabs to aeroplanes. Underneath this lies the half-conscious belief that language is a natural growth and not an instrument which we shape for our own purposes.

Now, it is clear that the decline of a language must ultimately have political and economic causes: it is not due simply to the bad influence of this or that individual writer. But an effect can become a cause, reinforcing the original cause and producing the same effect in an intensified form, and so on indefinitely. A man may take to drink because he feels himself to be a failure, and then fail all the more completely because he drinks. It is rather the same thing that is happening to the English language. It becomes ugly and inaccurate because our thoughts are foolish, but the slovenliness of our language makes it easier for us to have foolish thoughts. The point is that the process is reversible. Modern English, especially written English, is full of bad habits which spread by imitation and which can be avoided if one is willing to take the necessary trouble. If one gets rid of these habits one can think more clearly, and to think clearly is a necessary first step towards political regeneration: so that the fight against bad English is not frivolous and is not the exclusive concern of professional writers. I will come back to this presently, and I hope that by that time the meaning of what I have said here will have become clearer. Meanwhile, here are five specimens of the English language as it is now habitually written.

Activity 4.9

1   How would you describe the two different writing styles in Texts 4.6 and 4.7? Is one more serious than the other? Which one? Which phrases support your opinion?
2   Whose argument is the most interesting? What phrases keep you reading? Be specific: quote from both to support your assertions.
3   Can you sum up in one sentence each writer's argument?

Assessment: Sample student response

Now read the following opening of a presentation which involved a comparative analysis of both extracts, written by a student who presented on the following subject: 'Great essayists take extreme positions in order to tell us uncomfortable truths about ourselves'. The student had studied a number of essayists, including Orwell. The highlighted words were prompts which were referred to by the student to keep her focused.

All great essayists take _extreme positions_ to tell their societies _uncomfortable truths_. It is the _essayists, not the poets, who are the unacknowledged legislators of the world_, and nobody personifies this better than the English novelist George Orwell. His essays – clearly written, accessible, and filled with good sense – appear, on first reading, to be _uncompromising_ and extreme. Time has judged them to be, however, _perceptive and truthful_. His essay on _Politics and the English Language_, published in 1946, is one of the first essays on what we might today _call 'political correctness' and jargon_, and each generation should read it to remind them of Orwell's warnings. Orwell is the author of _Nineteen Eighty-Four_, and it was in this novel that he wrote at length about _Newspeak_ – a new political language which went beyond propaganda: this was a language which altered our thoughts before we know we have them. For him language should be an '<u>instrument for expressing and not for concealing or preventing thought</u>'. In *Politics and the English Language* Orwell writes about the dangers posed to our language from those who seek to control us for their own purposes. It is a masterpiece not just of substance but of style.

In the very first sentence Orwell's tone is marked by a <u>casualness</u> which belies the <u>seriousness</u> of his argument: his statement that '<u>most people who bother with the matter at all would admit that the English language is in a bad way</u>' suggests that there are many people who are not bothered by such things at all; and one could argue that those who are worried about the state of English are the sorts of people who will be convinced that it is in decline. The rest of his opening paragraph is a very condensed and clear explanation of the counter arguments: namely, that language is linked to society, and because <u>our society is in decline our language must be also</u>. There is a directness to Orwell's approach which engages us, even though we may not agree with what he says. For instance, his first sentence of the second paragraph – which states the <u>opinion</u> that economics affects language as a fact could be contentious, but it is stated in a way which convinces us …

The student continued to analyse Orwell's essay before referring to Belloc's essay:

In contrast to Orwell's serious – but never heavy – writing style we have the lightness of Belloc. His essay – *On Getting Respected in Inns and Hotels* – begins with a <u>sweeping and humorous</u> statement on language: that what we write – especially in those parts between the beginning and the end – doesn't really matter. But Belloc begins his essay in a style <u>reminiscent of a folk tale</u> ('To begin at the beginning') which suggests that what he writes is make-believe and not to be taken too seriously. The humorous quality of the writing is deceptive, however, and when Belloc writes that writing is 'a living art, the beginning being the motive and the end the object of the work, each inspires it: each runs through organically, and the two between them give life to what you do' we know that he has a love of language and a seriousness to his argument which, at this stage at least, is comparable to Orwell's.

Activity 4.10

Now read the student's conclusion to this presentation. Think about how successful an ending this is:

- Are the points clearly made?
- Does it bring points made earlier together?
- Is the tone used appropriate to the task?
- Do the highlighted phrases help as prompts?

How would you mark this presentation using the criteria you have already been provided with? Again, think about where marks are gained and lost.

Great essayists are unafraid of being criticised by others for being extreme, but what they should never be accused of is being boring. A great essay reveals something we might have already considered – the decline of guide books, the abuse of the English language, how to hit a home run or dance the polka – but they will do so in a direct way which never ceases to engage and surprise. <u>They should tell us something new, even if it is familiar</u>. Furthermore, the very best essayists will find in the everyday <u>eternal truths</u> which can be understood and transferred to all of us, regardless of our individual situations. As the number of voices competing for our attention grows, society <u>needs great essayists more than ever</u> to tell us what is really important and what can be discarded.

The following extracts (Texts 4.8 and 4.9) from two very different essays share journeying as a main theme. But both writers approach the theme very differently, and both use descriptive writing in quite distinctive ways. Hazlitt's description of nature is very general, providing a backdrop, or a context, for his main argument for the benefits of loneliness; and Camus' description, although geographically very specific, again uses setting as a means for exploring more profound ideas, such as identity.

Text 4.8 *On Going on a Journey*, William Hazlitt, 1822

William Hazlitt is one of England's finest political essayists. A friend of Wordsworth and Coleridge, he wrote on a huge range of subjects, and is the inspiration for many essayists who followed him. This essay was first published in the *New Monthly Magazine* in 1822.

One of the pleasantest things in the world is going a journey; but I like to go by myself. I can enjoy society in a room; but out of doors, Nature is company enough for me. I am then never less alone than when alone.

'*The fields his study, Nature was his book.*'

I cannot see the wit of walking and talking at the same time. When I am in the country, I wish to vegetate like the country. I am not for criticising hedgerows and black cattle. I go out of town in order to forget the town and all that is in it. There are those who for this purpose go to watering-places and carry the metropolis with them. I like more elbow-room and fewer incumbrances. I like solitude, when I give myself up to it, for the sake of solitude; nor do I ask for

'*... a friend in my retreat*
Whom I may whisper, solitude is sweet.'

The soul of a journey is liberty, perfect liberty, to think, feel, do, just as one pleases. We go a journey chiefly to be free of all impediments and of all inconveniences; to leave ourselves behind, much more to get rid of others. It is because I want a little breathing-space to muse on indifferent matters ... that I absent myself from the town for a while, without feeling a loss the moment I am left by myself.

Figure 4.7 William Hazlitt, (1778–1830).

Text 4.9 *The Wind at Djemila*, Albert Camus, 1967

Albert Camus (1913–60) was an Algerian-born novelist and essayist. His novel *L'Etranger (The Outsider)* is seen as one of the seminal existential texts. He was awarded the Nobel Prize in Literature in 1957. This essay was first published in English in 1968.

There are places where the mind dies so that a truth which is its very denial may be born. When I went to Djemila, there was wind and sun, but that is another story. What must be said first of all is that a heavy, unbroken silence reigned there – something like a perfectly balanced pair of scales. The cry of birds, the soft sound of a three-hole flute, goats trampling, murmurs from the sky were just so many sounds added to the silence and desolation. Now and then a sharp clap, a piercing cry marked the upward flight of a bird huddled among the rocks. Any trail one followed – the pathways through the ruined houses, along wide, paved roads under shining colonnades, across the vast forum between the triumphal arch and the temple set upon a hill – would end at the ravines that surround Djemila on every side, like a pack of cards opening beneath a limitless sky. And one would stand there, absorbed, confronted with stones and silence, as the day moved on and the mountains grew purple surging upward. But the wind blows across the plateau of Djemila. In the great confusion of wind and sun that mixes light into the ruins, in the silence and solitude of this dead city, something is forged that gives man the measure of his identity.

tip

Remember: you can highlight your notes, or take in props to your real presentation. When you have finished writing your presentation for this activity, highlight key words and phrases which would help you deliver your ideas should you get stuck: make sure the words are distinctive.

Activity 4.11

Read both Texts 4.8 and 4.9 twice and answer the following questions.

1 Which key themes can be found in these extracts?
   - The relationship between man and nature
   - The relationship between spirituality and faith
   - The relationship between liberty and isolation
2 To what extent would you agree with Hazlitt when he writes: 'The soul of a journey is liberty'? Explain your answer with examples from your own reading and your own experiences.
3 What does Camus mean when he writes: 'There are places where the mind dies so that a truth which is its very denial may be born'?

Preparing for a presentation

Using your answers to these questions, write a 5-minute presentation on one of the following:
   - 'All travel writing describes the inward journey as much as the outward journey.'
     Or
   - 'Travel writing explores the conflict between the individual and the collective, the known and the unknown: it tells us universal truths about our own society.'

Unit 4.4 **The 'new textualities' option**

In this option you will have the opportunity to explore the exciting ways in which English literature is developing and growing into new areas. You could give a presentation on graphic novels, hypertext narratives, fan fiction, or texts created through collaborative blogging. Some of these are developing so quickly that they are difficult to define or exemplify, and on the new frontiers of information technology the genres are being created by the users and sometimes defy easy categorisation (which is the case with collaborative creative and critical blogging).

Key term

Graphic novel A genre which combines visual and linguistic elements.

Graphic novels

Many people would share the British journalist Rachel Cooke's thoughts on the graphic novel. Writing in *The Guardian* she admitted:

> **I'm not proud of this but, for years and years, I thought that graphic novels were only read by geeky guys with long hair, fetid bedrooms and a serious fondness for thrash ... But then something changed. All of a sudden, a whole slew of books came my way that made me think graphic novels could be as satisfying, and even as literary, in their way, as a regular novel.**

Further resources

If you are interested in doing further research on graphic novels or cartoons you could begin by looking at this website: http://www.cartoonstudies.org/. You could also visit the Cartoon Museum in London, or go to their website: http://www.cartoonmuseum.org.

Cooke is not alone: what was once seen as a niche market for publishers is now a hugely popular and respected genre in its own right, appealing to young and old, male and female. You could get a great deal of pleasure, as well as rewarding study, from presenting on a favourite text from the many excellent graphic novels on sale in bookshops, or available online.

Remember: the graphic novels that you can study have to be original works, rather than adaptations of other texts. This means that you cannot study a graphic rendition of, say, Dickens's *Great Expectations*.

How literary is a graphic novel?

This is a difficult question to answer because of course one person's idea of what makes a text 'literary' might differ from another person's. But it may be possible to measure 'literariness' not only by the importance of the themes explored, but also by the sophistication of the method of conveying them. In this sense a film can be 'read', analysed and interpreted just like a written text, and so can the graphic novel, a genre which bridges visual and written media. Tom Wolf has written that 'the reading of words is but a subset of a much more general human activity ... the reading of words is one manifestation of this activity; but there are many others – the reading of pictures, maps, circuit diagrams, musical notes ...' and in studying this genre you should be aware of this understanding of the varieties of reading we are capable of doing.

The writers you will study over the two years for your English Literature course are serious artists (which of course does not mean that they don't write anything amusing). Serious artists – be they musicians, poets, playwrights, visual artists or novelists – try to explore important issues in their chosen medium, and very often they try to articulate themes which are almost beyond being easily represented and do so in an original way. It is this struggle with profound and universal truths, and a desire for a uniqueness of expression, which perhaps marks out great artists from good artists.

Read the following poem by Raymond Carver (Text 4.10), and then read the extract from *Sleepwalk and Other Stories* (Text 4.11) by Adrian Tomine, a collection of graphic stories published in 1995.

Text 4.10 *Yesterday, snow*, Raymond Carver, 1985

Yesterday, snow was falling and all was chaos.
I don't dream, but in the night I dreamed
a man offered me some of his whiskey.
I wiped the mouth of the bottle
and raised it to my lips.
It was like one of those dreams of falling
where, they say, if you don't wake up
before you hit the ground,
you'll die. I woke up! Sweating.
Outside, the snow had quit.
But, my God, it looked cold. Fearsome.
The windows were ice to the touch
when I touched them. I got back
in bed and lay there the rest of the night,
afraid I'd sleep again. And find
myself back in that dream...
The bottle rising to my lips.
The indifferent man
waiting for me to drink and pass it on again.
A skewed moon hangs on until morning,
and a brilliant sun.
Before now, I never knew what it meant
to 'spring out of bed'.
    All day snow flopping off roofs.
The crunch of tires and footsteps.
Next door, there's an old fellow shoveling.
Every so often he stops and leans
on his shovel, and rests, letting
his thoughts go where they may.
Staying his heart.
Then he nods and grips his shovel.
Goes on, yes. Goes on.

Text 4.11 *Sleepwalk and Other Stories*, Adrian Tomine, 1995

Page 84   Page 85

Activity 4.12

Read Texts 4.10 and 4.11 and then answer the following questions.

1   What are the main themes explored in each text?
2   Which text has the greater emotional impact on you?
3   Which text expresses the greater range of emotions?
4   Which text is the more open to different interpretations? Is this a strength or a weakness of this text?
5   Do you have a sense of the author's 'voice' in these texts? If so, how would you describe it? Reflective? Questioning? Uncertain? Assured?
6   Do you agree that both texts are original in what they are trying to say and how they say it?
7   What do both texts share?
8   How are the texts different?
9   Is the interplay of the words and images in the graphic novel very different from the interplay of words and images created in you by the poem?

Both Carver and Tomine take their subject matter very seriously, but both explore it in oblique and subtle ways. There are overlaps: we can sense from both that one of the main themes is transience, and even the fear of death; both texts are also ambiguous and open to interpretation; and, crucially, both have a distinctive 'voice', although both articulate that individual and distinctive method of expression using very different techniques. Both texts are literary, but it is your own personal opinion as to which is the more accomplished piece of literature. If you define your parameters – and your definitions – then a comparative analysis of this nature can be a rich area to explore. Understanding the key elements of a graphical text can help you considerably in your appreciation of the genre.

The key elements of the graphic novel

The graphic novel is a montage of different media, both written and visual. Much of this coursebook is concerned with analysing the written word, but an understanding of how visual media works is important in this unit. Remember, though, that your analysis should be essentially literary: you should focus on the elements of a graphic novel which you will find in a conventional 'novel': characterisation, plot, subplot, imagery, structure, and so on. But an awareness of a specialist vocabulary can only advance your insight into the graphic novels you are presenting on. The key elements include the text and the frame.

The text

When we read a novel we seldom think about the font: it works if it does not obstruct our enjoyment and understanding of the text itself. But in a graphic novel the style of text can convey very different meaning. Consider the sentences on the left.

To be, or not to be, that is the question

To be, or not to be, that is the question

To be, or not to be, that is the question

Each font conveys a slightly different mood: you could say that the font adds to the 'atmosphere' of the phrase itself. Do you think it adds anything to Shakespeare's original words? Or does the font distract us?

When you analyse your graphic texts do not overlook anything: each part of each frame conveys a certain unified meaning, and the words, in this context, function on the page visually: we 'read' them differently from the words you are reading now.

The frame

Graphic texts convey their narratives through words and pictures. In structure, of course, they are very different from a conventional text: they are broken down into segments which are called frames. But in order to preserve the 'flow' of the narrative the artist links and interconnects these frames in an endlessly inventive number of ways: indeed, the only limits placed on the number of permutations exists within the narrative itself. These frames are an integral part of the artistic form, rather than merely the medium (as the frames in cinematic film are). Think about each element in every frame you study:

- What happens in each one?
- Is the text contained entirely within the frame?
- Is the action contained entirely within the frame?
- Is there a frame border? What function does it serve? Is this border solid?
- If there isn't a frame border, why has the artist omitted it? How does this affect the narrative?
- Does anything happen *between* the frames? Is some of the action developed between each frame? How much time has passed between them? Seconds, minutes, hours, or years?

Key term

Frame In graphic texts the narrative is segmented into sequential scenes and these are enclosed by frames (also known as panels).

Activity 4.13

Preparing for a presentation

Your aim is to write a short presentation on a graphic narrative. Look at *A short history of America* by Robert Crumb (Text 4.12) and then answer the following questions:

1 What story is Crumb telling in this sequence?
2 Would it be possible to write a story to it? What would be lost if this was expressed through words only?
3 Is there a subtext to it that goes beyond the obvious series of representative images?
4 What happens between the frames?
5 The perspective remains consistent: why do you think this is so? How does this fixed perspective differ from the author's perspective in a conventional novel?

Text 4.12 *A short history of America*, Robert Crumb, 1979

You are now going to look at a longer extract from a graphic novel. *Persepolis* (2004) by Marjane Satrapi is the story of a young girl – also called Marjane – who grew up during the Islamic revolution in Iran. We watch her growing up and having traumatic experiences – the execution of her uncle, the Iran/Iraq war and her sense of growing isolation from a rapidly changing society. At the age of 14 she leaves Iran and goes to school in Austria but she is unable to settle in Europe. She eventually returns to her home country, but now finds that she is also at odds with the new Islamic Republic. She learns to accept her own cultural heritage, but realises that she cannot continue to live in a country that she no longer recognises. Eventually she decides to leave Iran for a new life in France. Satrapi deliberately chose a simple style of drawing in pen and ink – with very few identifying marks – in order to avoid the book's appearance dating, but also, perhaps, to show the timelessness of the story.

The following extracts (Text 4.13) are the final two pages of the story. Read them and then answer the questions in the activity which follows.

Text 4.13 *Persepolis*, Marjane Satrapi, 2004

Page 342   Page 343

Activity 4.14

1   Does the use of black and white drain the narrative of some complexity? Or does it add something starker?
2   What are the main themes explored in this part of the narrative?

Preparing for a presentation
Using your notes from Activities 4.12, 4.13 and 4.14, write a 10-minute presentation on one of the following subjects:

* The visual word: graphic novels as great literature. An analysis of technique and language.
* 'A second-rate sub-genre': the graphic text in a literary context.

If you choose to do your presentation on graphic text(s) it is important that the text(s) have a strong literary element. Adaptations of literary texts can be studied if they are distinctive, and add something new to the originals. You should analyse them as both literary and visual texts, and that means that elements such as pace and structure are explored in your presentation. The range of texts available is vast, and we have chosen two here which give you an insight in to the possibilities. These texts – based on Joseph Conrad's *Heart of Darkness* and Wilfred Owen's *Dulce et decorum est* – are included to help you explore the relationship between graphic texts and 'conventional' written texts. The process of adaptation, and of exploring and developing meaning within a text so that the original literary text is transformed into another new art form, is a rich area for analysis and can produce some fascinating responses.

Text 4.14 *Dulce et decorum est*, Wilfred Owen, 1917; graphic adaptation by Jason Cobley, 2010

Interview with Jason Cobley

Jason Cobley is the scriptwriter for the graphic version of Wilfred Owen's *Dulce et decorum est* (Text 4.14). The following interview should help you understand some of the decisions a scriptwriter makes when adapting a purely written text into a graphic text. If you choose to do your presentation on a graphic text it will be important to look at the technique of rendering ideas visually and linguistically. The choices made by the writer or artist are often highly creative interpretations in themselves, much like those made by a film or theatre director.

• What role do you play in turning a conventional literary text into a graphic narrative?

The best way to think of a graphic novel script is that it is very much like a screenplay, so the visuals have to come first. A comic book is all about conveying a story using words and pictures in conjunction with one another. At the same time, the integrity of the original text is very important – nothing of the original author's intent should be lost. In the case of Mary Shelley's *Frankenstein*, the key to the text is the relationship between Victor and the Monster, which is at once intellectual and highly emotional. The visuals have to support that, and add embellishments that deepen it – for example, when the two characters meet in a hut on a Swiss mountainside, they have a war of words, and I scripted the Monster hurling a copy of *Paradise Lost* into the fire as he talks about his feeling of kinship with Satan and the worthlessness of Man's achievements. Essentially, then, my job is to give the text a visual context that propels the narrative and provides symbols that enhance the reader's understanding of the themes and ideas.

• What is your working relationship with the artist?

Usually, I write the script in full, complete with descriptions of 'camera angles' and so on, and hand it over to the artist. Sometimes, the artist will share layouts and pages with me as they evolve, and I can add suggestions for amendments. This has to be filtered through the editor at that stage, but more often than not I don't see the artwork until it's finished.

• What are the major challenges you face when planning a graphic text?

Sometimes, it's because the original text just wasn't intended for any other medium. With *Dracula*, the biggest challenge was finding a way to present each of the narrators differently. This can be done with different fonts of course, but I suggested things like different colour palettes. Other times, the challenge is finding a way to make dialogue interesting visually. What I try to do is to preserve a multitude of meanings; I try to complement the meaning of text, because the danger is that it can impose a single meaning where there could be more than one. I try to allow for interpretation as much as possible, where the author intended it.

• Is a graphic text essentially literary or visual?

An acquaintance of mine who works for Marvel Comics insists that comics have more in common with film than novels, and I'm inclined to agree, but only up to a point. The interplay of the words and pictures is essentially visual, yet is the best aid to literacy that I've yet seen because it helps ideas and symbols to be associated with words for emerging readers. I learned to read through comics not novels. Overall, a graphic text is more literary than visual for that reason, and also because it helps develop the kind of literacy that we need more and more in the 21st century: reading onscreen and the interactivity of text and pictures is common to the comic form and the Internet.

• Does the act of 'visualising' a narrative limit the reader's imagination, or liberate it?

A bad adaptation will limit it. A good one will liberate it. When I adapted *Dulce et decorum est*, for example, I was eager to ensure that the message was foregrounded, not just the gory spectacle of men drowning in gas, so we have a framing sequence of people at a war memorial on Remembrance Sunday. An old man in a wheelchair looks up at a young man standing there, and the words of the poem then play out as the thoughts and memories of the old man, lecturing bitterly the young man about the waste of life that they are there to commemorate. It takes nothing away from the poem, and hopefully adds something, making it relevant to the reader now, rather than almost a hundred years ago.

Text 4.15 *Heart of Darkness*, Joseph Conrad, 1899; graphic adaptation by Catherine Anyango, 2010

Interview with Catherine Anyango

Catherine Anyango is an illustrator and film maker. She has rendered Joseph Conrad's classic novel, *Heart of Darkness,* as a graphic novel (Text 4.15). The following interview will help you focus on how an artist can re-create and adapt a well-known literary text and make something original in its own right. When reading the interview think about how, in your presentation, you will be able to analyse and explain the different elements which make up a graphic text such as Anyango's *Heart of Darkness.*

Figure 4.8 Catherine Anyango.

- Conrad's novel is a complex, challenging text: what attracted you to this particular text to adapt graphically?

I chose to adapt this text for two reasons: visually, I was drawn to the possibilities in the power of Conrad's dense, descriptive prose, and I also felt that the time and context he was describing unfortunately still have a relevance now. The power structures it describes are essentially the same, and Marlow as a hero is attractive because he is not your typical protagonist – he is not always likeable. The story still has power in the fact that I think colonial situations are a symptom of something more universal, which is why they recur in different guises. For me, it's about the idea of entitlement, and through the ages we enforce our feelings of entitlement in whatever way that age will allow.

- What were the major challenges you faced as an illustrator when you began working on this project?

A big technical challenge was getting all the historical details completely accurate, which I wanted to do to give the historical context the authority and gravitas it deserved. This meant researching uniforms, ranking details, graphic elements and even haircuts, as well as finding models of all the boats that appear in the book. The book also contains scenes of violence and callous treatment of the Congolese, which I felt it was important not to shy away from. I didn't want to make the drawing savage or ugly in any way, although that's the content, but to draw the reader in with seductive imagery, and then show them that even in the most beautiful of settings, terrible things can happen – as Marlow says –'*But as I stood on this hillside, I foresaw that in the blinding sunshine of that land I would become acquainted with a flabby, pretending, weak-eyed devil of a rapacious and pitiless folly.*'

- How do you react to critics who say that this process of 'visualisation', or rendering a text graphically, narrows a reader's imagination, rather than expanding it?

I would never suggest reading the graphic novel to the exclusion of the novel itself. However, I don't feel it narrows a reader's imagination, I feel the reading of a graphic novel is essentially different from reading text on its own. In this case, the reader is perhaps not invited to imagine, for example, the jungle, by himself – but he is invited, because of the way I have placed certain things on the page, to make connections or associations between things and thus put subliminal elements of the story together. An example – when Marlow sees for the first time the shrunken heads outside Kurtz's hut, his face and the head are matched on opposite pages. At this point his appreciation of the 'subtle horror' that separates 'pure, uncomplicated savagery' from the darker effects of colonial rule makes him understand that his position in the Congo may be on the wrong side of good and evil. In this moment, he and the head are not so unlike – he has also reached the end of something, he is also is doomed, and damned. They have been brought to this point by the same forces and he recognises himself in this thing. The visual of them side by side bring them together and we can sympathise and feel horror at both.

I think an artist will always try to leave some things unsaid in the drawings, so that the reader can fill in and guess at certain elements.

- Can you describe the creative process you go through when you read a text and begin to select the images which you think best represent the writer's aims? How much is lost, and what is gained?

It's a very intuitive process for me. On a first reading I'll come away with certain key images that I can see without doing any work at all. When I go through and storyboard it, I will be designing the pages to best bring the narrative across – a scene with a lot of action in it may have more panels, sometimes you need to set the scene with a double spread, etc. With the *Heart of Darkness* one of my main aims was to show the disintegration of both Marlow's beliefs and mental state as he went down the river, and I did this by making the drawings themselves increasingly fragmented. Certain things are lost in the process – plot details, even whole characters – which are not superfluous by any means – but would be too complicated to include in the number of pages available!

- To what extent do you think we read a graphic text differently from a conventional text (such as a novel or a poem)? How would you describe this difference?

A graphic text is almost something you have to learn how to read, or unlearn your reading of a conventional text while you are doing so. With the graphic novel, the words are not meant to be read in quite so linear a way – there's a sort of reciprocal relationship between the text, the images and the panels themselves. I like that it's a new or different type of reading, that you are reading words but also learning to understand different codes and shorthands for things. A graphic reading. For example, the outline of a panel can be used to convey time, in the same way that cinematically pace and frame can do so. It's for me a little like film, but in a way that you can take your time and savour each shot, as it were.

I like that the words and pictures work together. You can have the text saying one thing, with the picture saying something else, and the relationship between the two things at once serves up your story.

Further resources

For more information on Catherine Anyango's work visit these websites:

http://www.selfmadehero.com/news/2010/08/guest-blogger-catherine-anyango-on-the-subliminal-in-heart-of-darkness/

http:/news.selfmadehero.com/2010/09/guest-blogger-catherine-anyango-your.html

Hypertext narratives

Professor Jay David Bolter's book *Writing Space: Computers, Hypertext, and the Remediation of Print* (2010) includes a disk. When you put it into your computer a paragraph of text appears on your screen; within this paragraph certain words are highlighted and by pointing at them with your cursor you are able to open up a new window which expands the idea behind that word; this extension also might include highlighted words which allow you to explore further ideas. You are able to manoeuvre your way around the text, opening up different windows with new perspectives, and you are allowed to add to the texts as well, becoming, in effect, a co-author of a new text with Professor Bolter. You can then email it to your friends, or upload it to the Internet, where others will continue to amend and alter it; they, in turn, will become co-authors with you.

This raises interesting questions which you could discuss with a classmate or raise in your presentation:

- Who is the author?
- Can there be a coherent narrative?
- Who owns the text?
- Who owns the concept?

Interview with Professor Jay Bolter

• How would you describe hypertext narratives to a student new to the genre?

Hypertext is both a technology and a way of organising texts. In traditional writing for print, the author expresses her ideas as a series of paragraphs that are meant to be read from beginning to end. A hypertext, however, is stored in a computer and read on a screen. The text is divided into units, which may consist of words, images or even segments of video, and each unit may be 'linked' to several others. The reader moves through the text by following the links. The World Wide Web is a vast hypertext of linked pages. Most pages on the World Wide Web are informative or descriptive, rather than narrative. But it is possible to create a hypertext narrative (fiction or non-fiction) that is organised as a set of units and links. One of the first such hypertext fictions was Michael Joyce's *Afternoon*, published in 1990.

• How does this genre differ from other, more established forms of literature?

In traditional literature, the author is in complete control of the presentation of the text. The reader reads the narrative or the poem in the order that the author has determined in advance. A hypertext narrative does not have a fixed order. The reader determines the order, at least in part, as she reads, based on the links that she chooses. The meaning of the whole narrative may change in important ways depending on the order of reading, and this means that the reader herself becomes a partner with the author in the process of creation.

• If a hypertext narrative is inherently fluid, or unstable, should it be critically assessed?

Any text can be critically assessed. The methods of reading and assessing hypertext may differ somewhat from the methods for traditional literature, but that was also true of many forms of experimental literature in the 20th century, such as the cut-up poems of Tristan Tzara or the rambling narratives of Jack Kerouac.

• Should hypertext narratives be assessed differently from other genres and, if so, how? What criteria should we apply to evaluating this genre?

The reader or critic of a hypertext needs to read carefully and repeatedly in order to explore many of the pathways that the hypertext presents, although even then it may not be possible to exhaust the text. A critical reading of a hypertext should appreciate the potential of the text to generate diverse meanings. The author of a hypertext is writing not one narrative, but a family of narratives, and the critic needs to evaluate what that family of narratives has to offer both to a single reader who returns repeatedly to the text, and to different readers at different times.

• What do you think the future of hypertext narratives will be? What format might it take in ten years' time?

We have been talking about the 'classic' hypertext narrative that consists of text and links. In fact, that classic form is no longer widely practised. New forms of digital literature have supplanted hypertext. E-literature, as it is called, often consists of

Figure 4.9 Jay Bolter.

Key terms

Morph The process in which a word or image changes into something else (usually expressed as a verb).

Wiki Website or software constructed to promote collaborative writing and editing.

Further resources

For more information on the origins and structure of Wikipedia check out its own entry on itself here: http://en.wikipedia.org/wiki/Wikipedia

Sterne's *Tristram Shandy* is seen as the first text in English to be truly experimental. To read the whole book online, as well as read critical texts on Sterne's novel, go to this website first: http://www.tristramshandyweb.it/

dynamic forms of text that morph and change before the reader's eyes, sometimes in response to the reader's actions. This form of literature reminds us of the experimental visual poetry of the 20th century (such as concrete poetry), except that concrete poetry remained static on the page. Beyond E-literature, there are a variety of popular forms and genres that suggest the future of digital literature. Some videogames have the quality of interactive narrative, inserting the player into a story as he plays. Collaborative forms of writing using blogs or wikis are increasingly popular alternatives to traditional fiction. Furthermore, mobile phones now can present text and images and determine their own location. Mobile technology presents the opportunity for new kinds of narrative based on the writer's and reader's current location in the world. Writing practices are changing as these new technologies develop, and new forms of narrative are sure to follow.

Electronic literature

Perhaps the most frequently used reference website on the Internet is Wikipedia. Although it is overseen by a team of editors, its articles – over 16 million at the time of writing – are submitted by its users. Again, there is no conventional 'author' of this reference work but Wikipedia's easy access, as well as its relatively high levels of accuracy, suggests that collaborative texts on this scale are not only accepted by millions of people, but trusted to some degree as well. In *Here Comes Everybody* (2008) Clay Shirky argues that 'cooperation creates group identity … [and] the litmus test for collaborative production is simple: no one person can take credit for what gets created, and the project could not come into being without the participation of many.' But this presents inherent problems: namely, that agreeing something with a group is more difficult than agreeing something yourself (democracy takes more work than dictatorship). And there is another question to ask: what is to be gained by becoming involved in writing a story on a website such as http://storymash.com? The literature produced is not going to be intrinsically better than literature produced by one writer: indeed, some would argue that it could be considerably worse because it has no coherence. Such issues would have to be addressed in any presentation on this subject.

Hypertext fiction is a sub-genre of electronic literature which is rapidly growing in popularity on the Internet: as with Jay David Bolter's book, the reader is able to move from one link to another within the text, arranging the story as he or she wishes. This non-linear structure has its forebears in novels such as *Finnegans Wake* (1939) by James Joyce and *The Life and Opinions of Tristram Shandy* (1759) by Laurence Sterne: both writers subverted a conventional structure in favour of a narrative which 'jumps' back and forth across characters, perspectives and narratives.

Activity 4.15

If you are a member of a social networking site you can create a text and ask your friends to contribute to its ongoing composition: it's a good idea to set some parameters to stay within so that the content does not cause unnecessary offence. Set everyone a time limit, for example one week, and see where the narrative goes. You can then use this text as a resource for your presentation on hypertext narratives.

Of course people have worked together in the past to create art – be they musicians, artists or writers – but what is different about this relatively new genre is that the creative partnerships can be very extensive, and they very often consist of people who have never met together and have no shared or coherent sense of where the narrative will go.

In 2009 the Royal Opera House in London staged an opera which had its story (libretto) written on the microblogging site Twitter by the site's users. The story begins 'One morning, very early, a man and a woman were standing, arm-in-arm, in London's Covent Garden. The man turned to the woman and he sang …' and the rest of the libretto was then composed entirely of 'tweets' (the 140 character microblogs which make up a Twitter entry). The opera was performed live by two singers who had set the words to familiar songs, and it received good reviews.

Activity 4.16
Preparing a presentation
Write a short presentation on hypertext narratives. You could use one of these titles:
- Hypertext literature is the future of writing.
  Or
- Hypertext literature dilutes the writer's voice, rather than strengthens it.
  Or
- Hypertext literature is a genuinely new form of communication which defies categorisation and criticism.
  Or
- Hypertext literature has yet to produce one work that could be classed as a classic: until it does so it should not be taken seriously.
  Or
- Hypertext literature makes the individual a co-author: in that sense it liberates the imagination and engages the reader.

There is a key question to ask yourself before you decide to research hypertext literature: 'How well will I be able to prepare myself in this new area so that I am assessed using each of the three criteria?' The criteria used are:

Criterion A	*Knowledge and understanding of the work(s)* How much do you know about this new and rapidly developing genre? Which texts will you study? How reputable are they? Do they constitute good literature? Is there a body of secondary texts on them as there are for the other options?	10 marks
Criterion B	*Presentation* Will your presentation be able to exemplify the material you are talking about effectively? Will the medium be solely available on the Internet? If so, can this be adequately conveyed to your class and teacher? How will you structure your presentation? What is your argument?	10 marks
Criterion C	*Language* Are the texts you are presenting on sufficiently literary to require a literary analysis? Does this genre have its own specialist nomenclature? What is it?	10 marks
Total		**30 marks**

Further resources

For more information on hypertext fiction, check: http://en.wikipedia.org/wiki/Hypertext_fiction

If you're interested in the Royal Opera project go to http://twitter.com/youropera. You may be interested in how Twitter is inspiring new forms of communication and art: for example, http://twaggies.com turns tweets into 'graphic texts' or visuals. You could also go to the Electronic Literature Organisation's website: http://www.eliterature.org/

tip

Remember that you must use examples from legitimate sources in the real presentation: you should show these to your teacher and make a record of the exact website address, and the date you accessed it, before preparing your presentation.

TOK

Remember that film occupies a very different space within society from literature: it is often more highly visible and available in a number of different ways (DVD, download, Internet, television, as well as cinema). You should be aware of this position, as well as the social responsibility a film maker may have within society.

Does the film maker have any ethical responsibility? Do they ever change?

If you can answer these questions to your – and your teacher's – satisfaction then you are well on the way to giving a fascinating and perhaps even ground-breaking presentation. It is not a conventional option, but it could be one well worth taking: indeed, it could lead you into a field of technical and imaginative creativity that you may well want to develop an interest in beyond your Diploma studies.

Unit 4.5 **The 'literature and film' option**

We all love watching films, and many students are attracted to this option for that reason alone. But there are some important things to remember before you decide:

1 You should see yourself as a proactive critic of film, just as you are a serious student of literature. You will not do well in this option if the passive viewing habits that many of us adopt when we relax to watch a film are applied in your preparation for this presentation.

2 Secondly: as with each of the four options available it is important to remember that the focus for your presentation must remain with the *literary* element of the work, or works, you have researched. If there is a printed work available which you can use to help your understanding of the film then this will be acceptable.

The following activities will help you to understand the kinds of questions you will have to address before you begin to focus on a particular task. Although general in nature, these questions are important, and you should hope to address them – in relation to the films you are presenting on – in your final presentation.

Activity 4.17

Answer the following general questions about film; you could do this with a classmate, or in a group. These should act as preliminary notes for your presentation.

1 What is the function of film? Is it to:
   • entertain?
   • teach and educate?
   • represent reality?
   • create art?
   • make money?

For each answer you should be able to say more than 'yes' or 'no': support your answers with evidence from films you know. In preparing for a presentation on literature and film it would benefit you to write notes on each one as it is very likely that questions of this nature will arise after your presentation. It pays to research now.

2 What is the function of a literary adaptation? Is it to:
   • attract new audiences to the original text?
   • remain absolutely faithful to the original text?
   • modernise and make more accessible the original text?
   • make something entirely new from the original text?

Again, try to go beyond simple 'yes' or 'no' answers: if you feel that these questions are too difficult it may well be worth considering doing a presentation from one of the other options offered. Having said that, take time to consider them, and to reflect on what you have learned so far; it may also benefit you to talk to a classmate about these questions.

3   Who made this film? Why? What does this film tell us about the film maker's agenda?

4   Who did the film maker make the film for? How would you characterise its audience?

5   What outside influences are there? Does the company who made it impose its identity on it? Are there social, historical, political and cultural influences to be discerned in the film?

6   What tradition is it from? Just as you might find it essential to understand the conventions governing a certain literary text you are studying, you will also find it constructive to understand what tradition of film making your chosen film can be placed in (film noir? thriller? Bollywood? Ealing comedy?).

How do you bring the subject into focus?

In this option it would be tempting to give a presentation on a favourite film, or the work of a favourite film director, but this could be misguided. For example, one student was particularly interested in the films of the British film director David Lean. Originally he wanted the title of his presentation to be entitled 'Intercultural perceptions: the film making of David Lean'. In itself this sounds like a fascinating subject. Lean made classic 'British' films such as *Great Expectations* and *In Which We Serve*, but he also made films which were very international in perspective, such as *Lawrence of Arabia* and *A Passage to India*. However, even these films involve a very pronounced British perspective, and looking at this would be fascinating. The student's teacher, however, advised him against this for several reasons:

• Above anything else it is not literary enough: the focus has to be on how a film maker translates a book to the screen.

• It is not focused enough: the subject itself needs to be more clearly defined.

• It is too broad: Lean was a prolific film maker and there would be too much to pack in to the time allocated: which specific films would be referenced?

The student listened to the teacher's advice and returned with a different idea for a presentation on David Lean: '*Great Expectations*: from page to screen.' The student's teacher thought this was much better: there was a clear literary focus and, in restricting himself to a comparative analysis between one text and one film there seemed a much better chance of making an intelligent use of the allocated time for the presentation. It was not too ambitious, but it had enough depth to merit serious research.

However, the student submitted a third version of his title to his teacher: 'From page to screen: an analysis of David Lean's adaptation of Dickens's *Great Expectations*'. Because there have been so many film adaptations of Dickens's novel it was felt appropriate to clarify exactly which one was being assessed. The title also announces itself as an analysis, and although it may sound unnecessary by including the name of the author and the book the student makes the point very clearly that the presentation will be essentially literary in its emphasis.

Analysing a novel can be daunting enough, but analysing a complex film adaptation of that book as well might seem even more challenging, and then trying to squeeze everything into a short presentation might seem impossible. There are some things to keep in mind:

- You will not be able to cover everything, so keep your subject focused.
- You will be assessed using criteria that are matched to the task: it is understood that it is only possible to cover a certain amount of material in the time you have.
- You are capable of scoring very highly in this option, and, indeed, it could be a task that you enjoy doing and from which you gain a great deal.

How do you plan a presentation on literature and film?

Know and understand the book (and understand how it is different from the film adaptation): this may seem obvious, but it goes beyond simply knowing what happens and to whom. You should have a clear understanding of the following. The list is by no means exhaustive, but you should be able to decide, after reading it, whether you are suited to this sort of presentation. Many students are – and in fact it is one of the most popular options – so think carefully about each piece of advice.

- The plot: this means that you know the story and also the order of events. You should also be able to distinguish what happens in the book from what happens in the film – and when. Often they are not the same.
- The setting: you should not only know where the book is set geographically, but also its historical and social setting, and you should be able to talk about how the setting affects the development of the plot, the characters, and the main themes. Film makers often update the setting to make it more relevant to a modern audience, but how does this affect our interpretation of other elements of the book?
- The characters: you should have a very strong understanding of how the characters are represented in the book: in what ways has the writer developed a character? Remember, a writer can describe a character in a way that a film maker simply cannot so how does a film maker compensate for this?
- The themes: what are the most important themes in the book and are they developed or diluted by the film maker? How? Does the film maker sacrifice key themes for certain reasons? What factors might have influenced these changes?
- The technique: you have to understand the writer's technique before you can comfortably present a comparative analysis of the film adaptation. For instance, the writer's voice may be very distinctive in the text but this could be lost on the screen; if this is the case, what other elements are lost? Does the film maker attempt to compensate for this in another way, for example, by using a voiceover?

Key term

Voiceover The overplaying of a narrative voice in a film, often used to express a character's thoughts, or to summarise plot development.

You should also ask yourself the following questions before you begin to research a comparative analysis: **Why is this book considered suitable for adaptation? What cinematic qualities does it have**? In answering these you may wish to consider several factors:

- Have the themes the text explores retained their university and accessibility?
- Has the text remained popular and does it still appeal to a wide audience?
- Is the plot interesting and will it keep people watching?

- Are the characters strong and will they engage the audience?
- Is the setting suited to the cinema?

Making a film, unlike writing a novel (even a hypertext narrative) involves a lot of people and a significant amount of money, and any company that is looking to invest in adapting a text will have to be convinced that there is an audience for the film; of course, if the text has been popular then there is less of a risk than if the text has been relatively obscure.

When we analyse a text we are used to looking for certain elements which deepen our understanding and appreciation of the writer's aims: we explore the language, looking at the use of figurative language (including symbols, metaphors and similes), but this essentially linguistic process is denied us in film. However, if we think of film as another text – like a hypertext narrative or a graphic novel – we can begin to read it, albeit in a different way. We can, using different words and criteria, draw out meaning from frames and sequences.

Activity 4.18

Preliminary research

Look at the following frame taken from David Lean's adaptation of Charles Dickens's *Great Expectations*:

Symbolism of candles? Life and death? Transience?

Symbolism of cobwebs? Death? Being entrapped?

Light and darkness interplay here: is this symbolic?

Formal dress: what does this convey? Is it significant?

Use of facial expressions; position of figures: what does this tell us about their relationships?

Figure 4.10 A scene from David Lean's film *Great Expectations* (1946).

What do you think the film maker is conveying? We have to put this into context: this scene only lasts a matter of minutes, and this shot a couple of seconds, but, even so, it can be analysed as much as a written text can.

Some general questions to apply to single frames:

1   Why is it composed like this? Is there any significance to how the characters are positioned?
    In this shot the adult – Miss Havisham – is at the centre of the frame and both she and the young boy (Pip) are observing the other character (Estella) who is on the margins of the shot. Look at the positioning of Miss Havisham's and Pip's heads: they clearly seem to be talking about Estella, and Estella in turn seems unperturbed by this: she meets their gaze. The centrality of Miss Havisham suggests that she is at the heart of the narrative.

2   Why is the camera placed in this way?
    All the characters are included, but so, too, are other elements in the scene: the cobwebs, the candles, the furniture. The camera is placed not only to focus on the characters and their relationships, but also to establish their relationship within their setting.

3   Is symbolism used?
    Dress is very important and if you know the text you will know why the characters are dressed in this way (Miss Havisham's dress is very significant of course, but status is also conveyed in Pip's and Estella's dress); but even if you do not know Dickens's novel you should be able to see that the film maker has included symbols of life and death and entrapment (the candles and the cobwebs); the film was made before colour was extensively used but, even so, this is a scene that has a strong interplay between light and dark, and this further emphasises the conflict between life and death.

What questions should you ask about films?

By analysing literature we draw out an author's meaning, but the way in which this meaning can be conveyed by the author can be endlessly rich, ambiguous and open to different interpretations. A film maker loses the subtlety of expression that is available to a writer and one of the biggest challenges to anyone who has to adapt a text to the screen is how to retain the meaning. The scriptwriter will play a part in this, of course, as will set designers, cameramen, sound and light technicians, and other members of the team. But the director will have the ultimate say in which shots best convey the film main themes.

Activity 4.19

Further research

Find an important episode in the text you are studying for Part 4 of the course; now find a film adaptation of that scene (ideally lasting about 5 minutes). Read the extract in the text twice. Now look at the film adaptation. Play it through three times: in the first viewing simply watch it with the sound turned off; in the second viewing just listen to it (close your eyes, or turn the brightness down); in the third viewing watch it with sound and vision restored. Now answer the following questions (spend about 5 minutes on this):

- What is the writer's intention in this scene and how is it conveyed?
- What is the film maker's intention in this scene and how is it conveyed?
- What role does the soundtrack play in this scene?
- What role do the camera angles play in this scene?

Film makers use key shots to create meaning. Here is a list of key shots: read them through and then look again at your chosen scene and write notes on how the film maker has conveyed meaning using specific shots.

Shot	Effect
Extreme long shot	Used for views of landscapes, buildings, seascapes. It may also be a point of view shot by a particular character.
Long shot	A character is shown in the distance; the effect is to place that character into context, and for the surroundings to dominate our perception of that character.
Medium shot	The character is shown from the waist up: the audience will be able to see facial expressions, but also the background.
Close-up	Head and shoulders shot. Little background visible here: the audience focuses on the character's emotional response.
Extreme close-up	Used to show an important detail, moment or gesture.
High-angle shot	Used to convey the impression that a character is being watched; sometimes used to make the character appear less important.
Low-angle shot	Used to exaggerate the size of someone: for example, it may be employed as a point-of-view shot from a child looking up to a parent.

In addition, consider whether the camera is fixed or handheld. The latter technique has become increasingly popular with film makers and is often used to convey a certain character's point of view: for example, horror film fans are very used to seeing a victim being stalked from the attacker's point of view – the camera is shaky and mimics the attacker's perspective.

Each of these camera angles can convey meaning, but it is important to understand that just as these are conventions, a film maker can also subvert our expectations. The important point here is to think about each camera angle. Always ask yourself. 'Why is this happening?' Remember: don't be a passive viewer; instead, engage with the film critically, just as you would with a great work of literature.

There are many resources available online and in books, magazines and DVDs, and they will provide you with specific information on the making of certain films. But there are general considerations beyond framing and camera angles to keep in mind as you begin your preliminary research on this topic:

1   **Editing**: are there any transitional points which stand out? Has the film maker cut sharply from scene to scene, or do the scenes dissolve into each other? What's the difference? What effect does the one have over the other? How long is each shot held on screen? Some modern films have shots which last no longer than four seconds, whereas others may last considerably longer than this: why? How does this affect our interpretation of what we see? If appropriate, does it depart a great deal from the chapter breaks in the original text?

TOK

Consider some of these questions in relation to the films you are presenting on:

- What moral responsibilities does a film maker have to his or her audience?

- What is the function of film?

2   **Lighting**: is there anything significant about the lighting? How does the lighting affect the mood? Does a protracted use of shade create a gloomy atmosphere? Does much of the film take place in sunlight or artificial light?

3   **Dialogue**: look beyond what the characters say (although of course this is very important) and think about *how* they say it. Think about the clarity of their enunciation, the use of accent, colloquial or slang expressions. Do the characters ever talk directly to the audience (usually as a voiceover)? To themselves? To only one character?

4   **Sound effects**: we usually think of these as accompanying spectacular moments in the film, but they can also be subtle (a child crying, footsteps outside, rain falling). How do they affect your perception of a scene?

5   **Visual effects**: as with sound effects. We tend to think of spectacular effects, or CGI effects. But look for more subtle visual effects here, and ask how they enhance a scene.

6   **Music**: this is one of the chief ways a film maker can manipulate our emotions. Think carefully about the use of music in any film adaptation you are working with: what mood is the film maker trying to create with the music being used? How does this correspond with – or depart from – the original intentions of the writer?

7   **Setting**: how does this influence your understanding of the film? Does it remain faithful to the writer's own setting? How does it differ? What is lost as a result?

8   **Costume**: how does the way the characters are dressed influence our reaction to them? Is it period dress (in other words in keeping with the historical setting)? How is status conveyed through costume?

Activity 4.20

The presentation

Using the notes you have assembled from the previous activities in this unit, write a presentation on one of the following subjects. Because of the range of texts and films available these titles are generic, and can be adapted to your own choices. Remember these five important points:

1   The literary text is the primary focus for your presentation.
2   The film adaptation is the secondary focus for your presentation.
3   You have to be comparative in your analysis: explain how the film maker has adapted the text for the screen.
4   Always support your points with evidence from the text and the film.
5   Remember to keep asking yourself: 'How do I know this to be true?' Explain yourself clearly.

Suggested titles for presentations:
- Purity and dilution: how film making lessens the impact of all literary texts.
- Popularising the message: how film making widens the understanding of literary texts through adaptation.
- The lost voice: authorial absence in film making.
- Bringing new meaning to old texts: how film introduces new ideas to familiar texts.
- The importance of setting in texts and films.
- The creation of melancholy in texts and films.

- The eternal sunshine of humour and optimism in texts and films.
- The central protagonist in texts and films.
- Secondary characters in texts and films.
- The representation of evil in texts and films.
- There representation of femininity in texts and films.
- There representation of masculinity in texts and films.

More questions on the presentation

How many texts can I do the presentation on?

You can do it on one, two or three texts. Many students find it rewarding to compare and contrast two texts, but this is a personal choice (taken in consultation with the teacher). Comparing and contrasting three texts, given the time limitations, can be challenging, but making references to all the texts you have studied can strengthen a presentation.

Can I re-do the presentation if I make a mistake?

If you make a minor mistake in your presentation you should just carry on (and even acknowledge it): such things happen and you won't be penalised. Remember, though, that the presentation should be treated like an examination: you only have one go at it so make sure you prepare for it and do as well as you can on the day. Having said that, if you are ill, or there are other special circumstances, then your teacher can reschedule; once the presentation has been done, however, it cannot be attempted again.

If I can only do it once, how should I prepare for it?

Your teacher can allow your class to do 'trial' presentations on topics not chosen by students; another possibility is to do the presentation on texts from other parts of the course (for example, a text for Paper 2).

What do I do if I have no idea what to do for my presentation?

This rarely happens, but remember to take notes from the moment you start studying your texts; talk to your teacher, and discuss themes and ideas with your classmates. You will find a topic eventually: the challenge will be to get it sufficiently focused for the presentation.

Can I do my presentation on a favourite film?

You have to have a written source – such as a film script – to work from so that you can discuss the process of adaptation.

What do I do if I don't like speaking in public?

Lots of students feel the same way, but try to think of this as a process which allows you the opportunity to overcome this difficulty: you will find that your audience is really supportive. You should also talk to your teacher who will have various practical strategies and suggestions which will help. See this as a challenge that you are determined to meet.

What do I do if another classmate wants to do his presentation on exactly the same topic as mine?

This happens occasionally, and you should talk to each other and to your teacher. Here's a real example: two students wanted to do presentations on the representation of femininity in Joseph Conrad's *Heart of Darkness*. After consultation with the teacher it was agreed that this area was too vague: one student decided to do hers on 'Women as figures of mystery in *Heart of Darkness*' and the other student decided to focus on

'Misogyny and masculinity in *Heart of Darkness'*. Both were able to discuss the role of women in this work, but both considered different areas and put forward different arguments.

What if I completely freeze and my mind goes blank?
If you think this might happen, prepare for this in advance: you are allowed to take prompts – or short notes – into the presentation, and you're also allowed to use carefully chosen slides (or other methods of displaying information) to support your analysis. Some more advice: take the presentation seriously.

What if I go over my time?
Practise your presentation out of class and time it: if it is too long, try to cut it down. Your teacher should give you a warning of the time you have left, but try to avoid using up every last minute: nobody likes being rushed, so pace yourself accordingly, making sure that your main points are carefully explained.

Can I do my presentation with a friend?
You can certainly prepare for it with a friend (or friends) and, you can do it in groups (or a pair), but your teacher has to be able to assess you individually according to the criteria, and so you have to be speaking for enough time to allow this to happen. If you do your presentation in a group, but only speak for 3 minutes, then you will be assessed on that time, and, obviously, this will not advantage you.

How serious should I be?
Students sometimes find it difficult to adopt a suitably serious style of delivery when presenting to class: when they see their best friends in front of them some giggle, or speak too quickly (or too slowly), whilst others talk in a very casual way (as they might do with those friends out of class). This is understandable, but you will be marked down if you do this (Criteria B and C). Your teacher is partly responsible for establishing the appropriate atmosphere in the class, but so too are the students. Take it as seriously as a written examination in an examination hall: it's your qualification. The same goes when you are listening to others giving their presentations: listen to them as you would like to be listened to, don't try to put them off, and ask them relevant and informed questions once they have finished. If a mutually supportive atmosphere is established then everyone will benefit. Be sure to play your part in doing this.

Finally, when you are giving a presentation, remember:
• Maintain eye contact with your audience: only *refer* to notes.
• Highlight key words and phrases to make your glances to notes quick and effective.
• Think about your body language: remain calm and as still as you can, as this will be less distracting for your audience and will keep you calmer too.
• If you find that you don't know what to do with your hands, hold a pen, or a prompter for moving your presentation slides on.

- You may feel nervous, but that nervousness is not always noticeable to your audience. This is known as the 'illusion of transparency': you feel you are transparent, and that the audience can see your heart beating, or notice a nervousness in your voice ... but very often they can't see any of this.
- Make your voice interesting: go up at sentences when you are asking a question, and down to emphasise a point.
- Practise in front of others.
- Record yourself and listen to yourself.
- Be self-reflective and, where necessary, self-critical. You will improve by being honest about where you lose an audience.

You have to engage an audience: speaking in a monotone voice, and talking to the floor, will immediately distance you from those listening, regardless of the material you are talking about. Be aware of this as you prepare.

Chapter 4 summary

In the course of this chapter, we hope that you have:

- understood what you will study in Part 4 of the course and how it is assessed
- understood not only the different requirements for each of the four options, but also how they link with other parts of the English Literature course
- acquired a clear understanding of the importance of approaching each option from a literary perspective
- looked at a number of extracts and responded to them analytically
- developed a range of strategies to plan, prepare and deliver a successful presentation.

This part of the course is perhaps the most varied of all: the media you can study ranges from established (such as the essay) to emerging forms of creativity (such as the hypertext narrative); you are also able to analyse visual media such as the graphic novel and film. Whatever the choice for your presentation, you should have little difficulty finding something that interests and excites you.

Remember to be open-minded, inquisitive and a risk-taker; also remember to be well prepared and, importantly, to know and understand the texts and the genres they are shaped by. With enough preparation, and by approaching each task from a literary angle, you should enjoy this part of the course a great deal. You have the freedom to really stretch yourself here: make the most of it!

5 Paper 1: Commentary

This chapter follows the shape of Paper 1. At the end of your course you will take an unseen literary analysis (sometimes known as a commentary) examination. For SL students it is entitled the guided literary analysis, and for HL students this paper is entitled the literary commentary. As these titles suggests, you cannot 'revise' for this paper by getting to know the texts because you will be assessed on texts you have never seen before. This paper tests the skills and knowledge you will develop throughout your two-year study of literature; how you prepare for it before the exam, together with how you plan your answer in the exam itself, will be crucial to your success.

In Paper 1 you will write a commentary on unseen poetry or prose. This chapter will prepare you to do this and is divided into three units. Unit 5.1 aims to give you an overview of the course and the skills you will need to write a successful essay in the examination. Units 5.2 and 5.3 deal with poetry and prose respectively. Unit 5.3 covers both fiction and non-fiction texts. The exam itself will include both a prose extract and a poetry extract; you will choose which one to write about.

Unit 5.1 **What is Paper 1: Commentary?**

It is important to understand what you will need to be able to do in this exam so, firstly, let's look at how you will be assessed for Paper 1: Commentary. You should pay particular attention to the differences between SL and HL:

Standard Level		Higher Level	
Paper 1 (1.5 hours) Analysis of one unseen text in response to guiding questions	Worth 20%	**Paper 1 (2 hours)** Literary commentary on of one unseen text	Worth 20% of your final mark

There are four assessment criteria for SL and HL:

Criterion A	*Understanding and interpretation* How well does your interpretation show an understanding of the ideas behind the passage? How successfully are your ideas supported by references to the passage?	5 marks

Criterion B	*Appreciation of the writer's choices* To what extent do your ideas show an appreciation of the writer's choices of language, style, technique and structure?	5 marks
Criterion C	*Organisation (and development at HL only)* How well organised is your answer? How coherent is your presentation of your ideas?	5 marks
Criterion D	*Language* Is your language clear and precise? Is your register, style and your use of terminology appropriate?	5 marks
Total		**20 marks**

What do you need to do to prepare for this exam?

When you open the exam paper you will find two sections: one will contain a poetry extract, one a prose extract. You will need to choose which one you write on. This chapter will support you in making that choice and in writing effectively about poetry and prose so that you can keep your options open.

Before you start to write, remember:

- Read each text on the paper carefully: making the right choice is crucial.
- Ask yourself: 'Does the poem have greater complexity of language than the prose piece?' If so, perhaps you should choose the poem.
- Once you have chosen which piece you will write on, work through the text and mark it up. Think carefully about the effect of the language. Remember that you should always try to analyse; don't just describe.
- When you are planning your answer you should be thinking about an argument: what are the main points you are going to make about this text? Have you got five or six key ideas that you can expand upon? At SL you should be marking up and planning for at least 15 minutes; at HL you should mark up and plan for at least 20 minutes.

What do you need to remember when writing the essay?

In your English Literature course 70% of your marks will come from the essays you will write. It is important, therefore, that you understand the key features of essay writing. The following advice applies to virtually every English essay you will write (and may help your essay writing in other subjects too). When writing the essay, remember – the 'little things' really do matter:

- Use the writer's surname.
- Write about literature in the present tense.
- Use formal, precise language: aim to say something sophisticated but express it very simply.
- Use the correct terminology for the text you are writing about. You need to be clear about the differences between prose and poetry and use the correct technical vocabulary for each.

Look again at the guidance on writing essays that you will find in Unit 1.4, on pages 28–9 in Chapter 1. It is important that you remember this advice about essay writing as you work through the rest of this chapter. Some of the activities will ask you to write your own essays in response to poetry and prose texts, as you will have to do this in the exam.

Figure 5.1 A marked-up book with handwritten Chinese translations.

Unit 5.2 Poetry

Why choose the poem in Paper 1: Commentary?

There are many good reasons to choose to write your commentary on a poem. Indeed, poetry is often an excellent choice in a Paper 1: Commentary exam. Poets tend to use language in heightened and carefully crafted ways which can make it easier for you to interpret (Criterion A) and to show appreciation of the ways in which the writer's choices shape meaning (Criterion B). However, you should always make an informed choice on the day of the examination.

In order to write an effective commentary on a poem, you need to recognise that writers make very careful choices about the language they use, about the form and about the structure of their poems. If you can write with accuracy and clarity about these choices and show effectively how and why the poet makes them, then you will produce an impressive commentary.

One of the tools you will need to help you to write about poetry is a knowledge of literary terms and features. One obvious set of choices a writer makes is when, how and why they use features such as alliteration, metaphor and rhyme, amongst many others. However, whilst effective commentaries might be able to pick out a range of literary features from a poem, the best will go on to interpret the ways in which the poet chooses to use them. Equally, whilst convincing commentaries may identify interesting uses of language, the best will go on to show how and why the poet uses particular forms and structures.

We will look at literary features specifically in the first text and show you how you might go about identifying and analysing these features in the Paper 1: Commentary exam. It is worth remembering that to score highly in Paper 1: Commentary you should know the four assessment criteria you are being marked against. Here they are again:

	Summary of description	Marks available
Criterion A	*Understanding and interpretation* How well do you understand the poem? Do you get its basic sense? How effectively have you interpreted its meaning?	5

Criterion B	*Appreciation of the writer's choices* How does the writer's choice of language and linguistic techniques influence our reading of the poem? How do the structure and the form the poet has chosen affect our understanding of the poem?	5
Criterion C	*Organisation* Is your essay well organised? Does it have a clear opening, development and conclusion?	5
Criterion D	*Language* Are your language choices accurate? Do you use appropriate literary terms effectively (and correctly)? Is the tone appropriate?	5
Total		**20**

How should you approach the poem in the exam?

Firstly, you need to read the poem carefully a number of times and mark it up. When you are doing this you might work through these stages:

- **Mark up**: this can take whatever form you feel comfortable with – coloured pencils, circling, etc.
- **Reflect on the poem's title**: circle the title and draw a quick 'map' of the various ideas the poem suggests to you. Underline the words in the poem you think are likely to prove interesting or important. The title is our first way in: how does the writer use it?
- **Summarise the basic sense of the poem**: who is speaking (who is the narrator)? To whom? About what? For what purpose? When and/or where (if relevant)? And how (tone)? *in intro paragraph*
- **Paraphrase any problematic lines or sentences**: a 'problematic line' could present an opportunity for exploring ambiguity. An ambiguous word or line is one that has more than one possible meaning or whose meaning is not immediately obvious. Don't ignore words and lines that are ambiguous; often they hold an important key to understanding the poem.
- **Paraphrase any key words or phases**: some poems written in a modern idiom don't require much paraphrasing; other poems may require more. An important part of the process is to analyse with precision the exact meaning of key words: verbs, for example, act as 'hinges' of meaning.
- **Note the poet's use of language**: remember that the basic building blocks are words. How would you assess the poem's **diction** overall? Is the poem's language formal or casual? Does it have **jargon** and **slang**? Why? Is it more concrete, or abstract? Precise or ambiguous? How does tone appear as a function of diction? How does the poet manipulate syntax (sentence structure)? Why?
- **Map the poem's tensions and contrasts**: you will often find many oppositions and tensions, and many poets use contrasts of various sorts with which they 'move' the poem's meaning. It has been said that poetry is 'moment, movement, and meaning'; in other words, a poem establishes a moment, or an occasion, an issue, an image, a dilemma, a voice, and then moves from this initial state. The overall effect of that movement on the reader indicates or otherwise suggests the poem's meaning. Tensions and oppositions may come in the form of contrasts between:
  - o speaker and situation
  - o reader's view and speaker's view
  - o sides of a dilemma or problem

o sets of images
o past and present
o levels of diction, even before form and content.

- Often, **irony** is present in some form or another. Identify any uses of an ironic voice within the poem (remember that irony is when your intended meaning is the opposite of what you actually say).

- **Scan the poem for structure**: is there a rhyme scheme? What other rhythmic features are present? Look for half rhymes. Identify traditional patterns (fixed forms such as sonnet, ballad) that are defined, in part, by rhyme. Remember: poets writing in closed form craft their own structures which they then adhere to.

- **Interpret**: be clear from the start of your response how you interpret the poem; don't withhold your interpretation until the last paragraph.

We will now look at a number of different poems; you should aim to keep in mind the points above when looking at any poem or text for the first time.

Figure 5.2 The British poet Ted Hughes, 1930–1998.

Text 5.1 *Wind*, Ted Hughes, 1962

The first example here is a poem by the British poet Ted Hughes (1930–98) called 'Wind'. Ted Hughes, who was Britain's Poet Laureate from 1984 until his death, and was also married to the American poet Sylvia Plath, often wrote about the power and beauty of the natural world.

We will look at how you might approach this poem by identifying and writing about a number of obvious literary features. Even before you read the poem you should notice key features of the writer's choices. For instance, before you read the first word of 'Wind' you will notice that the poet has chosen to organise his poem into six stanzas of four lines each. This is an important choice, and something we will return to when we think about how Hughes presents the passage of time in his poem.

The mark-ups here do one simple thing: they point out some of the examples of literary techniques Hughes uses. In your commentary, it is not enough merely to list features – you will need to organise your analysis into a clear thesis or argument – but this can be a useful way to start. Don't worry if some of the key terms included here are unfamiliar: they will be explained immediately after the poem.

Wind

This house has been far out at sea[1] all night,[2]
The woods crashing[3] through darkness, the booming[4] hills,
Winds stampeding[5] the fields under the window
Floundering black astride and blinding wet[6]

Till day rose;[7] then under an orange sky   5
The hills had new places, and wind wielded[8]
Blade-light, luminous black and emerald,
Flexing like the lens of a mad eye.[9]

At noon[10] I scaled along the house-side as far as
The coal-house door.[11] Once I looked up –   10
Through the brunt wind that dented the balls of my eyes
The tent of the hills drummed and strained its guyrope,[12]

1	Metaphorical language
2	Time
3	Onomatopoeia
4	Onomatopoeia
5	Anthropomorphism
6	Enjambement
7	Time
8	Alliteration
9	Simile
10	Time
11	Caesura
12	Metaphor

The fields quivering, the skyline a grimace,
At any second to bang and vanish with a flap;
The wind flung[13] a magpie away and a black-   **15**
Back gull bent like an iron bar slowly.[14] The house

Rang like some fine green goblet in the note
That any second would shatter it.[15] Now deep
In chairs, in front of the great fire, we grip
Our hearts and cannot entertain book, thought,   **20**

Or each other.[16] We watch the fire blazing,
And feel the roots of the house move, but sit on,
Seeing the window tremble[17] to come in,
Hearing the stones cry out[18] under the horizons.

13	Anthropomorphism
14	Simile
15	Simile
16	Enjambement
17	Anthropomorphism
18	Anthropomorphism

The mark-up on this poem draws attention to several key features the writer has used; you could point out many more. However, in order to write well about these, it is important to remember that you're not just pointing them out, but showing *how* and *why* you think the writer uses them. In the next section we explain some of the features the poet uses here and suggest ways in which you might interpret them. You need to understand how the features work and then provide a convincing analysis of how and why the writer uses them. Remember that when you write your commentary you will need to organise these ideas carefully into a structure that responds to a clear thesis which you will set out in the first paragraph of your essay.

How do you write effectively about the features the writer uses?

The title
Too often, students fail to pick up on some of the most obvious and interesting clues. It is always worth commenting on the title. Hughes's title is remarkably simple: 'Wind'. His poem is a description of the wind. This is an important starting point.

Time references
You will have noticed that the mark-up draws attention to a time reference in each of the first three stanzas: 'all night' (2); 'Till day rose' (7); 'At noon' (10). It is interesting to note that these references are introduced into consecutive stanzas. There is a fairly basic, but nonetheless important, structural point to be made here about how Hughes is demonstrating how time is passing while the storm continues to rage. He chooses to use consecutive stanzas to represent a new period as we move from the night to morning to midday.

Enjambement
Enjambement just means a run-on line. Because poetry is ordered into lines, the sense or meaning is often completed at the end of a line. However, when the poet makes a choice to run the meaning into the next line (or sometimes – and even more interestingly – the next stanza) then this is something you can identify and analyse. It can be difficult to write convincingly about enjambement; in order to do so, think

tip

Don't be tempted to overcomplicate or over-analyse in an unnecessary way. Don't use long words for the sake of it. Say something clever but say it as clearly and simply as possible.

about what the poet is trying to do. Look at the transition from stanza one to stanza two in this poem. The meaning is carried from one stanza to the next: 'blinding wet/Till day rose'; indeed, there is a slight pause whilst the eye flicks back across and down the page. Time literally passes.

But look back to what we've just noticed about how Hughes is using the stanzas to represent the passing of time. When we remember this, we can write about how the enjambement underlines the sense of time passing slowly and how the storm, like the form of the poem itself, moves without any interference from night to the morning of the next day.

Metaphor

Metaphor is a key element in many literary works. Students tend to be very good at spotting metaphorical language but not so good at writing about how and why the writer is choosing to use it. Perhaps this is because they overlook how metaphor actually works. The word *metaphor* comes from the Greek word meaning 'transfer' or 'carry across'. When we use metaphor we are carrying across a different idea and applying it to the thing we're trying to describe.

So, in the poem *Wind*, Ted Hughes wants to describe a house in a storm. However, he wants the reader to appreciate the house's fragility and the power of the natural world. In order to do this he asks what would create just such an image in his reader's mind, and settles upon the idea of a ship at sea. The metaphor he uses ('This house has been far out at sea all night') forces us, the readers, to hold two ideas in our head at the same time. Firstly, we have the idea of the house and, secondly, the transferred idea of the ship at sea. By carrying across the idea of a ship, Hughes is asking us to associate its qualities (its fragility and smallness in comparison to the power of the sea and the danger it is potentially in) with the house. In this way he transfers this idea and uses metaphor to suggest how the house is delicate and provisional compared to the natural world.

Onomatopoeia

Onomatopoeia is when a word sounds like the action it is describing. If you say the word 'plop' out loud, for instance, you hear exactly the sound that a stone makes on being dropped into water. You will have noticed that Ted Hughes chooses to use two onomatopoeic words in the second line of this poem. He describes the woods as 'crashing' and the hills as 'booming'. You need to ask yourself why he would choose to do this. To answer this question, we need to go back to what he's doing in the poem. This poem is describing the awful power of wind and of the natural world. In order to make that world even more powerful and convincing, Hughes uses onomatopoeia to give an extra dimension to our sensual experience of the poem. The words 'crashing' and 'booming' help to create a vivid soundscape so that the poem comes to life in the ear as well as on the page and in the mind of the reader.

Anthropomorphism

If a poet chooses to apply the qualities of a human being or an animal to something we wouldn't usually expect to have human or animal qualities then this is called **anthropomorphism**. In line 3 of the poem, Hughes describes 'Winds stampeding the fields'. We need to notice Hughes's choice of the verb 'stampeding'. It is an interesting and unusual use of this word. We wouldn't normally describe the wind in these terms. This is usually a term that is used to describe animals, perhaps horses which are out

Key term

Anthropomorphism The attribution of human characteristics to a god, animal or object.

of control. Similarly, in the final two lines of the poem, Hughes describes 'Seeing the window tremble' and 'Hearing the stones cry out'. The verbs 'tremble' and 'cry out' suggest an emotional response and we wouldn't normally expect these to be applied to inanimate or non-human objects such as windows and stones. Hughes chooses to use these techniques because he wants his reader to think of the natural world in human or animal terms: it is out of control and Hughes is also suggesting that it has emotions and that it can trigger the emotional response of fear in other objects.

(creates sympathy sometimes).

Alliteration

In line 6, Ted Hughes uses the phrase: 'wind wielded'. This is an example of alliteration which is where a writer uses words which start with the same letter in the same line. This is a technique that some students are good at spotting but find difficult to say anything convincing about. The answer, as always, lies in thinking about why the writer chose to use these words in this order. Look at the phrase in context; the sense continues: 'Blade-light' perhaps suggesting that the wind has the effect of a knife. It we think about the context of Hughes's presentation of nature, and of wind in particular, as dangerous and threatening, perhaps this helps us to understand why he chooses to use the phrase 'wind wielded'. Can you hear, in the repetition of the 'w' sound, the slicing or cutting motion of a blade?

Simile

The easiest way to think about simile is as a very specific type of metaphor. It works in just the same way as a metaphor but the link between the thing being described and that being 'carried across' is made explicit through the use of the words 'like' or 'as'. Hughes chooses to use a simile in stanza two when he describes the wind as: 'Flexing like the lens of a mad eye'. What idea is being transferred here? The sense is powerfully clear: Hughes is suggesting that the wind is dangerous, out of control and hugely disconcerting – we fear for our safety.

Caesura

A caesura is an obvious break in a line of poetry. Poets sometimes choose to insert a pause into a line. It often has an important or interesting effect. Look at the first two lines of stanza three, for instance: 'At noon I scaled along the house-side as far as/ The coal-house door. Once I looked up'. You will notice the break in the second line where the sentence ends (indicated by the full stop). We need to think about what is happening at this point in the poem. The speaker is walking around the house and has stopped for a moment to look up at the storm. It is the act of stopping that is important: the poet uses the structure of the line to imitate the actions of the speaker. The caesura is that pause or break in the line.

TOK

Do the metaphors we use affect the way in which we think about the world around us? Why is personification a literary feature often associated with creating fear? If you are interested in these ideas you should read George Orwell's 'Politics and the English Language'.

Activity 5.1

You need to practise writing essays as often as possible. If you feel confident enough now, have a go at writing your own essay. Remember that whilst you should refer to literary features throughout, you must not simply list them in an essay. Refer to them to support your main argument or thesis. Perhaps you could find some more poems by Ted Hughes and write essays in response. Have a look at *Hawk roosting* or *The Thought-Fox* (Text 3.24, page 108).

1 The title gives us a hint that the poem is about listening to the radio, but 'tuning in' is also used metaphorically to suggest 'making sense of'.

2 The first word suggests something happening immediately, like the radio being suddenly switched on.

3 The register of the language here is different – the voices from the radio spill into the poem.

4 This clearly picks up on the image of the ship at the start of the line but it also works on a metaphorical level: the 'new mooring' is a new station to tune into.

Key term

Register The level of formality used in a text (defined by the vocabulary and syntax employed).

Text 5.2 *Tuning in*,[1] Moniza Alvi, 1996

Moniza Alvi was born in Pakistan in 1968 and grew up in England. She is particularly interested in writing about issues of identity and belonging. For a long time she was a secondary school teacher; she now lives in London.

Figure 5.3 Moniza Alvi's poem is concerned with communication.

Now[2] for the morning story,
or in the afternoon that tale
of adventurous, practical children.
Ship ahoy![3] Time for a new mooring.[4]

With no special interest in boats
I tune in to the vivid location.
Something disappears on the airwaves.
Tendrils of spring are twining

across the electromagnetic field.
Comedy bubbles up from the archives.
Some of us listen, heads bent
as if in search of a lost item –

until a voice whirls and grips us.
We eat it up like an apple.
We are the indoor people, all ears –
disturbance is detected from afar.

Leaves crackling at the window.
The vibration of tremendous journeys.

TOK

• How is our view of the world shaped by the different media we watch, listen to and read?

• How critical are we of the various biases which may be inherent in these media?

• To what extent does your cultural and/or geographical situation affect the way you read, watch or listen to language?

Activity 5.2

The title and the first stanza of *Tuning in* are marked up for you. After you've read the poem a couple of times, try to mark up the remaining stanzas yourself, remembering to look out for interesting ways in which the writer has used language and structure.

There are many things you could say about the language of the poem. Here are some of the things you might have considered.

• In the penultimate stanza the poet uses an interesting simile when she describes how the listeners to the radio eat up the voices 'like an apple'. On one level this suggests their hunger for more programmes and enjoyment of the pleasure of listening; however, the apple perhaps also suggests temptation (think of the biblical story of the fall and the Garden of Eden): this is also a guilty pleasure.

- The poet makes an interesting use of onomatopoeia: this is a poem about sound – the sound of the radio – and the noises of the radio are represented through the onomatopoeic words 'bubbles', 'whirls' and 'crackling'.
- The poem starts with a first person singular narrator: 'I tune in to the vivid location.' However, by the third stanza, the poet has started to use the first person plural ('us' and 'we'). Perhaps she is showing how, as a listener to the radio, she has become part of a community of listeners. This point is most obviously apparent in the line: 'We are the indoor people'. Here, Alvi associates herself with a whole culture of other listeners who are, nevertheless, experiencing a similar experience, just as we are when we read this poem.

What did you pick out to say about the structure of the poem? Again, there are many things you could say. The following are some ideas which you may already have thought about:

- There is an interesting use of enjambement between stanzas two and three. The sense of the poem moves across the stanza break: 'Tendrils of spring are twining/ across the electromagnetic field.' What is interesting here, though, is that the process of bridging a gap ('twining … across') is represented as bridging the literal gap between the stanzas on the page.
- The final stanza is only two lines long, in contrast to all the other four-line stanzas. This is a structurally interesting decision which the writer has clearly made for effect:
    o The movement into the final stanza is triggered by the word 'afar'.
    o The last stanza is two separate phrases: 'Leaves crackling at the window./The vibration of tremendous journeys.'
    o The movement of the poem's argument takes us from the individual listener to the outside world.
    o The radio is a medium which conveys to us, through sound, knowledge of the wider world.

tip

Always comment on the structure and form of the poem. Good responses analyse the writer's choice of language; the very best responses analyse the writer's choices of structure and form as well as language.

EE **Extended essay**

Compare the ways in which modern poets from a range of different cultural backgrounds explore issues of identity. Look at these web pages to compare two poets:
http://en.wikipedia.org/wiki/Moniza_Alvi
http://en.wikipedia.org/wiki/Sujata_Bhatt
http://www.contemporarywriters.com/

Text 5.3 *A far cry from Africa*,[1] Derek Walcott, 1992

Derek Walcott was born in Saint Lucia, in the Caribbean, in 1930. He is a playwright and poet whose works have often focused on the interplay between myth, culture and a sense of belonging. He was awarded the Nobel Prize in Literature in 1992.

A wind is ruffling the tawny pelt[2]
Of Africa, Kikuyu,[3] quick as flies,
Batten upon the bloodstreams of the veldt.
Corpses are scattered through a paradise.
Only the worm, colonel of carrion,[4] cries: **5**
'Waste no compassion on these separate dead!'[5]
Statistics justify and scholars seize
The salients of colonial policy.
What is that to the white child hacked in bed?
To savages, expendable as Jews?[6]   **10**
Threshed out by beaters, the long rushes break
In a white dust of ibises[7] whose cries
Have wheeled since civilization's dawn
From the parched river or beast-teeming plain.
The violence of beast on beast is read   **15**

1   Think about the ambiguity of the title: 'far cry' means both a call and message from a long way away and, colloquially, simply 'very different from'.
2   An animal skin – why do you think Walcott uses this metaphor?
3   Kenya's most populous ethnic group.
4   Why do you think Walcott uses a military term here?
5   Is this a worm speaking?
6   Why do these questions have so much power?
7   A wading bird found in warm climates.

> 8 Can you explain how 'upright man' might be a clever pun? What are the meanings of 'upright'?
> 9 Why does Walcott introduce a napkin at this point?
> 10 What do you make of all the rhetorical questions at the end of this poem?

As natural law, but upright man[8]
Seeks his divinity by inflicting pain.
Delirious as these worried beasts, his wars
Dance to the tightened carcass of a drum,
While he calls courage still that native dread   20
Of the white peace contracted by the dead.

Again brutish necessity wipes its hands
Upon the napkin[9] of a dirty cause, again
A waste of our compassion, as with Spain,
The gorilla wrestles with the superman.   25
I who am poisoned with the blood of both,
Where shall I turn, divided to the vein?
I who have cursed
The drunken officer of British rule, how choose
Between this Africa and the English tongue I love?   30
Betray them both, or give back what they give?
How can I face such slaughter and be cool?
How can I turn from Africa and live?[10]

Figure 5.4 The Kikuyu people are the largest ethnic group in Kenya.

Activity 5.3

Read text 5.3 *A far cry from Africa*. Make detailed notes and mark up the text as you read the poem. Think about: structure, purpose, place, use of questions and interesting vocabulary choices. You should use the mark-ups and the questions to help you. You should then have the following discussion:

- Who do you think is narrating this poem? What do we learn about them, about their state of mind and about their feelings about the places and events described in the poem?
- What do you make of all the rhetorical questions? Could you use these as a starting point to think about structuring your commentary?
- What do you think the 'message' of this poem is? What is its mood and tone?

Then write an essay in response to the poem in order to practise for the Paper 1: Commentary exam.

Assessment: Sample student response

Now read the following example of a student's analysis of *A far cry from Africa*. Ask yourself how well you think this answer addresses the various assessment criteria. Make sure you have a copy of the criteria in front of you as you read.

- How well does it show a good understanding of the text and how valid is the interpretation (Criterion A)?
- How well does the response show a clear appreciation of the writer's choices (Criterion B)?
- Is the essay well organised and is the analysis clearly developed (Criterion C)?
- How sophisticated and accurate is the language used by the student (Criterion D)?

'A far cry' is a phrase that, colloquially, means a long way away and so we can assume that this is a poem about distance and separation. However,

Think like the examiner! Make sure you know exactly how you will be assessed; this will make it much easier to write the sort of response the examiner is looking for.

A far cry from Africa is also a calling from a different continent, a pleading request; perhaps this is a poem about coming to terms with history and guilt. Derek Walcott ends *A far cry from Africa* with a series of powerful rhetorical questions. He is struggling for answers and feels a huge sense of guilt about writing in English, which he sees as the language of the colonisers whose policies cause such devastation in Africa. The final line invites us to look back at the argument of the poem with its haunting cry: 'How can I turn from Africa and live?'

Africa is metaphorically represented as a living beast: its land is a 'tawny pelt'. This metaphor is extended to give a powerful sense of a living landscape when Walcott describes the 'bloodstreams of the Veldt'. The image of Africa as full of life is contrasted, however, with the dead bodies which are 'scattered through a paradise'. In a poem of powerful contrasts, this is particularly suggestive: a world that should be teeming with life is, in fact, full of death. Walcott foregrounds this paradox by focusing on the worm which he describes as the 'colonel of carrion'. The image of nature feasting on the dead is disturbing in itself; however, the military terminology is also important. Perhaps Walcott is suggesting that the worm is a symbol of the militaristic colonisers who benefit from suffering and death. The ironically charged line given to the worm ('Waste no compassion on these separate dead!') we could easily imagine being said by a literal colonel in a compassionless imperial army.

There is a noticeable change of tone in line 7 where, after a surreal exclamation from the worm, Walcott writes: 'Statistics justify and scholars seize/The salients of colonial policy.' The register here is formal, cold and bureaucratic. Word choices such as 'salients' highlight the detached nature of the language; indeed, the alliteration ('Statistics'; 'scholars'; 'seize'; 'salients') underlines the pedantic tone. Walcott wants to show how unthinking and inhumane much of the 'colonial policy' really is; he does this through his language choices. However, this is in sharp contrast to the emotive rhetorical questions which follow. The emotively charged verb 'hacked' is a direct challenge to the reader to confront the horrors of colonialism. In addition, Walcott's use of the simile 'expendable as Jews' immediately suggests the brutal history of the 20th century and forces the reader to elide in their minds the holocaust with the continuing suffering on the continent of Africa.

In lines 15–16, we are told that: 'The violence of beast on beast is read/As natural law'. This statement appears uncomplicated on first glance but it is made problematic by the way in which Walcott has already used metaphor to suggest the ways in which human beings are sometimes like beasts: the Kikuyu are 'quick as flies' and the worm is the 'colonel of carrion'. However, the beasts are set in direct contrast with 'upright man'. Walcott's choice of the word 'upright' is interesting because it is ambiguous. On the one hand, it refers to the physical state of humans who walk on two legs rather than on four; however, it also has a clear moral dimension: it suggests that humans ought to be morally good, a thought further underlined in the next line with the idea that man 'Seeks his divinity'. Nevertheless,

EE

Extended essay

You could write a study of how a historical legacy (perhaps colonialism, for instance) has inspired the work of a particular writer such as Derek Walcott. See, for instance:
http://nobelprize.org/nobel_prizes/literature/laureates/1992/walcott.html

Timed essay

Write a commentary on the poem 'Island man' (Text 5.4).
HL students: take 2 hours to do this.
SL students: take 1 hour 30 minutes to do this.
Remember: only SL candidates will have guiding questions in the exam.

Figure 5.5 The North Circular road in London and the Los Pinos Beach in Puerto Rico.

he is also 'Delirious as these worried beasts'. The first stanza ends with a note of unease, accentuated by the rhyming, in the final couplet, of the two powerful and troublingly similar words 'dread' and 'dead'.

The second stanza starts with the word 'Again': 'brutish necessity', Walcott would seem to be suggesting, is ongoing and unending. The image of wiping hands (we think of washing our hands of a deed) is strengthened by the use of the napkin. A napkin is traditionally white and starched; perhaps it is being suggested as a symbol of the colonising powers who have the ability to wipe away any 'dirty cause'. 'Again' is repeated at the end of the second line of the second stanza. The suffering continues; indeed, the enjambement pushes it into the next line where we have a strange re-working of the words put into the mouth of the worm in stanza one. This time Walcott describes 'A waste of our compassion'. A command ('Waste no compassion') has been modulated into a desperate observation ('A waste of our compassion'). The perspective is shifted from the ironic voice of the colonising powers to the plangent cry of the colonised, the victims and those who are suffering.

The end of the poem is characterised by the use of the first person pronoun: Walcott shifts from the impersonal to the personal, the objective to the subjective when he acknowledges: 'I who am poisoned with the blood of both'. He is referring to the 'gorilla' and the 'superman', which could, perhaps, represent natural and unnatural or even colonised and coloniser. Walcott ends by articulating two paradoxes he has to live with: he has to 'face such slaughter and be cool' and 'turn from Africa and live'. The fact that he expresses these as questions demonstrates his uncertainty and ongoing unease; perhaps the poem is ultimately an assuaging of guilt.

Text 5.4 *Island man*, Grace Nichols, 1993

Grace Nichols was born in Guyana, South America, in 1950. She was a teacher and a journalist before moving to the UK in 1977. She writes about the links between her new life in England and her old life in the Caribbean.

It might help, when you read this poem, to know that the North Circular is a long and very busy road that cuts across the north of London.

Morning
and island man wakes up
to the sound of blue surf
in his head
the steady breaking and wombing

wild seabirds
and fishermen pushing out to sea
the sun surfacing defiantly

from the east
of his small emerald island
he always comes back   groggily groggily

Comes back to sands
of a grey metallic soar
                              to surge of wheels
to dull North Circular roar

muffling muffling
his crumpled pillow waves
island man heaves himself

Another London day

Once you've written your commentary, look again at how you might be marked by the examiner; ask yourself how successful you've been at meeting all the assessment criteria.

We would advise you to read as much poetry as you can over the course of the two years. If you have access to a good anthology of poetry, you could make it a regular activity to read a poem, mark it up and write an essay in response to it. It will be particularly important to practise doing this several times in the run-up to the exam, particularly if you intend to write about poetry in Paper 1: Commentary.

Unit 5.3 **Prose**

How should you approach the prose text in the exam?

Many students choose to write their commentaries on poetry in the exam believing that there is more to say on form and structure in verse than in prose. But prose can be just as rich as poetry, and, as with poetry, the right approach can make for a perceptive, penetrating essay that unpicks the meaning of the piece, rather than a descriptive essay that does not. Look again at the assessment criteria on pages 178–9 so that you know how this paper will be marked.

This unit is divided into two sections: fiction and non-fiction texts. Although the skills you will need to write about both are very similar, we hope that you will find it clearer to look at these two different styles of prose separately. You will need clear strategies in place when writing about prose so that you are prepared for a variety of forms. You could be asked to write an unseen commentary on a text from a novel, diary, letter, or article from a newspaper or magazine. Each of these requires a different approach, and a different understanding of what the writer intended to achieve when the piece was first written. A journalist writing a piece of reportage writes in a very different context, with different aims, from a novelist or writer of a private diary. Understanding the writer's aims, as well as the word choices and audience, will help you write an insightful analysis.

You will have 5 minutes' reading time, and you should use this constructively. Try to clarify as many key themes and ideas in this first reading as you can; you should try to read the piece at least twice in the reading time you have.

Prose fiction

If the text is a piece of fiction you should think about a number of different aspects: setting, character, plot, language, tone, structure and theme. By doing this you will give a structure to your analysis.

Key term

Reportage The writing and reporting of the news in the media; a style of journalistic writing.

tip

Remember that you cannot write anything in the reading time. You should practise reading and running through ideas in your head whenever you have a chance. Take any text and time yourself reading it for 5 minutes. Order your ideas, and then write down key themes when the time is up. How much did you remember? How effectively did you use the time?

Key terms

Atmosphere The mood, or feeling, of a piece.

Interior monologue a technique in which the author articulates the internal thoughts of a character.

Secondary characters Characters that play a less important part than the main, or primary, characters.

Direct/indirect speech Direct speech is when the exact words someone says are quoted (i.e. *'I'm leaving,' she said*). In indirect speech, the words someone says are reported but without using the exact words (e.g. *She said she was leaving*).

Colloquial language Informal language used in everyday and familiar conversations or exchanges.

Stream of consciousness A writing style that claims to be unprepared and unedited; it is 'free form' in order to access the mind of the author.

Setting

- Is the setting significant in this passage?
- Is there one setting, or several?
- What part does setting play?
- Are the characters in harmony with the setting, or in opposition?
- Does it carry particular connotations, or create a certain atmosphere?
- Can the setting be described as psychological (that is, the landscape seems an extension of the narrator's thoughts, rather than something more objectively defined)?

Character

- Is there a central character?
- What do we learn about him/her? How do we learn this – through other characters' comments, through descriptions, through interior monologue?
- Is there anything significant about his/her relationship with another character? How do we feel about other character(s)?
- What about secondary characters? If there are several, what is the relationship between them? Is there conflict or tension? Of what kind? What effect does this have?
- From what point of view is the passage told? Is there a shift in perspective? If so, where and why does this happen?

Plot

- On the surface, what is the passage about? Is it about a key event? A decision a character takes? A secret revealed?
- Find a focus and underline any section that exemplifies it. Now begin to drill down into its meaning.

Language

- What part does description play? Does it provide setting, add atmosphere, tell us about the characters, or what?
- How are images used, and what effect do they create?
- Comment on how the diction enhances meaning. Think about dialogue: what purpose does it serve? Does it develop character and plot?
- If there is direct or indirect speech you should pay particular attention to it – why do you think the writer chose to use it? Also, is it dialect, colloquial language, slang, or is it more formal than these?

Tone

- Is it humorous or bleak? Is it forward-looking or reflective?
- Which words and phrases add to the tone?
- How are we being invited to read this passage? With empathy, experiencing the feelings and thoughts of the characters or narrator? Critically? Or with curiosity? Ask questions of the language.

Structure

- How is the passage structured?
- Does it fall into several sections, or is it one unbroken stream of consciousness?
- What effect does the structure have? On what rationale is the structure based? (e.g. Different stages of a journey? A progression of thought? Something else?)

- Look closely at the beginning and ending: is there anything striking about either or both of these? Also, do not overlook the mechanics of structure: sentence length, paragraphing and punctuation all affect our reading of a text.

Theme
- What are the main themes explored in this passage?
- How does the writer develop these themes? What images are used to make these themes vivid and memorable?

You are now going to look at a variety of different prose texts, and you will consider them from a range of different perspectives. Essential to this process is learning how to 'mark up' – or annotate – a text. The aim is for you to become not just a stronger reader of a text but also a more organised reader, so that the good ideas you have become linked and developed. Marking up a text provides you with a firm foundation for constructing a coherent analysis.

Text 5.5 *The Great Gatsby*, F. Scott Fitzgerald, 1925

Look at this short – but rich – passage from F. Scott Fitzgerald's (1896–1940) novel, *The Great Gatsby*. The narrator, Nick Carraway, visits a desolate area of New England with his companion, Tom Buchanan. Tom is looking for his mistress, who lives in the garage with her husband. Overlooking the whole, dismal scene, is a fading billboard advertising Dr T.J. Eckleburg's services. Look closely at how this passage has been marked up, and concentrate on *understanding* and *interpretation* (Criterion A).

Figure 5.6 Dr T.J. Eckleburg looking out over the valley of ashes in *The Great Gatsby*.

1 Unusual name: suggestive of what? Birth? New life?

2 Very specific location.

3 Language: archaic.

4 Intensifiers such as 'desolate' affect the mood of the piece.

5 Has connotations of hell, of death.

6 Oxymoronic: how can ashes grow?

7 A corrupted representation of nature.

8 Again, adjectives such as this affect mood.

9 The use of the word 'transcendent' seems ironic; there is no rebirth here: these men seem like shadows of men, crumbling, dead.

10 A powerful image of contrasts between the tangible and the intangible.

11 Look at the use of colour in the passage: it is de-saturated, colourless; 'ash' and 'grey' are repeated elsewhere in the passage.

12 'Crawls' and 'creak': anthropomorphism, but what is the effect?

13 The key words and phrases here are 'ash-grey men', 'swarm', 'leaden spades', 'impenetrable cloud' and 'sight'. They are like gravediggers caught in a hellish landscape.

14 Suggestive of a lack of control, of ill health and deterioration.

15 Dust is reminiscent of graves: 'dust to dust, ashes to ashes', and this endless drift suggests torpor, aimlessness.

16 Perception is again linked to seeing, to vision.

17 A motif: vision, seeing.

18 This is an image closer to a god looking out over a ruined landscape.

19 The irony is that in this place vision is obscured, and even a god needs spectacles to see.

About half-way between West Egg[1] and New York[2] the motor road[3] hastily joins the railroad and runs beside it for a quarter of a mile, so as to shrink away from a certain desolate[4] area of land. This is a valley of ashes[5] – a fantastic farm where ashes grow[6] like wheat into ridges[7] and hills and grotesque[8] gardens; where ashes take the forms of houses and chimneys and rising smoke and, finally, with a transcendent effort,[9] of ash-grey men who move dimly and already crumbling through the powdery air.[10] Occasionally a line of grey[11] cars crawls[12] along an invisible track, gives out a ghastly creak, and comes to rest, and immediately the ash-grey men swarm up with leaden spades and stir up an impenetrable cloud, which screens their obscure operations from your sight.[13]

But above the grey land and the spasms[14] of bleak dust which drift endlessly[15] over it, you perceive,[16] after a moment, the eyes[17] of Doctor T. J. Eckleburg. The eyes of Doctor T. J. Eckleburg are blue and gigantic – their retinas are one yard high.[18] They look out of no face, but, instead, from a pair of enormous yellow spectacles[19] which pass over a non-existent nose. Evidently some wild wag of an oculist set them there to fatten his practice in the borough of Queens, and then sank down himself into eternal blindness,[20] or forgot them and moved away. But his eyes, dimmed a little by many paintless days,[21] under sun and rain, brood on over the solemn dumping ground.[22]

The valley of ashes is bounded on one side by a small foul river,[23] and, when the drawbridge is up to let barges through,[24] the passengers on waiting trains can stare at the dismal scene for as long as half an hour. There is always a halt there of at least a minute, and it was because of this that I first met Tom Buchanan's[25] mistress.

The fact that he had one was insisted upon wherever he was known. His acquaintances resented the fact that he turned up in popular cafés with her and, leaving her at a table,[26] sauntered about, chatting with whomsoever he knew. Though I was curious to see her, I had no desire to meet her[27] – but I did. I went up to New York with Tom on the train one afternoon, and when we stopped by the ashheaps he jumped to his feet and, taking hold of my elbow, literally forced me from the car.

'We're getting off,' he insisted. 'I want you to meet my girl.'

I think he'd tanked up[28] a good deal at luncheon, and his determination to have my company bordered on violence.[29] The supercilious assumption was that on Sunday afternoon I had nothing better to do.

20 Again, the reference to sight, and its loss, and the use of 'eternal' reiterates the universal nature of this scene; but there is a balance here, and the next part of the sentence undermines the profundity of the statement with something more everyday.

21 Again, a reference to the lack of colour.

22 Another reference to death – the dumping ground suggestive of a mass grave.

23 Possibly an allusion to the River Styx which, in Greek mythology, formed the boundary between Earth and the underworld.

24 Drawbridge and barges makes this resemble an ancient land, of myth and mystery.

25 First introduction of a character using a name; a mistress is something illicit.

26 Like a possession: something to show off?

27 A curious statement in itself: why would you wish to meet somebody but not meet them? Again, this emphasises the importance of sight here because he wants to 'see' her.

28 Drunk? Blurred vision?

29 Nature of friendship is questionable here: lovers, friends, acquaintances … none of them seems sincere.

I followed him over a low whitewashed railroad fence, and we walked back a hundred yards along the road under Doctor Eckleburg's persistent stare.[30] The only building in sight was a small block of yellow brick sitting on the edge of the waste land,[31] a sort of compact Main Street ministering to it, and contiguous to absolutely nothing.[32] One of the three shops it contained was for rent and another was an all-night restaurant, approached by a trail of ashes; the third was a garage-repairs.[33] GEORGE B. WILSON. Cars bought and sold. – and I followed Tom inside.

30 There is judgement here: this god is watching them have this illicit meeting.
31 Hellish imagery again.
32 Nothingness, nihilism.
33 It is appropriate that this garage seeks to repair things in this broken world.

You will notice that these mark-ups are not complete sentences or fully formed ideas: they are quickly written responses to the words on the page, and shaping them into coherent, linked points will come later. Marking up a text in this way directly relates to Criterion A (it is fundamental to understanding and interpretation), Criterion B (it makes you more clearly appreciate the writer's choices), and Criterion C (it forms the basis of a well-organised literary essay).

Intensifier A word that makes meaning more intense (such as an adverb or an adjective).

Setting
The setting plays a key part in our understanding of the main themes: this is a moral and material 'wasteland'. It is modern America, industrial, urban, unearthly.

Character
There are two main characters: the narrator and Tom Buchanan. Dr T.J. Eckleburg is also a presence in the text, but does not develop beyond being a motif, a symbol of impotence; some minor characters are referred to, but the focus is on setting, the narrator, and Tom Buchanan. The effect is that the characters seem secondary and insubstantial.

Plot
The passage is about a meeting between Tom Buchanan, the narrator and Tom's mistress. We learn that the two central characters are going to a garage to meet Tom's mistress, but beyond that very little is revealed.

Language and tone
This is a passage which is rich in imagery. The language creates an apocalyptic atmosphere: words such as 'grey' and 'ash' are repeated, adding to an overwhelming sense of unreality and despair. The small amount of dialogue is in contrast with this: it is conversational and realistic. Fitzgerald's word choices are bleak: there is, throughout the text, an overwhelming sense of hopelessness. The narrator is judgemental, critical of what he sees and what others say and do. Also, the fact that it is written in the past tense adds a sense of reflection to it, which in turn contributes to the sense that the characters, and the action, are being judged.

Structure
The passage has a simple narrative structure. This is clearly divided into two sections: the first sets the scene, the second introduces us to the narrator, and the reason why he and Tom Buchanan have gone to the valley of ashes.

Theme
Death seems the most dominant theme: the setting immediately creates an ominous, gloomy atmosphere, and the imagery vividly adds to this. There is also the theme of judgement, symbolised by T.J. Eckleburg's gaze, watching these characters move across this hellish, damned environment.

1   Good opening: links
    setting with language.
2   Comfortably using literary
    terms.
3   Embedded quotations.
4   Good development of
    ideas: clearly understands
    relationship between
    setting and theme.
5   Strong statement.
6   Supported by quotations.
7   Point is developed.
8   Strong development,
    and has secure grasp of
    both the text and her own
    essay structure, linking
    points, looking ahead.

tip

Spending some time marking
up a passage, and getting your
initial responses into some sort of
shape, can really help clarify your
commentary. Once you have done
this try to write a synopsis of your
argument in one or two sentences.
If you can do this before you begin
your essay it will help you stay
focused. Keep your synopsis in
view throughout the exam so that
you retain a very clear idea of your
argument and you know where your
essay is going.

TOK

Look at the different forms of
perception here: we have the
narrator's and T.J. Eckleburg's. Are
they different and distinct? When
you read a passage, ask yourself
whether the narrator's observations
can be trusted. Why would a writer
create an unreliable narrator?

Assessment: Sample student response

The following is the opening of an HL student's response to this passage (Text 5.5),
written under timed conditions. As you read it, think about the assessment criteria.
How well has the student understood the passage? Is this a convincing interpretation?
How well organised is this opening? The comments at the side were made by the
student's teacher.

In this first paragraph we can see how Fitzgerald establishes the setting, and,
with it, the mood.[1] This is a bleak environment, and is described using imagery[2]
suggestive of hell; it is populated by strange creatures, human-like, but also 'ash-
grey',[3] swarming like insects around the anthropomorphised cars. The landscape
is unreal, but Fitzgerald has located it specifically in New England (just outside
New York), adding to the surrealism of the scene: here, in a fixed – and supposedly
affluent – place we have this impoverishment.[4] The narrator's voice is equal to this
apocalyptic vision,[5] using as he does powerful imagery of ashes growing 'like wheat
into ridges';[6] if the New World was supposed to be a new Eden this is a corruption
of that ideal (the gardens here are 'grotesque').[7] The final word of this paragraph
is 'sight', and this theme of seeing is developed in the second section of the text
when the writer employs the image of T.J. Eckleburg overseeing everything.[8]

Now look at the second section of this analysis. Where do you think the student gains
more marks? What are the essay's obvious strengths? You should think about Criterion
A (understanding and interpretation) – how does the candidate show that not only
does she understand what the passage is about, but that her interpretation is perceptive
and persuasive?

This second section of the passage further develops the hellish setting, but
also introduces characters, dialogue and plot, and each deepens Fitzgerald's
description of the scene. The most striking image is that of Dr T J Eckleburg:
he seems to be a god, overseeing this valley of ashes. Crucially, though, this
is a short-sighted deity, who needs glasses to see, and he is also one who is
fragmenting and disintegrating, sinking into 'eternal blindness'. Crucially, he is
there and not there: a facade behind which there is nothing but emptiness. He is
indifferent: Fitzgerald writes of him 'moving on', leaving his subjects adrift, morally
and spiritually. And yet Fitzgerald makes it clear that in this world of seemingly
empty relationships – where 'acquaintances' judge others, where other men's wives
are exhibited like trophies, and where company is violently grabbed at, Dr Eckleburg
still stares, watching but powerless to stop what is happening in this 'dumping
ground'. This is a broken world where Main Street backs on to nothing, and where
the two main characters, tellingly, head for the 'garage-repairs'.

Read this synopsis and discuss it: does this sound like a strong argument which would
make you want to read on?

Fitzgerald describes a hellish landscape; it seems the ultimate corruption of the
American Dream, and it is watched over by an impotent, blind god who was himself
a materialist, and a failure. Into this world two characters are presented, searching

for some sort of 'repair', but here it seems that everything – sight, relationships, the spirit of man – is broken.

Text 5.6 *Enduring Love*, Ian McEwan, 1997

Ian McEwan (1948–) has many different themes that he often returns to in his novels. His work reveals a fascination with the macabre and he is often accused of deliberately writing to shock. His stories often involve cruelty, violence and humiliation, but he is also a deeply moral writer concerned with ethical issues and profound conflicts relevant to everyone, such as the nature of faith and the different qualities of love. His more recent novels have concerned themselves with our relationship with nature and science. McEwan often chooses real situations, unusual 'cases' and controversial issues as the starting points for his novels.

Figure 5.7 McEwan's novel begins with a dramatic accident involving a hot air balloon.

The opening of *Enduring Love* describes a remarkable scene: a hot air balloon is seen floating overhead by Joe Rose. In it is a young boy, and dangling from a rope is a man who is desperately trying to bring the balloon back down. Within a few minutes a number of other men rush to try to help him. These actions have many consequences, but one is that one of the main characters – who suffers from a rare psychological condition – becomes obsessed with the narrator. Read the following opening passage of the novel.

The beginning is simple to mark.[1] We were in sunlight under a turkey oak, partly protected from a strong, gusty wind.[2] I was kneeling on the grass with a corkscrew in my hand,[3] and Clarissa[4] was passing me the bottle – a 1987 Daumas Gassac.[5] This was the moment, this was the pinprick on the time map:[6] I was stretching out my hand, and as the cool neck and the black foil touched my palm, we heard a man's shout. We turned to look across the field and saw the danger.[7] Next thing, I was running towards it. The transformation was absolute:[8] I don't recall dropping the corkscrew, or getting to my feet, or making a decision, or hearing the caution Clarissa called after me. What idiocy, to be racing into this story and its labyrinths,[9] sprinting away from our happiness among the fresh spring grasses by the oak. There was the shout again, and a child's cry, enfeebled by the wind that roared in the tall trees along the hedgerows. I ran faster. And there, suddenly, from different points around the field, four other men were converging on the scene, running like me.[10]

I see us from three hundred feet up, through the eyes of the buzzard we had watched earlier, soaring, circling and dipping in the tumult of currents: five men running silently towards the centre of a hundred-acre field. I approached from the south-east, with the wind at my back. About two hundred yards to my left two men ran side by side. They were farm labourers who had been repairing

the fence along the field's southern edge where it skirts the road. The same distance beyond them was the motorist, John Logan, whose car was banked on the grass verge with its door, or doors, wide open. Knowing what I know now, it's odd to evoke the figure of Jed Parry directly ahead of me, emerging from a line of beeches on the far side of the field a quarter of a mile away, running into the wind. To the buzzard Parry and I were tiny forms, our white shirts brilliant against the green, rushing towards each other like lovers, innocent of the grief this entanglement would bring. The encounter that would unhinge us was minutes away, its enormity disguised from us not only by the barrier of time but by the colossus in the centre of the field that drew us in with the power of a terrible ratio that set fabulous magnitude against the puny human distress at its base.

What was Clarissa doing? She said she walked quickly towards the centre of the field. I don't know how she resisted the urge to run. By the time it happened the event I am about to describe, the fall – she had almost caught us up and was well placed as an observer, unencumbered by participation, by the ropes and the shouting, and by our fatal lack of co-operation. What I describe is shaped by what Clarissa saw too, by what we told each other in the time of obsessive re-examination that followed: the aftermath, an appropriate term for what happened in a field waiting for its early summer mowing. The aftermath, the second crop, the growth promoted by that first cut in May.

1 Can anything be simple to mark? How do we define a beginning?
   The passage goes on to show how difficult it is to 'mark' it.
2 Highly detailed.
3 An almost forensic attention to detail: why?
4 Context: what does the name suggest to you in terms of class and culture?
5 A telling detail: again, reveals a lot about social context.
6 Use of metaphor emphasises the drama of the moment.
7 The moment of revelation is withheld: the suspense builds, carefully and skilfully.
8 Hyperbole or simple description?
9 Reflective: the narrator is reviewing this episode which is now in the past, adding a judgement to it. There is a knowingness about the narrative, and a sense of inevitability in the action.
10 The theme of fate is developed here: all five men are running towards their destiny.

Activity 5.4

This is an exercise which you should do with another student or in a group.

1 Have the assessment criteria in front of you and, as you read Text 5.6, mark up paragraphs two and three (your teacher can provide you with a copy of the extract to mark up). The aim of this reading is to focus on Criteria A and B:

Criterion A	Understanding and interpretation How well do you understand the passage? How effectively have you interpreted its meaning?	5
Criterion B	Appreciation of the writer's choices How does the writer's choice of vocabulary influence our reading of the text? How does structure affect our understanding of the text?	5

2 Now make notes on the opening of the passage:
   • the effect the first sentence has on you
   • the narrator's voice: how would you describe it?
   • the development of the characters
   • the action: how is it developed?
3 The writer is exact about the species of the tree, the make and year of the bottle of wine, the size of the field, etc. Why is it so detailed? Does McEwan deliberately make the narrator pretentious? Why would a writer do this?

On a first reading we seem to learn little about the characters in this text. There are hints about their class or status (perhaps in Clarissa's name and the fact that it is a vintage bottle of wine), but what else do you discover? What picture can you build up of the narrator and Clarissa? Are there any telling details included? The narrative technique could be described is one of avoidance: the narrator teases the reader by avoiding a quick, early description of what has happened. Though he seems to begin directly enough he also spends a great deal of time describing everything in detail. He also asks us to think about how the scene might look through the eyes of a buzzard, and pauses in his own narrative to ask, rhetorically, what Clarissa is doing at the time.

Activity 5.5

Continue to make notes on paragraphs two and three of Text 5.6. This time think about setting, character, plot, language, structure and theme. Consider the passage in relation to Criteria A and B: ask questions of the text, exploring its meaning, but in doing so stay focused on where and how you will be assessed.

Criterion A	*Understanding and interpretation* How does the setting influence our understanding of the text? Do you understand what is happening with the plot? What are the main themes in this text?
Criterion B	*Appreciation of the writer's choices* How would you describe the narrator's voice? How does he develop the mood of the piece? Look closely at the language: which words and images shape his meaning? Which images are the most vivid? Which could be described as significant, or turning points? Why? How is character developed here? What key details influence our reading of character? How is the passage structured? Look at the sentence lengths, the paragraphs, but also look at the way suspense is built up: meaning is withheld for a specific effect; perspective is altered so that different viewpoints can be explored. How does this influence our reading of the text?

Figure 5.8 Justin Torres, author of *Lessons*.

Text 5.7 *Lessons*, Justin Torres, 2008

Justin Torres is a young American writer. This short story, published in *Granta* magazine in 2008, gives a graphic description of a working-class family dominated by the father.

1 We wanted more

We wanted more.[1] We knocked the butt ends[2] of our forks against the table, tapped our spoons against our empty bowls; we were hungry. We wanted more volume, more riots.[3] We turned up the knob on the TV[4] until our ears ached with the shouts of angry men. We wanted more music on the radio; we wanted beats, we wanted rock.[5] We wanted muscles on our skinny[6] arms. We had bird bones,[7] hollow and light, and we wanted more density, more weight. We were six snatching hands, six stomping feet; we were brothers, boys, three little kings locked in a feud for more.[8]

When it was cold, we fought over blankets until the cloth tore down the middle. When it was really cold, when our breath came out in frosty clouds,[9] Manny crawled into bed with Joel and me.

'Body heat,' he said.

'Body heat,' we agreed.[10]

We wanted more flesh, more blood, more warmth.

When we fought, we fought with weapons – boots and garage tools, snapping pliers – we grabbed at whatever was nearest and we hurled it through the air; we wanted more broken dishes, more shattered glass. We wanted more crashes.[11]

And when our Paps came home, we got spankings.[12] Our little round butt cheeks were tore up: red, raw, leather-whipped. We knew there was something on the other side of pain,[13] on the other side of the sting. Prickly heat radiated upward from our thighs and backsides, fire consumed our brains,[14] but we knew that there was something more, some place our Paps was taking us with all this. We knew, because he was meticulous,[15] because he was precise, because he took his time.

And when our father was gone, we wanted to be fathers. We hunted animals. We drudged[16] through the muck of the creek, chasing down bullfrogs and water

1   Inclusive opening, immediately introducing a collective voice, an expression of a group. This short, opening sentence could introduce the theme of longing for fulfilment.

2   Colloquial expression: American?

3   A strange word: is this the riot of childhood? Unruliness? High spirits?

4   Does this signify a modern setting?

5   Modern setting emphasised again.

6   Transfer from the materialistic to the physical: the theme being developed here is that of ageing: growing up, longing not just for food but for adulthood.

7   An image of fragility, but also suggestive of flying nests, of moving.

8   The pace of the writing is fast, reflecting of the speed and energy of youth; the narrative voice is also young, with vocabulary choices being simple and direct. The opening paragraph emphasises the physicality of the relationship, the competitiveness and urgency.

9   Figurative language: poetic, beautiful, and in this moment of extremity we see the brothers move close together.

10   There is possibly something darker here: more visceral and parasitic.

11   Again, links to the first paragraph; the structure of the language adds to the urgency of what is being described, and the voice is closely tied to this youthfulness.

12   A transitional point: 'Paps' is a familiar term, colloquial, as is 'spankings' and 'butt cheeks were tore up': this is the language of brutal intimacy.

13   The tone changes here: this is an adult's voice articulating how the pain induced by the father was different from what they experienced between themselves.

14   A psychological pain as much as a physical pain.

15   In contrast to the children he is methodical, and in taking the time to analyse the father's different approach the writer cleverly develops character and introduces the theme of time.

16   Onomatopoeic: what is the effect?

snakes. We plucked the baby robins from their nest. We liked to feel the beat of tiny hearts, the struggle of tiny wings. We brought their tiny animal faces close to ours.

'Who's your daddy?' we said, then we laughed and tossed them into a shoebox.[17]

Always more, always hungrily scratching for more. But there were times, quiet moments, when our mother[18] was sleeping, when she hadn't slept in two days, and any noise, any stair creak, any shut door, any stifled laugh, any voice at all, might wake her – those still, crystal mornings, when we wanted to protect her, this confused goose of a woman, this stumbler, this gusher, with her backaches and headaches and her tired, tired ways, this uprooted Brooklyn creature, this tough talker, always with tears when she tells us she loves us, her mixed-up love, her needy love, her warmth – on those mornings, when sunlight found the cracks in our blinds, and laid itself down in crisp strips on our carpet, those quiet mornings, when we'd fixed ourselves oatmeal, and sprawled on to our stomachs with crayons and paper, with glass marbles that we were careful not to rattle, when our mother was sleeping, when the air did not smell like sweat or breath or mould, when the air was still and light, those mornings, when silence was our secret game and our gift and our sole accomplishment – we wanted less: less weight, less work, less noise, less father, less muscles and skin and hair. We wanted nothing, just this, just this.[19]

2 Heritage

When we got home from school Paps was in the kitchen, cooking and listening to music and feeling fine. He whiffed the steam coming off a pot, then clapped his hands together and rubbed them briskly. His eyes were wet and sparkled with giddy life. He turned up the volume on the stereo and it was mambo, it was Tito Puente.

'Watch out,' he said, and spun, with grace, on one slippered foot, his bathrobe twirling out around him. In his fist[20] was a glistening, greasy metal spatula, which he pumped in the air to the beat of the bongo drums.

My brothers and I, the three of us, stood in the entrance to the kitchen, laughing, eager to join in, but waiting for our cue.[21] He staked staccato[22] steps across the linoleum to where we stood and whipped Joel and Manny on to the dance floor, grabbing their wimpy arms and jerking them behind him. Me he took by the hands and slid between his legs and I popped up on the other side of him. Then we wiggled around the kitchen, following behind him in a line, like baby geese.[23] We rolled our tiny clenched fists[24] in front of us and snapped our hips to the trumpet blasts.

There were hot things on the stove, pork chops frying in their own fat, and Spanish rice foaming up[25] and rattling its lid. The air was thick with steam and spice and noise, and the one little window above the sink was fogged over.

this paragraph contrasts with the opening sentence: this places it at a point of conflict, and we can see here how a writer can use structure to develop themes. The narrator is at a turning point: he wants to gain in strength, to be male, but he also wishes to remain the child, and to be with his mother.

20 Even when happy there is an element of threat present when the father is in the house.

21 The spatula is reminiscent of a baton, with the father conducting the music, and the children.

22 Continues the reference to music.

23 Reference to the mother, the 'confused goose': they are her children.

24 And the imagery of violence links them to their father.

25 Emphasising the vibrancy of the scene. This is a description of life: steaming, foaming, noisy, fogged up and frying. There is confusion and controlled exuberance here.

17 They have learned from the father: there is a desire to protect, but also harm, and a casualness in treatment of those weaker than them.

18 First mention of the mother in this male-dominated household.

19 Most of this paragraph is one sentence: look at how the punctuation – and lack of it – adds to the mood of the passage. What does it tell us about the narrator's relationship with his mother, and of the mother herself? What words stand out as being unusual? Which phrases are the most illuminating about the mother and the narrator ('confused goose of a woman', 'mixed-up love')? Look also at how

26	There is succession here: the older child usurping the father, pointing towards the future.
27	Again, this emphasises the tentative, uncertain relationship the children have with the father: free to dance, but only on tiptoe.
28	The final image is of liberation, but one which, again, hints at a concealed violence at its heart: the children's freedom is clearly prescribed and controlled by the father.

Paps turned the stereo even louder, so loud that if I screamed no one would have heard me, so loud that my brothers felt very far away and hard to get to, even though they were right there in front of me. Then Paps grabbed a can of beer from the fridge and our eyes followed the path of the can to his lips. We took in the empties stacked up on the counter behind him, then we looked at each other. Manny rolled his eyes and kept dancing, and so we got in line and kept dancing too, except now Manny was the Papa Goose, it was him we were following.[26]

'Now shake it like you're rich,' Paps shouted, his powerful voice booming out over the music. We danced on tiptoes,[27] sticking up our noses and poking the air above us with our pinkies.

'You ain't rich,' Papi said, 'Now shake it like you're poor.'

We got low on our knees, clenched our fists and stretched our arms out on our sides; we shook our shoulders and threw our heads back, wild and loose and free.[28]

Look for points of tension in a text. In this extract, there is obvious tension within the family, not only between the father and sons, but also between the mother and sons. The tension is also in evidence thematically: the children are at the crossroads between childhood and adulthood.

Marking up can help begin to make sense of an extract; in doing it you will start to unearth the main themes the writer is concerned with, as well as other areas, such as the development of the characters, the importance of the setting, and the word choices the writer uses to make each of these as effective as possible. This is the basis of your response, but how do you move on from this to write an analytical essay?

Assessment: Sample student essay

The following commentary on the extract from *Lessons* by Justin Torres (Text 5.7) was written by a student under timed conditions; the comments on the side were made by his teacher.

From the very first sentence, Justin Torres introduces us to a close group ('we') which longs for something else beyond what they already have.[1] Key themes in the first paragraph are developed later on in the passage (violence, love, hunger, and, perhaps most importantly, the clash between childhood and adulthood[2]). Furthermore, the vocabulary, and the structure of the sentences, add to the sense of urgency, and innocence. Torres's narrator is impatient: the rattling of cutlery articulates a desire not just for food ('we were hungry'), but for adulthood: these are children who want 'muscles on our skinny arms', they want to be men. But as the rest of the text shows, being a man is not an unambiguous pleasure: like the 'angry' men[3] on the television, the children's father is violent, as well as loving, and this conflict between the aggressive masculinity and the more vulnerable femininity of the mother is central to the passage. These are boys at the crossroads of their lives:[4] they are boys, but also 'kings'. The language, too, reflects an urgency: each sentence in the opening paragraph is direct, words are simple, sometimes colloquial ('butt ends', 'beats'), and clearly convey the excitement – and noise – of the scene and the three brothers.[5]

Torres is careful to avoid sentimentality: these are boys who, although close, seek out each other's 'body heat' when it gets cold, fight with 'weapons', as if it is a domestic war. However, this aggression is seen, through the repetition of 'more'

1	Not just a summary statement, but actually says something about the text itself.
2	Shows an understanding of the text.
3	Good attention to detail.
4	Sets out a clear argument.
5	A concise opening paragraph.
6	Good use of embedded quotations

(which links it to the first paragraph) as a part of the indiscriminate need for more experience; indeed, it seems almost impersonal, rather like the violence they watch on television. It is only when the father returns home that we see a different, adult form of violence, and this in turn develops the theme of violence in the passage, but makes it darker.

The father is the most complex – and developed – character in the piece …

Now continue with this essay: write two paragraphs which could link between this and the next paragraph. What linking words and phrases might you use? You could include, for example: 'In addition to this', 'similarly', 'from this it is clear' – or others of your own choosing.

The mother is the opposite of the father: in contrast to the noise and violence which surrounds him, the mother is introduced as sleeping; her world is one of 'quiet moments'. This fragility brings out the compassionate qualities of the boys: they creep around the house, aware that 'any voice at all, might wake her'. And with this sensitivity comes a more fluent, emotional language from the narrator. Tellingly, this passage is one long sentence – like a sudden gush of love and care – and contains some of the most striking imagery in the text: there are 'still, crystal mornings',[6] again emphasising the brittleness of the memory, and the mother. And the language used to describe her is a mixture of affection and pity: she is a 'confused goose', a 'tough talker' of a woman, capable of 'warmth', but also of 'needy love'. She is not idealised: the children 'fixed their own oatmeal' and amused themselves, but it is her presence which banishes the masculine world of 'sweat or breath or mould', it is her who the narrator associates with light, and with a 'silence [which] was our secret game and our gift and our sole accomplishment'. It is the mother who shows them the importance of less, of wanting nothing more than to be with her, as children. The contrast with the father could not be clearer.

Now consider how you could develop your argument at this point: look at the original markings and think about what has been forgotten, or what can be drawn into your essay. Is there anything that has been overlooked?

Now look at the concluding part of this assessed essay: again, what are its strengths? Could it be improved in some way?

Torres cleverly develops the complexity of relationships which exists within all families. The mother is seen as light compared to the father's dark, she is silence to his noise, she is peace in contrast with his anger. However, the writer also shows us how the father is able to manipulate them, and even direct them, or guide their movements like a conductor: they wait for their 'cue', eager to dance, but also waiting 'in line' for the father to give them permission to join in with him. He controls them, but, for the first time, we see his successor, Manny, gaining in confidence, and, importantly, he is described as the 'Papa Goose', a term which brings both the father and the mother together. Perhaps in him the family will have a combination of both; perhaps in the next generation there will be more hope, and less division.

Extended essay

A favourite area for research for an extended essay is behavioural psychology and child psychology. Writers, scientists and philosophers have argued about whether we are born free and innocent and acquire our personalities through our upbringing and backgrounds, or whether we inherit much that determines our future lives. (You may also want to explore this debate, often referred to as 'nature versus nurture' for your Theory of Knowledge presentation.)

TOK

The narrator in this story is recalling what happened when he was a child, but is it true that we all, to a great extent, edit our pasts, and create new ones to suit our own narratives? Think about your own past: write down some very clear memories and then talk to others who were there to see if you recall them in different ways. You may wish to think about who is the most reliable narrator. A child? A parent? Or somebody less emotionally involved? This is just a starting point to thinking about bigger issues about identity and the reliability of the past.

Quick commentaries

In completing these exercises you will:

- focus on developing your close reading skills with very concentrated short bursts of analytical writing and discussion
- become increasingly confident in talking and writing about a range of different writing styles.

Read the following extracts from seven different texts; they are all considered classics. Some extracts are marked up but some are left as 'clean' texts. Practise reading them, without taking notes, in 5-minute periods of intense concentration: order your thoughts before marking up each one. Each extract is suitable for both SL and HL students.

After you have spent 5 minutes reading each text, consider the following:

- How important is setting in the extract?
- What do we learn about the main characters in this extract? How does the writer develop them?
- What happens in this extract? How does the plot develop?
- What language choices made by the writer are significant? Which images are the most powerful? What is the tone of the extract?
- How is the text structured?
- What are the main themes explored in this extract?
- How does all this shape our understanding of the text?

Text 5.8 *Emma*, Jane Austen, 1815

Emma Woodhouse, handsome, clever, and rich, with a comfortable home and happy disposition, seemed to unite some of the best blessings of existence; and had lived nearly twenty-one years in the world with very little to distress or vex her.

She was the youngest of the two daughters of a most affectionate, indulgent father; and had, in consequence of her sister's marriage, been mistress of his house from a very early period. Her mother had died too long ago for her to have more than an indistinct remembrance of her caresses; and her place had been supplied by an excellent woman as governess, who had fallen little short of a mother in affection.

Sixteen years had Miss Taylor been in Mr Woodhouse's family, less as a governess than a friend, very fond of both daughters, but particularly of Emma. Between *them* it was more the intimacy of sisters. Even before Miss Taylor had ceased to hold the nominal office of governess, the mildness of her temper had hardly allowed her to impose any restraint; and the shadow of authority being now long passed away, they had been living together as friend and friend very mutually attached, and Emma doing just what she liked; highly esteeming Miss Taylor's judgment, but directed chiefly by her own.

The real evils, indeed, of Emma's situation were the power of having rather too much her own way, and a disposition to think a little too well of herself; these were the disadvantages which threatened alloy to her many enjoyments. The danger, however, was at present so unperceived, that they did not by any means rank as misfortunes with her.

Text 5.9 *Wuthering Heights*, Emily Brontë, 1847

1801 – I have just returned from a visit to my landlord – the solitary neighbour that I shall be troubled with. This is certainly a beautiful country! In all England, I do not believe that I could have fixed on a situation so completely removed from the stir of society. A perfect misanthropist's heaven: and Mr Heathcliff and I are such a suitable pair to divide the desolation between us. A capital fellow! He little imagined how my heart warmed towards him when I beheld his black eyes withdraw so suspiciously under their brows, as I rode up, and when his fingers sheltered themselves, with a jealous resolution, still further in his waistcoat, as I announced my name.

'Mr Heathcliff?' I said.

A nod was the answer.

'Mr Lockwood, your new tenant, sir. I do myself the honour of calling as soon as possible after my arrival, to express the hope that I have not inconvenienced you by my perseverance in soliciting the occupation of Thrushcross Grange: I heard yesterday you had had some thoughts –'

'Thrushcross Grange is my own, sir,' he interrupted, wincing. 'I should not allow any one to inconvenience me, if I could hinder it – walk in!'

The 'walk in' was uttered with closed teeth, and expressed the sentiment, 'Go to the Deuce': even the gate over which he leant manifested no sympathising movement to the words; and I think that circumstance determined me to accept the invitation: I felt interested in a man who seemed more exaggeratedly reserved than myself.

Figure 5.9 Emily Brontë (1818–48), author of *Wuthering Heights.*

Figure 5.10 Melville's (1819–91) *Moby Dick* is concerned with one man's search for the legendary white whale of the title.

Text 5.10 *Moby Dick*, Herman Melville, 1851

Call me Ishmael.[1] Some[2] years ago – never mind how long precisely[3] – having little or no money in my purse, and nothing particular to interest me on shore,[4] I thought I would sail about a little and see the watery part of the world. It is a way I have of driving off the spleen and regulating the circulation. Whenever I find myself growing grim about the mouth;[5] whenever it is a damp, drizzly November in my soul;[6] whenever I find myself involuntarily pausing before coffin warehouses, and bringing up the rear of every funeral I meet;[7] and especially whenever my hypos[8] get such an upper hand of me, that it requires a strong moral principle[9] to prevent me from deliberately stepping into the street, and methodically knocking people's hats off – then, I account it high time to get to sea as soon as I can.

1	An unreliable narrator? Why not call him by his real name? Is there anything significant about this choice of name? Ishmael is viewed by some as a prophet, by others as an outsider, cast into the wilderness. Either way, this choice of name complicates the narrative: why would writer do this?
2	Is this deliberately vague?
3	Again, is this deliberately vague?
4	How would you describe the tone of this extract so far? The voice of the narrator is deliberately aimless and vague.
5	A striking image: what is its effect?
6	Figurative language, which develops a sense of the spiritual, and this is developed in the next part of the sentence.
7	A mixture of dark, even absurd, humour: the character seems drawn to the ceremonies of death.
8	What do you think this means? What do you do if you encounter a word that you do not know in the exam?
9	Again, absurdly comic.

Remember that it is important to have a structured approach to the unseen literary analysis. Once you have read these extracts through you could break your analysis down into different areas. The following is a suggested structure which could be used to clarify and order your thoughts after you have marked up your text and before you start writing your essay. This example relates to Text 5.10.

Setting

How important is setting in the extract?

The physical setting is not clearly established to begin with, but the psychological setting certainly is, and it is a dark place. The narrator – who calls himself Ishmael (a figure shrouded more than most in mystery and disputed heritage) – longs for the sea, but only because it allows him to escape his murderous thoughts. By the end of the passage the sea grows as a presence, as a future setting.

Character

What do we learn about the main characters in this extract?

We learn a great deal about the psychology of the narrator, but not who the narrator is: he adopts a pseudonym and, in doing so, tellingly conceals his identity from us. In adopting the name 'Ishmael' he associates himself with an outsider (most of Melville's audience would have come from a Judaeo-Christian heritage). The writer carefully describes a character who is motivated by a 'damp, drizzly November in [his] soul'. His desire to go to sea allows the writer to introduce key themes: this is a character who cannot be held by anything of permanence – of the physical – but instead longs for the transient – the sea. Ishmael is very aware of himself: he reflects on his situation, but does not try to explain it. The tone is also resigned, as if his actions are inevitable.

Plot

What happens in this extract?

Character is established and themes introduced, but beyond a sense that the plot will be linked to the sea, there is little in the way of plot development here.

Language

What choices made by the writer are significant?

The very first sentence establishes the writer's style: it appears clear and simple, but is actually deceptively complex and dark. The writer describes Ishmael's actions, his symptoms, but not necessarily the reasons why he acts the way he does. The imagery is often vivid (not only the 'November in [his] soul' but also the 'stepping into the street, and methodically knocking people's hats off') and archaic ('spleen', 'hypos'). The tone is gloomy, but there is also a liveliness to the language, and an inevitable movement towards the sea.

Structure

How is the text structured?

The abrupt opening sentence is both intimate and distancing, and this ambiguous position develops in the second sentence. But the movement is towards greater openness, with the tempo of the text building increasingly to the final pronouncement that it is 'high time' to go to sea. The whole text consists of only three sentences, with the first being in obvious contrast to the long, complex sentences that follow it. In these sentences the character of Ishmael is introduced and developed, and the language used creates a character who is both confessional and secretive.

Theme

What are the main themes explored in this extract?

Appearance and reality are key themes in this passage, and the conflict between the two exists within the narrator: he appears to be discontented, even violent, and is drawn to darkness (he is attracted to funerals and coffins). Above all, he seems alienated from others, and, paradoxically, it is this urge to escape that pulls him towards a community of outsiders: those who live on the sea, those who wish to escape the certainty of land for the possibilities of water. The themes of alienation, identity, death, appearance and reality, escape and hope are introduced here in a complex, compact opening.

Text 5.11 *Hard Times*, Charles Dickens, 1853

'Now, what I want is, Facts. Teach these boys and girls nothing but Facts. Facts alone are wanted in life. Plant nothing else, and root out everything else. You can only form the minds of reasoning animals upon Facts: nothing else will ever be of any service to them. This is the principle on which I bring up my own children, and this is the principle on which I bring up these children. Stick to Facts, sir!'

The scene was a plain, bare, monotonous vault of a school-room, and the speaker's square forefinger emphasized his observations by underscoring every sentence with a line on the schoolmaster's sleeve. The emphasis was helped by the speaker's square wall of a forehead, which had his eyebrows for its base, while his eyes found commodious cellarage in two dark caves, overshadowed by the wall. The emphasis was helped by the speaker's mouth, which was wide, thin, and hard set. The emphasis was helped by the speaker's voice, which was inflexible, dry, and dictatorial. The emphasis was helped by the speaker's hair, which bristled on the skirts of his bald head, a plantation of firs to keep the wind from its shining surface, all covered with knobs, like the crust of a plum pie, as if the head had scarcely warehouse-room for the hard facts stored inside. The speaker's obstinate carriage, square coat, square legs, square shoulders, – nay, his very neckcloth, trained to take him by the throat with an unaccommodating grasp, like a stubborn fact, as it was, – all helped the emphasis.

'In this life, we want nothing but Facts, sir; nothing but Facts!'

The speaker, and the schoolmaster, and the third grown person present, all backed a little, and swept with their eyes the inclined plane of little vessels then and there arranged in order, ready to have imperial gallons of facts poured into them until they were full to the brim.

Figure 5.11 A Victorian education, a subject which concerned Charles Dickens in *Hard Times*.

Text 5.12 *North and South*, Elizabeth Gaskell, 1855

'Edith!' said Margaret, gently, 'Edith!'

But, as Margaret half suspected, Edith had fallen asleep. She lay curled up on the sofa in the back drawing-room in Harley Street, looking very lovely in her white muslin and blue ribbons. If Titania had ever been dressed in white muslin and blue ribbons, and had fallen asleep on a crimson damask sofa in a back drawing-room, Edith might have been taken for her. Margaret was struck afresh by her cousin's beauty. They had grown up together from childhood, and all along Edith had been remarked upon by every one, except Margaret, for her prettiness; but Margaret had never thought about it until the last few days, when the prospect of soon losing her companion seemed to give force to every sweet quality and charm which Edith possessed. They had been talking about wedding dresses, and wedding ceremonies; and Captain Lennox, and what he had told Edith about her future life at Corfu, where his regiment was stationed; and the difficulty of keeping a piano in good tune (a difficulty which Edith seemed to consider as one of the most formidable that could befall her in her married life), and what gowns she should want in the visits to Scotland, which would immediately succeed her marriage; but the whispered tone had latterly become more drowsy; and Margaret, after a pause of a few minutes, found, as she fancied, that in spite of the buzz in the next room, Edith had rolled herself up into a soft ball of muslin and ribbon, and silken curls, and gone off into a peaceful little after-dinner nap.

Figure 5.12 A still from the BBC adaptation, (1994) of George Eliot's *Middlemarch*.

Text 5.13 *Middlemarch*, George Eliot, 1871

Miss Brooke had that kind of beauty which seems to be thrown into relief by poor dress. Her hand and wrist were so finely formed that she could wear sleeves not less bare of style than those in which the Blessed Virgin appeared to Italian painters; and her profile as well as her stature and bearing seemed to gain the more dignity from her plain garments, which by the side of provincial fashion gave her the impressiveness of a fine quotation from the Bible, – or from one of our elder poets, – in a paragraph of to-day's newspaper. She was usually spoken of as being remarkably clever, but with the addition that her sister Celia had more common-sense. Nevertheless, Celia wore scarcely more trimmings; and it was only to close observers that her dress differed from her sister's, and had a shade of coquetry in its arrangements; for Miss Brooke's plain dressing was due to mixed conditions, in most of which her sister shared. The pride of being ladies had something to do with it: the Brooke connections, though not exactly aristocratic, were unquestionably 'good:' if you inquired backward for a generation or two, you would not find any yard-measuring or parcel-tying forefathers – anything lower than an admiral or a clergyman; and there was even an ancestor discernible as a Puritan gentleman who served under Cromwell, but afterwards conformed, and managed to come out of all political troubles as the proprietor of a respectable family estate. Young women of such birth, living in a quiet country-house, and attending a village church hardly larger than a parlour, naturally regarded frippery as the ambition of a huckster's daughter. Then there was well-bred economy, which in those days made show in dress the first item to be deducted from, when any margin was required for expenses more distinctive of rank. Such reasons would have been enough to account for plain dress, quite apart from religious feeling; but in Miss Brooke's case, religion alone would have determined it; and Celia mildly acquiesced in all her sister's sentiments, only infusing them with that common-sense which is able to accept momentous doctrines without any eccentric agitation.

Text 5.14 *The Return of the Native*, Thomas Hardy, 1878

A Saturday afternoon in November was approaching the time of twilight, and the vast tract of unenclosed wild known as Egdon Heath embrowned[1] itself moment by moment.[2] Overhead the hollow[3] stretch of whitish cloud shutting out the sky was as a tent which had the whole heath for its floor.[4]

The heaven being spread with this pallid screen[5] and the earth with the darkest vegetation, their meeting-line at the horizon was clearly marked. In such contrast the heath wore the appearance of an instalment of night which had taken up its place before its astronomical hour was come: darkness had to a great extent arrived hereon, while day stood distinct in the sky.[6] Looking upwards, a furze-cutter[7] would have been inclined to continue work; looking down, he would have decided to finish his faggot[8] and go home.[9] The distant rims of the world and of the firmament seemed to be a division in time no less than a division in matter. The face of the heath by its mere complexion added half an hour to evening; it could in like manner retard the dawn, sadden noon, anticipate the frowning of storms scarcely generated, and intensify the opacity of a moonless midnight to a cause of shaking and dread.[10]

Figure 5.13 Egdon Heath is the setting for Thomas Hardy's *The Return of the Native*.

1	Interesting verb: it describes a lack of colour, a time of the day where nature loses some of its vividness. Will this affect the themes the writer is going on to develop?
2	This opening sentence establishes the setting, both in time and place. Connotations of ill-health pervade.
3	Comparing the cloud cover to a tent. The atmosphere is brooding, being both open and enclosed.
4	Here there is a juxtaposition of the global and the domestic: the wild heath becomes almost contained, adding a sense of perspective against the sky.
5	'Pallid' means lacking in colour, further developing the imagery of ill-health, of the landscape *lacking something*.
6	Element of threat, and unease, in this setting.
7	An agricultural worker.
8	A slice of peat to burn on a fire.
9	The man is positioned here both at one with nature, and distanced from it: the divide between night and day, land and sky, is unnatural, and he is caught in this divide.
10	This long, complex sentence anthropomorphises the heath and invests it with a gloomy, sombre character: it retards, saddens and causes 'shaking and dread'. The setting has become a character, and has begun to develop the themes of loss and death.

Text 5.15 *The Adventures of Huckleberry Finn*, Mark Twain, 1885

You don't know about me without you have read a book[1] by the name of *The Adventures of Tom Sawyer*; but that ain't no matter.[2] That book was made[3] by Mr Mark Twain, and he told the truth, mainly.[4] There was things which he stretched, but mainly he told the truth. That is nothing.[5] I never seen anybody but lied one time or another, without it was Aunt Polly, or the widow, or maybe Mary. Aunt Polly – Tom's Aunt Polly, she is – and Mary, and the Widow Douglas is all told about in that book, which is mostly a true book, with some stretchers, as I said before.[6]

1	Grammatically incorrect: what effect does this have?
2	Dialect how important is this choice of language? Context?
3	'Made' not 'written'? It is unusual that the central character is referring to the writer, and casting doubt on his reliability.
4	Surely he told the truth or he did not: is the narrator telling the truth?
5	Does the truth count as nothing?

Extended essay

Each of the writers Hardy and Twain provides ample material for an extended essay: the challenge, as with all extended essays, is to narrow the focus to something that interests you, but which also provides enough material to sustain a lengthy piece of analysis. The title should be comprehensive and clear, so avoid: 'The novels of Thomas Hardy' or 'How important is the weather in the novels of Thomas Hardy?' A better title would be 'An investigation into Hardy's use of weather in "The Return of the Native"' as it narrows the focus to a particular novel.

TOK

To what extent is knowledge implicit in language? How successfully do each of the writers here represent reality? Is it possible to answer that question? Do we get closer to the knowledge they are trying to impart through the language they use? Or do we imagine it in purely visual terms? This leads to another question: in what ways does written language differ from spoken language and other forms of communication (gestures, pictures, sounds)?

Figure 5.14 A still from the 1939 adaptation of Mark Twain's *The Adventures of Huckleberry Finn* which is set on the Mississippi River.

Now the way that the book winds up is this: Tom and me found the money that the robbers hid in the cave, and it made us rich.[7] We got six thousand dollars apiece – all gold. It was an awful[8] sight of money when it was piled up. Well, Judge Thatcher he took it and put it out at interest, and it fetched us a dollar a day apiece all the year round – more than a body could tell what to do with. The Widow Douglas she took me for her son, and allowed she would sivilize me;[9] but it was rough living in the house all the time, considering how dismal regular and decent the widow was in all her ways; and so when I couldn't stand it no longer

6   By the end of the first paragraph we have doubts about the main character's reliability as a narrator, and it is clear that the writer wishes to introduce this doubt into our minds.

7   The narrator is again subverting our understanding of his role within the novel: the conventional narrative development is upset by the assumption that the reader knows the background to the novel.

8   Archaic language: what is its effect?

9   There is a conflict here between childhood and adulthood, with childhood apparently classed as uncivilised.

I lit out.[10] I got into my old rags and my sugar-hogshead again, and was free and satisfied.[11] But Tom Sawyer he hunted me up and said he was going to start a band of robbers, and I might join if I would go back to the widow and be respectable. So I went back.[12]

10 Dialect phrase, but the meaning is clear enough. The voice, although that of a child, is independent and experienced.
11 A key theme: freedom.
12 The conflict between childhood and adulthood is in evidence here: the idea of 'a band of robbers', together with the ease with which the narrator exchanges his dream of freedom for respectability, is strongly suggestive of a child's imagination.

Text 5.16 *Sister Carrie*, Theodore Dreiser, 1900

As a matter of fact, no man as clever as Hurstwood — as observant and sensitive to atmospheres of many sorts, particularly upon his own plane of thought — would have made the mistake which he did in regard to his wife, wrought up as she was, had he not been occupied mentally with a very different train of thought. Had not the influence of Carrie's regard for him, the elation which her promise aroused in him, lasted over, he would not have seen the house in so pleasant a mood. It was not extraordinarily bright and merry this evening. He was merely very much mistaken, and would have been much more fitted to cope with it had he come home in his normal state.

After he had studied his paper a few moments longer, he felt that he ought to modify matters in some way or other. Evidently his wife was not going to patch up peace at a word. So he said:

'Where did George get the dog he has there in the yard?'

'I don't know,' she snapped.

He put his paper down on his knees and gazed idly out of the window. He did not propose to lose his temper, but merely to be persistent and agreeable, and by a few questions bring around a mild understanding of some sort.

'Why do you feel so bad about that affair of this morning?' he said, at last. 'We needn't quarrel about that. You know you can go to Waukesha if you want to.'

'So you can stay here and trifle around with some one else?' she exclaimed, turning to him a determined countenance upon which was drawn a sharp and wrathful sneer.

He stopped as if slapped in the face. In an instant his persuasive, conciliatory manner fled. He was on the defensive at a wink and puzzled for a word to reply.

'What do you mean?' he said at last, straightening himself and gazing at the cold, determined figure before him, who paid no attention, but went on arranging herself before the mirror.

'You know what I mean,' she said, finally, as if there were a world of information which she held in reserve — which she did not need to tell.

'Well, I don't,' he said, stubbornly, yet nervous and alert for what should come next. The finality of the woman's manner took away his feeling of superiority in battle.

She made no answer.

'Hmph!' he murmured, with a movement of his head to one side. It was the weakest thing he had ever done. It was totally unassured.

Mrs. Hurstwood noticed the lack of colour in it. She turned upon him, animal-like, able to strike an effectual second blow.

'I want the Waukesha money to-morrow morning,' she said.

He looked at her in amazement. Never before had he seen such a cold, steely determination in her eye — such a cruel look of indifference. She seemed a thorough master of her mood — thoroughly confident and determined to wrest all control from him. He felt that all his resources could not defend him. He must attack.

Timed essay

Write a timed commentary on Text 5.16, the extract from *Sister Carrie*.

SL students: take 1 hour 30 minutes to do this.

HL students: take 2 hours to do this.

Look at the guiding questions which are given after the text; you can use them if you wish, but remember that only SL candidates have two guiding questions in the exam. The aim of this exercise is to get you writing with more confidence, rather than practising writing under strict exam conditions.

Remember to use 5 minutes before you start writing as reading time. Try to find the key ideas in the passage during this time, so that when you begin marking up the passage you are able to do so quickly and effectively.

'What do you mean?' he said, jumping up. '*You* want! I'd like to know what's got into you to-night.'

'Nothing's *got* into me,' she said, flaming. 'I want that money. You can do your swaggering afterwards.'

'Swaggering, eh! What! You'll get nothing from me. What do you mean by your insinuations, anyhow?'

'Where were you last night?' she answered. The words were hot as they came. 'Who were you driving with on Washington Boulevard? Who were you with at the theatre when George saw you? Do you think I'm a fool to be duped by you? Do you think I'll sit at home here and take your "too busys" and "can't come," while you parade around and make out that I'm unable to come? I want you to know that lordly airs have come to an end so far as I am concerned. You can't dictate to me nor my children. I'm through with you entirely.'

'It's a lie,' he said, driven to a corner and knowing no other excuse.

'Lie, eh!' she said, fiercely, but with returning reserve; 'you may call it a lie if you want to, but I know.'

'It's a lie, I tell you,' he said, in a low, sharp voice. 'You've been searching around for some cheap accusation for months, and now you think you have it. You think you'll spring something and get the upper hand. Well, I tell you, you can't. As long as I'm in this house I'm master of it, and you or any one else won't dictate to me — do you hear?'

He crept toward her with a light in his eye that was ominous. Something in the woman's cool, cynical, upper-handish manner, as if she were already master, caused him to feel for the moment as if he could strangle her.

Activity 5.6

Read Text 5.16 twice and comment on its effectiveness. In your response you should consider:

- How does the writer use detail to indicate his attitude to the situation described here?
- What do we learn about the relationship between both characters in this extract?
- Comment on the point of view of the narrative voice.
- Evaluate the significance of the contrast between the first and final paragraphs.
- Compare and contrast what is conveyed in the descriptive passages, and in the dialogue.

Prose non-fiction

Many students choose to write a commentary on prose non-fiction in the Paper 1: Commentary exam. Non-fiction offers many opportunities for a strong analysis, as we shall see in this section; but you should also be aware that the rich ambiguity and imagery of fiction (as well as plot, theme and character) are often less developed in non-fiction. Writers of prose non-fiction have many different purposes and audiences in mind. Some are journalists, others are diary writers or travel writers, for example. Understanding that there are differences is vital to writing an effective response.

Journalism

Although there are many sub-genres which could be included in the exam as non-fiction texts, journalism remains one of the most popular choices simply because the calibre and the range of texts available is so wide. The writers are professional, the themes often local as well as universal, the episodes described powerful and vivid. You may be asked to analyse a piece of reportage – as you will do shortly with an article by George Orwell – or some travel writing, or an opinion piece which argues very directly one side of an argument. All are different forms of journalism.

Activity 5.7

Read the following article by George Orwell (Text 5.17), first published in 1931. It is an eye-witness account of a public execution. Spend about 30 minutes reading it and making notes. As you read it, mark it up, looking for anything that you think is interesting and significant.

It might help to keep the PALS mnemonic in your mind as you read (Purpose, Audience, Language, Structure).

Purpose

What are the writer's intentions? Does he want to describe? Educate? Arouse emotion? Inform? Or does he wish to persuade us to accept his argument? How effective is he in achieving his purpose?

Audience

What sort of readership do you think this piece was originally aimed at? Was it a specialist group or the general public? How did the context (cultural, social, historical) influence the writer and how does it influence us, the readers?

Language

How would you describe the mood of this article? What words support this judgement? How would you describe the writer's voice? Is it first person ('I'), second person ('you') or third person ('we')? Does the tone change or develop? Are there any figures of speech here? If so, what images or phrases stand out as unusual or significant? Why? Is it written in the past or present tense? Is the choice of tense significant?

Structure

How does this develop? Look at the sentencing (simple, complex), paragraphing, vocabulary, and syntax.

Text 5.17 *A Hanging*, George Orwell, 1931

It[1] was in Burma, a sodden[2] morning of the rains. A sickly[3] light, like yellow tinfoil,[4] was slanting over the high walls into the jail yard. We were waiting outside the condemned cells,[5] a row of sheds fronted with double bars, like small animal cages.[6] Each cell measured about ten feet by ten and was quite bare within except for a plank bed and a pot of drinking water. In some of them brown silent men[7] were squatting at the inner bars, with their blankets draped round them. These were the condemned men, due to be hanged within the next week or two.[8]

Figure 5.15 Capital punishment is a highly controversial and emotive issue. Does this extract suggest Orwell is for or against it? What evidence is there in the text?

One prisoner had been brought out of his cell. He was a Hindu, a puny wisp of a man,[9] with a shaven head and vague liquid[10] eyes. He had a thick, sprouting moustache, absurdly too big for his body,[11] rather like the moustache of a comic man on the films. Six tall Indian warders were guarding him and getting him ready for the gallows.[12] Two of them stood by with rifles and fixed bayonets, while the others handcuffed him, passed a chain through his handcuffs and fixed it to their belts, and lashed his arms tight to his sides. They crowded very close about him, with their hands always on him in a careful, caressing grip, as though all the while feeling him to make sure he was there.[13] It was like men handling a fish which is still alive and may jump back into the water. But he stood quite unresisting, yielding his arms limply to the ropes, as though he hardly noticed what was happening.[14]

Eight o'clock struck and a bugle call, desolately thin[15] in the wet air, floated from the distant barracks. The superintendent of the jail, who was standing apart from the rest of us, moodily prodding the gravel with his stick, raised his head at the sound. He was an army doctor, with a grey toothbrush moustache and a gruff voice. 'For God's sake hurry up, Francis,' he said irritably. 'The man ought to have been dead by this time. Aren't you ready yet?'[16]

Francis, the head jailer, a fat Dravidian[17] in a white drill suit and gold spectacles, waved his black hand. 'Yes sir, yes sir,' he bubbled.[18] 'All iss satisfactorily prepared. The hangman iss[19] waiting. We shall proceed.'

'Well, quick march, then. The prisoners can't get their breakfast till this job's over.'[20]

We set out for the gallows. Two warders marched on either side of the prisoner, with their rifles at the slope; two others marched close against him, gripping him by arm and shoulder, as though at once pushing and supporting him. The rest of us,[21] magistrates and the like, followed behind. Suddenly, when we had gone ten yards, the procession[22] stopped short without any order or warning. A dreadful thing had happened – a dog,[23] come goodness knows whence, had appeared in the yard. It came bounding among us with a loud volley of barks, and leapt round us wagging its whole body,[24] wild with glee[25] at finding so many human beings together. It was a large woolly dog, half Airedale, half pariah[26]. For a moment it pranced round us, and then, before anyone could stop it, it had made a dash for the prisoner, and jumping up tried to lick his face. Everyone stood aghast, too taken aback even to grab at the dog.[27]

'Who let that bloody brute[28] in here?' said the superintendent angrily. 'Catch it, someone!'

A warder, detached from the escort, charged clumsily after the dog, but it danced and gambolled[29] just out of his reach, taking everything as part of the game.[30] A young Eurasian[31] jailer picked up a handful of gravel and tried to stone the dog away, but it dodged the stones and came after us again. Its yaps echoed from the jail walls. The prisoner, in the grasp of the two warders, looked on incuriously, as though this was another formality of the hanging. It was several minutes before someone managed to catch the dog. Then we put my handkerchief through its collar and moved off once more, with the dog still straining and whimpering.

It was about forty yards to the gallows. I watched the bare brown back of the prisoner marching in front of me. He walked clumsily with his bound arms, but quite steadily, with that bobbing[32] gait of the Indian who never straightens his knees. At each step his muscles slid neatly into place, the lock of hair on his scalp danced up and down, his feet printed themselves on the wet gravel.[33] And once, in spite of the men who gripped him by each shoulder, he stepped slightly aside to avoid a puddle on the path.

It is curious, but till that moment I had never realized what it means to destroy a healthy, conscious man.[34] When I saw the prisoner step aside to avoid the puddle, I saw the mystery, the unspeakable wrongness,[35] of cutting a life short when it is in full tide. This man was not dying, he was alive just as we were alive.[36] All the organs of his body were working – bowels digesting food, skin renewing itself, nails growing, tissues forming – all toiling away in solemn foolery[37]. His nails would still be growing when he stood on the drop, when he was falling through the air with a tenth of a second to live. His eyes saw the yellow gravel and the grey walls, and his brain still remembered, foresaw, reasoned – reasoned[38] even about puddles. He and we were a party of men walking together, seeing, hearing, feeling, understanding the same world; and in two minutes, with a sudden snap, one of us would be gone – one mind less, one world less.[39]

1   Even the first word is ominous.

2   Tone is established early on: sombre, dark.

3   Theme: unhealthy.

4   Striking image, both unnatural and unhealthy.

5   The subject is now made clear.

6   This links the condemned men to animals.

7   Context: cultural differences – what does it tell you about the audience and the period?

8   What effect does this clear, sparsely written sentence have at this point? Why not begin the article in this way? How does it influence the mood? The final sentence of the first paragraph is often significant: think about its effect.

9   Emphasises the fragility of the man, his impermanence.

10   Again, emphasises transience.

11   This emphasises fragility.

12   Orwell stresses the absurdity of the situation: the contrast in size and number of the guards and the man. The final word in this sentence, 'gallows', is charged with significance.

13   A fascinating oxymoron: the guards are shown to be, through Orwell's language choices, both his captors and his protectors ('caressing grip').

14   Emphasises the unreal, 'absurd' atmosphere, and also the inevitability of his fate.

15   Emphasising, again, fragility.

16   Contrast between the focus on the human and the mechanical procedure we are about to witness.

17   Context.

18   Onomatopoeic, conveying the servility and confusion of the exchange.

19   This protracted sibilance conveys a snake-like quality in the language.

20   Mechanical, a process, inhuman.

21   Involved narrator, not just a dispassionate spectator, but one involved in this act.

22   Connotations: a ceremony, sombre, dutiful.

23   Pathos: something dreadful is undercut by the dark humour of the inappropriate interruption of the dog on to the scene.

24   Hyperbole.

25 More hyperbole, anthropomorphism.

26 Context. Explain?

27 Why are they aghast? Because it shows the prisoner some affection: the irony is clear – it is the last sign of affection the prisoner will experience, and it comes from a dog.

28 Again, ironic: the dog is not brutish, but affectionate, a contrast to the superintendent and what is about to be sanctioned.

29 Orwell emphasises the innocence of the creature; connotations of a lamb (to the slaughter).

30 To what extent does Orwell construct this process as a game, with rules which make sense only to those taking part in it, but which to the outsider seem absurd and arbitrary?

31 Context: how does this influence our reading?

32 Contrasts with the sombre context.

33 The miracle of life, its precision and complexity, next to its imminent extinction.

34 The key sentence in the extract, and a pivotal point in the narrator's moral position.

35 A powerful, emotive phrase; the writer takes a very strong moral position on this issue.

36 For the first time the man is seen as fundamentally equal to the others.

37 A striking oxymoron: the body is ignorant of the reality of what will happen.

38 Close repetition for effect, emphasising man as a reasoning creature.

39 Again, a powerful image. Orwell emphasises the event but, contrasts this with the fact that one man in this group will be executed. Although it is only one man, Orwell emphasises the universality of the action in the last three words.

Activity 5.8

Now analyse this passage using the PALS mnemonic: Purpose, Audience, Language, Structure. The following notes may help you clarify your ideas.

Purpose	The purpose of the article is not only to describe a hanging; it is also to inform us of what is happening, and to persuade us that this is wrong.
Audience	The audience is broad and informed: there is little explanation of context, and this is typical of reportage: there is an immediacy to what is described, as well as a compassionate tone which the writer no doubt hopes will influence his readership.
Language	The language is clear and unambiguous, but there are some striking images which make the moral message powerful and humane. It is not overly emotive, though: at all times Orwell retains a dispassionate objectivity, even when he explores, in detail, what it means to kill a man. The incident with the dog acts as an absurd, bleakly humorous, interjection which throws the horror of what is to happen into sharper relief.
Structure	This is a cleverly structured article: Orwell takes some time to establish the scene, but there is development, both of plot and character, and themes suggested right at the start are explored more fully as the narrator looks more closely at what he is witnessing.

Extended essay

EE

George Orwell remains a hugely influential writer: his most famous books are *Nineteen Eighty-Four* and *Animal Farm*. Students who are considering writing their extended essays on totalitarianism or the Cold War would be well advised to read some of Orwell's novels and his journalism. Search for links on the Internet, and use Wikipedia as a starting point: http://en.wikipedia.org/wiki/George_Orwell

Activity 5.9

Read the following article (Text 5.18) and assess it according to Criteria C and D.

Criterion C	*Organisation* How effectively is it organised? Does it have a clear opening, development, and conclusion? What are its weaknesses?	5
Criterion D	*Language* Do you think the language choices are appropriate? Does the language effectively convey the necessary information in a succinct way?	5

Text 5.18 *Programme in turmoil after shuttle tragedy* in *The Guardian*, Alex Brummer, 29 January 1986

On 28 January 1986 the United States' space shuttle, *Challenger*, exploded during its launch. All seven crew members were killed. The following appeared in the British newspaper *The Guardian* the following day.

The future of America's ambitious space shuttle programme was in complete turmoil last night after a devastating mid-air explosion, just one minute after takeoff, which killed the crew of seven, including the first ordinary citizen on the programme, a New Hampshire school teacher, Mrs Christa McAuliffe.

Nasa said last night that it had suspended operations of the shuttle indefinitely, pending the findings of a board of inquiry. But in a televised address to the American people, President Reagan stressed that the space programme would go ahead.

A spellbound nation watched with high expectations as *Challenger* lifted cleanly off the launch pad at 11.38 am, trailing the normal blazing geyser of fire behind it.

Some 60-seconds into the launch, as the elegant spacecraft soared nine miles into the deep blue sky above Cape Canaveral, it turned into a ferocious fireball as a bolt on the main fuel tank exploded, detonating an eruption with the power of what was described by Nasa scientists as a 'small nuclear weapon.'

For a lingering moment there was stunned silence across the country from the Concord, New Hampshire, school – where some 1,200 people had gathered to watch the launch on a giant television screen – to the VIP viewing room at the Cape where Christa McAuliffe's six and nine-year-old children were watching with her husband, Steve.

At the White House, the First Lady, Nancy Reagan, watching the shuttle launch quietly on her own, let out a scream of 'Oh My God'. The Vice-President, Mr George Bush, and the National Security Adviser, Admiral John Poindexter, burst in on President Reagan, alone in the Oval Office, with the report from Cape Canaveral, The President was stunned into silence before saying it was a 'horrible thing.'

Figure 5.16 The *Challenger* disaster, 28 January 1986.

Further resources

Footage of this disaster is available on a number of different websites: search for 'Challenger + shuttle + disaster' to find contemporary records of this event.

Discussion

After you have watched film clips of the disaster, discuss in pairs (or in a group) the following questions:

- How successful is the newspaper report?
- What does it provide us with that a television report does not? Are the facts reported objectively or does the writer's voice affect our understanding of the event?

The President then hastily consulted leaders on Capitol Hill and requested that his fifth State of the Union message – which was to have been delivered to a joint session of Congress last night – be cancelled. Mr Reagan immediately sent Mr Bush to Cape Canaveral to express condolences to the families, and it was announced that the President would go on television to explain the tragic turn of events.

Mr Reagan was particularly affected by yesterday's disaster since it was his own idea that a national competition be held to find a teacher to be sent into space so that children across the country could learn the wonders of the universe at first hand. Christa McAuliffe was to have delivered two lectures from space to be broadcast to schools across the country by public television stations.

In his televised address yesterday evening, President Reagan, who is committed to the shuttle because of its significance in his Star Wars program, said: 'There will be more shuttle flights, more shuttle crews, more volunteers, more teachers … nothing ends here. Our hopes and journeys continue.' He praised the seven dead astronauts for their 'daring and their bravery.' Mr Reagan looked grave and sombre but sought to keep alive the spirit of space exploration which he likened to the efforts of Sir Francis Drake, who died off the coast of Panama 390 years ago.

'Today their dedication, like Drake's, remains incomplete,' the President said. Mr Reagan, who was to have delivered an optimistic State of the Union message, last night closed his televised broadcast by saying, 'They slipped the surly bonds of earth to touch the face of God.' He said that it was a day for mourning and remembering what was truly 'a national loss.' He sent a special message to the millions of schoolchildren who had witnessed the disaster on television.

They had witnessed the fearsome sight of *Challenger* breaking up against the Florida skies, sending two huge streamers of white smoke into the atmosphere. For a brief moment the country held its breath as a large parachute opened and headed towards the Atlantic. But then there was national sorrow and disappointment as it was explained that the parachute was for paramedical staff who had followed the craft as a normal safety precaution.

The explosion happened as Nasa was sending instructions to the shuttle commander, Francis Scobee, to boost the rockets from 64 per cent power to 104 per cent power as the craft was entering the period of maximum aerodynamic pressure. It was the first disaster in the air in 56 manned space missions for the United States, although three American astronauts died on the launch pad in the *Apollo 1* craft 17 years ago on Monday.

Soon after the explosion a forlorn voice rang out from mission control saying 'We are checking with recovery forces to see what can be done at this point … contingency procedures are in effect.'

The voice added 'Vehicle has exploded … we are awaiting word from any recovery forces down range.' But as the search and rescue squads began combing the area it quickly became clearer that the shuttle crew – which included two women, Mrs McAuliffe and Judith Resnick – could not have survived.

Last night, after examining video film of the takeoff, Nasa experts said that the first sign of trouble came when small flames began to leak out from one of the two giant solid rocket boosters which propel the *Challenger* orbiter into space. One of the solid rocket boosters fell away and the hydrogen fuel exploded.

The commander and crew of the space shuttle may have been able to see that something was wrong from the computers and equipment in the small crew capsule at the front of the shuttle. But the explosion came so quickly that it was unlikely they had time to take any precautionary action. This shuttle mission, unlike some of the earlier craft, carried no ejector seats. They had been considered an unnecessary safety precaution.

As the accident occurred radio communications and telemetry fell silent. There was shock and disbelief among the thousands of observers at the Cape who had given the rocket a huge cheer as it lifted off the ground carrying the smiling schoolteacher. 'I can't believe it,' said one weeping woman.

Activity 5.10

Now answer the following questions about Alex Brummer's article:
- What did you grade it (out of 10)? Explain your assessment.
- Where did it gain marks? Be specific, pointing to key areas of the text.
- Where did it lose marks? Be specific, pointing to key areas of the text.

Discussion

The *Challenger* disaster forced many people to ask if scientific knowledge was worth risking such a loss of life. Others argued that to broadcast this sort of event live – with family members and children – watching was unethical. Discuss these issues with your class: is such research worth the risk? Is it worth the money? What counterclaims might be made to support such projects?

We are now going to look at another article from a newspaper, but this is very different in style and subject matter. This article, by Tanya Gold, is an opinion piece about the 'overnight' success of the singer Susan Doyle. Reading this article will help you to further explore how a journalist:
- uses emotive language to shape meaning
- provokes a strong response from readers.

Text 5.19 'It wasn't singer Susan Boyle who was ugly on Britain's Got Talent so much as our reaction to her' in *The Guardian*, Tanya Gold, 16 April 2009

Figure 5.17 Susan Boyle became famous in the UK after appearing on the television programme *Britain's Got Talent*.

Discussion

1 Discuss with a friend whether you found it difficult to remain objective, and to separate the quality of the writing from the emotive story it is describing.
2 Mark up this article using the skills you have developed with other activities (5.7 and 5.8):
   Purpose   Audience
   Language   Structure
3 What guiding questions (for an SL paper) could you write for this article? You may wish to do this with a friend, or in a group.

Susan Boyle was an unknown singer before she appeared on the talent show *Britain's Got Talent*. Within hours of appearing she had become one of the most famous women in the world. She was interviewed on chat shows and got more 'hits' on the Internet than other, more established stars. She went on to be the runner-up in the show's final but has since established a successful recording career.

As you read this article remember the mnemonic PALS: Purpose, Audience, Language and Structure.

Is Susan Boyle ugly? Or are we? On Saturday night she stood on the stage in Britain's Got Talent; small and rather chubby, with a squashed face, unruly teeth and unkempt hair. She wore a gold lace dress, which made her look like a piece of pork sitting on a doily. Interviewed by Ant and Dec beforehand, she told them that she is unemployed, single, lives with a cat called Pebbles and has never been kissed. Susan then walked out to chatter, giggling, and a long and unpleasant wolf whistle.

Guiding questions

1 What effect do the two rhetorical questions have on the reader? What tone do they set?
2 How would you describe the writer's attitude to Susan Boyle? Support your point with embedded quotations.
3 What do the details about Susan Boyle's private life add to our picture of her? Why has the journalist included them?

Why are we so shocked when 'ugly' women can do things, rather than sitting at home weeping and wishing they were somebody else? Men are allowed to be ugly and talented. Alan Sugar looks like a burst bag of flour. Gordon Ramsay has a dried-up riverbed for a face. Justin Lee Collins looks like Cousin It from The Addams Family. Graham Norton is a baboon in mascara. I could go on. But a woman has to have the bright, empty beauty of a toy – or get off the screen. We don't want to look at you. Except on the news, where you can weep because some awful personal tragedy has befallen you.

Guiding questions

4 The writer uses a rhetorical question to begin the second paragraph: explain the effect that this has on the reader.
5 She mentions several British celebrities (you do not need to know who they are): what is the purpose of contrasting these men with the statement she makes about women?
6 Do you agree with what she says? Think of the purpose of the final two sentences: what effect do they have on the reader?

Simon Cowell, now buffed to the sheen of an ornamental pebble, asked this strange creature, this alien, how old she was. 'I'm nearly 47,' she said. Simon rolled his eyes until they threatened to roll out of his head, down the aisle and out into the street. 'But that's only one side of me,' Susan added, and wiggled her hips. The camera cut to the other male judge, Piers Morgan, who winced. Didn't Susan know she was not supposed to be sexual? The audience's reaction was equally disgusting. They giggled with embarrassment, and when Susan said she wanted to be a professional singer, the camera spun to a young girl, who seemed to be at least half mascara.

She gave an 'As if!' squeak and smirked. Amanda Holden, the female judge, a woman with improbably raised eyebrows and snail trails of Botox over her perfectly smooth face, chose neutrality. And then Susan sang. She stood with her feet apart, like a Scottish Edith Piaf, and very slowly began to sing Les Miserables' I Dreamed A Dream. It was wonderful.

Guiding questions

7 The writer is attacking stereotypical views of women: do you think her description of Amanda Holden is a contradiction of her position? Why might it not be?

8 Which sentence marks a turning point in this article? Comment on its structure and its effect.

9 The final sentence is unambiguous and clear: do you think this makes it more effective?

The judges were astonished. They gasped, they gaped, they clapped. They looked almost ashamed. I was briefly worried that Simon might stab himself with a pencil, and mutter, 'Et tu, Piers, for we have wronged Susan in thinking that because she is a munter*, she is entirely useless.' How could they have misjudged her, they gesticulated. But how could they not? No makeup? Bad teeth? Funny hair? Is she insane, this sad little Scottish spinster, beloved only of Pebbles the Cat?

* British slang for an unattractive woman

Guiding questions

10 The writer uses hyperbole here: where, and to what effect?

11 The writer uses allusion at one point: where, and to what effect?

12 The writer uses a slang term here: why do you think she does this, and what effect does it have?

13 The writer uses several rhetorical questions: why and to what effect?

14 The last sentence introduces a note of pathos: what effect does this have?

When Susan had finished singing, and Piers had finished gasping, he said this. It was a comment of incredible spite. 'When you stood there with that cheeky grin and said, "I want to be like Elaine Paige", everyone was laughing at you. No one is laughing now.' And it was over to Amanda Holden, a woman most notable for playing a psychotic hairdresser in the Manchester hair-extensions saga Cutting It. 'I am so thrilled,' said Amanda, 'because I know that everybody was against you.' 'Everybody was against you,' she said, as if Susan might have been hanged for her presumption. Why? Can't 'ugly' people dream, you flat-packed, hair-ironed, over-plucked monstrous fool?

Guiding question

15 This is the most emotive paragraph in the article: can you summarise the writer's argument, and why the language becomes so personal about the judges? What effect does this have on us as readers? Do we sympathise more with the argument?

I know what you will say. You will say that Paul Potts, the fat opera singer with the equally squashed face who won Britain's Got Talent in 2007, had just as hard a time at his first audition. I looked it up on YouTube. He did not. 'I wasn't expecting that,' said Simon to Paul. 'Neither was I,' said Amanda. 'You have an incredible voice,' said Piers. And that was it. No laughter, or invitations to paranoia, or mocking wolf-whistles, or smirking, or derision.

We see this all the time in popular culture. Do you ever stare at the TV and wonder where the next generation of Judi Denchs and Juliet Stevensons have gone? Have they fallen down a Rada wormhole? Yes. They're not there, because they aren't pretty enough to get airtime. This lust for homogeneity in female beauty means that when someone who doesn't resemble a diagram in a plastic surgeon's office steps up to the microphone, people fall about and treat us to despicable sub-John Gielgud gestures of amazement.

Guiding questions

16 How has the writer extended her argument to make more general points than those which have occupied her so far in the article?

17 How convincing is this extension of her argument? Is it too culturally specific? Is the point lost on an audience that does not understand her references? Is this a weakness in her article?

Susan will probably win Britain's Got Talent. She will be the little munter that could sing, served up for the British public every Saturday night. Look! It's 'ugly'! It sings! And I know that we think that this will make us better people. But Susan Boyle will be the freakish exception that makes the rule. By raising this Susan up, we will forgive ourselves for grinding every other Susan into the dust. It will be a very partial and poisoned redemption. Because Britain's Got Malice. Sing, Susan, sing – to an ugly crowd that doesn't deserve you.

TOK

Some questions: is fame intrinsically degrading, both for the famous and for those who make them famous? To what extent should those who elect to be famous be protected from the media? Does every society get the celebrities it deserves? Should reality television be banned on ethical grounds? Can we test the moral health of a society by measuring the value that society places on fame?

Activity 5.11

- What is the purpose of this article? To persuade? To inform? To state an opinion?
- Who do you think the audience is? Informed and sophisticated? Young or old? What evidence do you have to make such a judgement?
- How would you describe the language in this article? Is it balanced, or over-emotive? Does the language clearly explain the main points the writer wants to make?
- Comment on the structure of the article: how is the argument developed? What phases does the article go through? Is the conclusion effective?